The Practical
SQL
Handbook

Third Edition

The Practical
SQL
Handbook

Using Structured Query Language

Third Edition

Judith S. Bowman
Sandra L. Emerson
and Marcy Darnovsky

ADDISON-WESLEY DEVELOPERS PRESS

An imprint of Addison Wesley Longman, Inc.

Reading, Massachusetts • Harlow, England • Menlo Park, California
Berkeley, California • Don Mills, Ontario • Sydney
Bonn • Amsterdam • Tokyo • Mexico City

Many of the designations used by manufacturers and sellers to distinguish their products are claimed as trademarks. Where those designations appear in this book, and Addison–Wesley was aware of a trademark claim, the designations have been printed in initial capital letters or all capital letters.

The authors and publisher have taken care in preparation of this book, but make no expressed or implied warranty of any kind and assume no responsibility for errors or omissions. No liability is assumed for incidental or consequential damages in connection with or arising out of the use of the information or programs contained herein.

Library of Congress Cataloging-in-Publication Data

Bowman, Judith S.
    The practical SQL handbook : using structured query language /
Judith S. Bowman, Sandra L. Emerson, and Marcy Darnovsky. —3rd ed.
        p.   cm.
    Includes bibliographical references and index.
    ISBN 0-201-44787-8
    1. SQL (Computer program language)   2. Relational databases.
I. Emerson, Sandra L., 1947– . II. Darnovsky, Marcy. III. Title.
QA76.73.S67B69 1996
005.75'6—dc20   96-20301
                                                        CIP

Sponsoring Editor: Kathleen Tibbetts
Project Manager: John Fuller
Production Assistant: Melissa Lima
Cover design: Trish LaPointe
Set in 10-point Trump Mediaeval by Octal Publishing, Inc.

1 2 3 4 5 6 7 8 9–MA–00 99 98 97 96
First printing, August 1996

Addison-Wesley books are available for bulk purchases by corporations, institutions, and other organizations. For more information please contact the Corporate, Government, and Special Sales Department at (800) 238-9682.

Find A–W Developers Press on the World-Wide Web at
http://www.aw.com/devpress/

Contents

Foreword

The SQL language has metamorphosed from a database language known only to computer specialists to a broadly used, worldwide standard of the PC industry. The number of SQL-92–compatible databases shipping each year now totals in the millions. It is safe to say that if you are accessing corporate information from the Internet or from an internal network, SQL is probably involved. However, what seems like an obviously good idea today wasn't always so obvious.

Back at the beginning of relational time, when SQL was being designed at the IBM Research Laboratory, I was involved in implementing a database language meant to compete with SQL. Our language could handle more complex queries than SQL could, and had fewer special cases, but it was harder to learn. After seven years and two complete product developments with the non-SQL language, I became an enthusiastic convert to SQL.

The reasons were simple: SQL is easy to learn, is powerful enough and getting more powerful all the time, and—most important—has been implemented by every surviving DBMS vendor. Therefore, my third DBMS design (at Sybase) was based entirely on SQL.

It's easy to lose sight of the fact that the previous generation of databases were nonrelational, and each had its own special language. Implementation costs were prohibitive, and learning to use another database management system was an ordeal.

We have now entered an age in which all DBMSs support SQL. Even the prior generation of databases can be accessed through SQL translators that join data between different databases. In client-server and Internet computing, databases are accessed in SQL. Therefore, a working knowledge of the SQL language is a valuable skill, no matter which DBMS you ultimately use.

Given SQL's academic origins, it's easy to understand why many people are intimidated by SQL and relational database management systems. Terms such as "normal forms," "correlation variables," and "referential integrity" are not intuitive and do nothing to convey the meaning of what are basically simple concepts. They make database management seem like a branch of higher mathematics—which only makes for more doctoral dissertations and more Ph.D.'s (myself included).

Despite its underlying simplicity, SQL is a powerful language. Such power can produce unexpected pitfalls: even DP professionals are sometimes fooled. Several years ago, for example, I was involved in a competitive benchmark with another DBMS company. We performed well in every case except one, in which we took sixty hours (yes, hours) to perform a command that a different system completed in two minutes.

We agonized over the situation for days, until someone asked the customer to tell us in English what question the query was supposed to answer. That exercise made it clear that the customer's SQL statement had a right parenthesis in the wrong place. When the parenthesis was moved, the query ran in under a minute!

I'll never forget the customer's lament: "Relational languages are more sensitive to parentheses than FORTRAN!" Today, I could rescue such a customer, and save a lot of wear and tear on the benchmarkers, with a copy of *The Practical SQL Handbook*.

Having worked with relational database management systems since 1976, I was quite happy to read *The Practical SQL Handbook*. It covers not only SQL, but also database design and normalization in a manner that can be described—as the title says—as practical. That means that this book will get you up and running in a hurry.

The examples in *The Practical SQL Handbook* always make clear the practical significance of the concepts being explained. For example, *The Practical SQL Handbook* makes it clear that enforcing "referential integrity" can mean something as straightforward as putting a "no-vaporware rule" into your DBMS application: the system will then refuse to allow you to ship a product that doesn't exist. Nor will it let you ship to a customer who doesn't exist (this could be called the "no-fraud rule").

The Practical SQL Handbook also prepares you for the SQL future. SQL is not a static language, and both DBMS vendors and the SQL standards committees are busy extending it. Many of the changes are being driven by the need to develop increasingly complicated systems that require the database to play a stronger role in governing application programs. SQL extensions to enforce central database administration are particularly important for systems in which personal computers and workstations communicate with the DBMS over a network architecture known as client-server computing. *The Practical SQL Handbook* covers some of these extensions to SQL, as seen in the Transact-SQL language developed by Sybase for the SQL Server and SQL Anywhere.

In summary, this is the book for the "intelligent amateur." It is for someone who has little or no knowledge of SQL and who needs a broad introduction to relational database management. This book provides a vendor-independent introduction to everything you need to know to start using SQL and relational databases.

Robert Epstein
Executive Vice President
Sybase, Inc.

Preface to the Second and Third Editions

WHY NEW EDITIONS?

Many things have changed since this book was first published in 1989, and SQL is no exception. It has expanded tremendously, both in numbers of users and in numbers of commands. Sales of relational databases are steadily growing.

When we wrote the first edition of *The Practical SQL Handbook*, the American National Standards Institute (ANSI) had already passed the 1986 standard. The International Standards Organization (ISO) adopted it in 1987. Both ANSI and ISO were working on the 1989 version. The 1986 standards were skimpy, lacking features that most commercial vendors offered. The 1989 standards were more complete, but still left many important elements undefined.

What actually mattered at that time was the de facto industry standard: each vendor kept a wary eye on what the others were doing and made core offerings similar enough to attract (with claims of compatibility) both customers migrating from competitors and new users looking for database systems they could build on. Because of this, we left both the not-quite-jelled ANSI standards and particular vendor implementations to the experts in those fields and concentrated on the common ground: generic or "industry-standard" SQL. Our goal was to offer the intelligent amateur practical information on how to use the actually available SQL of that time.

The 1992 ANSI standard (often called SQ-2 or SQL-92) represents a new stage in SQL development. It's much fuller than the 1989 standard, containing more than four times as many pages as the earlier version. Database vendors have adopted large parts of the 1992 standard. The industry and the ANSI/ISO standards are converging.

Nonetheless, there is still a general, industry-wide core of SQL commands that all users need to understand. Adopting standards doesn't happen overnight; it is a long process. At any point, vendors will have varying levels of conformance. SQL users can still benefit from mastering the fundamentals of the language before investigating the specifics of particular implementations.

THE SECOND EDITION

In reviewing what was available for SQL users, we found the same holes in 1993 as in 1989: very little practical advice on how to use the language. There are a number of good books on specific implementations (check your local library or bookstore for a list) and several complete treatments of the language from a standards point of view (notably Date and Darwin's *A Guide to the SQL Standard,* Third Edition (Addison-Wesley, 1993) and Melton and Simon's *Understanding the New SQL: A Complete Guide* (Morgan Kaufmann, 1993). It looked as if both vendor-specific information and standards explications were well covered.

But talking to new and developing SQL users, we heard over and over of their need for examples to follow, change, narrow, and broaden. Accordingly, the bulk of the added material in the second edition is in two completely new chapters. Both of them are composed largely of code "recipes." Reported errors in the original chapters have also been corrected.

Chapter 11, "Solving Business Problems," is a selection of code samples based on questions and answers that came over the popular NETNEWS/ USENET computer networks. We reproduced interesting problems and solutions in terms of the sample *bookbiz* database used throughout the book. The chapter includes examples of formatting results, finding data, working with multitable queries, using the GROUP BY clause, and creating sequential numbers.

A few samples fell into a different category. They weren't so much solutions to problems as indications of common errors. These items went into Chapter 12, "Mistakes and How to Avoid Them." They include GROUP BY, HAVING, and WHERE interactions, DISTINCT, and misunderstandings of what SQL can do.

THE THIRD EDITION

The third edition has a different goal: to bring basic SQL grammar up to date and to incorporate those SQL-92 changes that most vendors have adopted. These include new datatypes, additions to the CREATE TABLE statement that allow built-in integrity constraints, modifications to the ORDER BY and GROUP BY clauses, the new escape character for the LIKE keyword, and changes to GRANT and REVOKE, among others. We looked at the syntax of the most common commands for Sybase SQL Server, Sybase SQL Anywhere, Microsoft SQL Server, Informix, and Oracle. All of the examples were run on both Sybase SQL Server and SQL Anywhere.

The third edition of *The Practical SQL Handbook* is also more than just a book: a CD containing a run-time version of SQL Anywhere with the sample *bookbiz* database now comes with it. This means you can run the examples (and your variants) on a PC. We've always felt that the secret to learning SQL is practice. Now you can experiment to your heart's content, trying out code samples with data you know and checking the results to see if they are what you expect. When you're stumped by complicated code, break it into small, meaningful pieces and run them separately to make sure you understand what each segment does. Then put them together in increasingly complex combinations—and have fun!

ACKNOWLEDGMENTS

We would like to thank the following people for their contributions to this book:

Donna Jeker and Stu Schuster for supplying timely support and encouragement;

Jeff Lichtman and Howard Torf for offering advice, examples, anecdotes, and reality checks;

Tom Bondur, Susie Bowman, John Cooper, and Wayne Duquesne for providing resource materials and other information;

Paul Winsberg for reviewing the database design chapter in the first edition;

Robert Garvey for technical review of the second edition;

Karen Ali for making the SQL Anywhere CD possible; and

Theo Posselt for technical review of the third edition.

Introduction

THE BEGINNINGS OF SQL

In the beginning was IBM, and IBM created SQL.

SQL, originally an acronym for "Structured Query Language," is a unified language for defining, querying, modifying, and controlling the data in a relational database. Its name is officially pronounced "ess-cue-ell" (according to the American National Standards Institute), but many people say "sequel." In this book, we use the term SQL as if it were pronounced "sequel."

The relational model of database management was proposed in 1970 by Dr. E. F. Codd at the IBM Research Laboratory in San Jose, California, and developed during the following decade in universities and research laboratories. SQL, one of several languages that grew out of this early work, has now almost completely taken over the world of relational database languages. Vendors of relational database management systems who initially chose other languages have flocked to SQL; national and international standards organizations have proposed a codified version of the language.

During the early years (roughly 1970–1980), the poor performance of relational database management systems hampered their commercial viability. The relational model's important strengths—mathematical soundness and intuitive appeal—could not overcome the fact that the management of large databases with early relational systems was slow and difficult—practically speaking, sometimes impossible. Two factors changed this situation: the availability of faster, larger-capacity computers, and the development of superior data retrieval, data storage, and data access methods to support the "back end" functions of relational systems.

In 1981, IBM announced its first commercial SQL-based product, SQL/DS. Oracle, Relational Technology, and several other vendors also announced SQL-based relational database management systems during the early 1980s. By 1989, there were more than seventy-five SQL or SQL-like database management systems, running on computers of all sizes and shapes—from single-user micros to machines that handle hundreds of users. SQL is now entrusted with "mission-critical" information management and data processing tasks in corporate, government, and public interest organizations.

The emergence of a highly competitive marketplace for relational database management systems has produced an array of SQL implementations, representing years of effort to develop a complete and highly expressive language for the relational model. But a problem remains: there are as many dialects of SQL as there are relational systems on the market. Although all the dialects are recognizably SQL, none is identical to another in syntax or semantics. Furthermore, many vendors regularly extend their versions of SQL, which makes the language a moving target as well as a multiple target.

SQL will continue to evolve—in part because its original design was vague in a number of areas (and the database industry didn't wait for those fuzzy areas to be cleared up), and in part because the industry is striving to develop database systems that fulfill more of the capabilities of the relational model.

The flexibility of SQL and the ease with which it can be extended means that it will keep on changing to meet the demands of the market.

The Commercialization of SQL

The first commercial implementations of SQL had much the same experimental flavor as the research versions developed in university settings and industry labs, in part because the pioneer SQL vendors were working without the benefit of a finished standard. Early implementations such as Oracle, SQL/DS, and DB2 have grown and changed remarkably since their first appearance. Still, commercial SQL implementations continue to differ from each other—and from the ANSI SQL standard (first drafted in 1983 and most recently issued in 1992)—in many respects.

The situation could become a Babel of mutually incomprehensible SQL dialects competing for market share. Fortunately, however, market forces, as well as the standards movement, encourage commercial implementations to become more and more like each other as time goes on.

Competition promotes cross-fertilization and imitation on the commercial SQL scene for two reasons. First, companies try to offer prospective customers the same "checklist" of functions and extensions. Second, companies are constantly trying to attract customers of other relational systems and need to minimize the cost of converting from one SQL-based system to another.

These forces are pushing commercial implementations closer together. After all, both commercial interests and the standards committees are defining a SQL that

- Implements an increasingly complete relational model;
- Minimizes incompatibility and implementation dependence; and
- Adds language for new functions carefully, in order to maintain compatibility with early versions of SQL.

This book (and the CD containing a run-time version of SQL Anywhere) can help you teach yourself basic SQL. Then you can apply what you've leaned to other SQL dialects you have access to. Once you understand the fundamentals, you'll find it easy to make adjustments for different versions.

WHO SHOULD USE THIS BOOK

The Practical SQL Handbook is meant for you if you use a relational database system—whether you're sharing that system with other users or going it alone on a single-user personal computer. It assumes that you're an intelligent amateur—whether you're an end user in a large company, government office, or nonprofit agency; the owner of a small business; the manager of a small organization; a home computer user working on a personal project; or a student learning about database technology. You may be moving to a relational database system from a PC file manager, making the transition to SQL from a non-SQL–based database management system, or taking up database management for the first time.

We do take for granted that you have a nodding acquaintance with computers and computer tools. Of course, some degree of familiarity with database systems will help.

If you're planning to develop a sophisticated database application, you'll need to embed SQL in a programming language or use it with a "fourth-generation application language" (4GL). But you need never have written a single line of programming code in order to use *The Practical SQL Handbook* successfully to learn both the basics of SQL and to get a good grasp on a variety of more advanced topics.

Theoreticians are not our intended audience; we assume that the fine points of relational theory and the intricacies of the ISO-ANSI debates are not of primary interest to our readers. On the other hand, we think you should be aware of the major SQL controversies—at least in their broad outlines—so that you'll be alert to the tricky areas of SQL use. In short, we think you want to know what really works, or at least the fastest way to find that out.

Accordingly, this book concentrates on teaching you to use SQL interactively—typing the commands and receiving results directly on a screen, as opposed to embedding them in a programming language. Every commercial implementation of SQL has an interactive interface for use in learning the language initially and writing ad hoc queries. Many provide report writers or 4GLs that can be used in association with SQL to develop applications of moderate complexity.

THE FOCUS OF THIS BOOK

In spite of the messiness involved, this book focuses on the real world of commercial SQLs—which we also refer to as "industry SQLs"—rather than on the current ANSI standard version of SQL. We made this choice because the industry SQLs provide a better teaching tool in the areas of notation, target audience, and overall functionality:

- The syntax notation used to document most industry SQLs is reasonably clear and intuitively understandable. The ISO-ANSI publications, on the other hand, use BNF (Backus Naur Form) notation, which is very precise but difficult to read and understand.
- All the industry SQLs support an interactive interface for the beginning or casual user; the ISO-ANSI standard is largely concerned with the embedded SQL interface for programmers and applications developers.
- Vendors of relational database systems implement the features their customers ask for, including some originally offered only by competitors. Adoption of ANSI SQL features varies from SQL to SQL. By taking the industry standard (rather than the ANSI standard) as the basis for this book, we can focus on features available today.

The ANSI standard is a forbidding document, bristling with clauses, caveats, and footnotes; its BNF notation is best suited for capturing the function of each language element, rather than its exact syntax. If you want to undertake your own investigations, we recommend that you take a guide along: C. J. Date's *A Guide to the SQL Standard*. Date is one of the major theoreticians of the relational model and one of the most prolific writers on relational matters. His book explains how to read BNF and serves as a useful collection of his opinions on the merits and deficiencies of the standard and of SQL in general.

After ruminating on the ISO-ANSI document for a while, even with the assistance of Date's *Guide*, you're likely to turn for enlightenment to the closest relational database management system's user's manual. But user's manuals have their own drawbacks and limitations.

While some user's manuals are adequate for learning the basics of SQL, a great many are either overly simplistic or overly obscure. Perhaps more problematic, user's manuals (including several written by the authors of this book) unavoidably focus on the details of syntax and the eccentricities of one particular dialect—often at the expense of the conceptual picture.

The Practical SQL Handbook is meant to take up where even the best SQL user's manual leaves off. It takes you step by step through the basics of SQL and then introduces you to the issues involved in designing SQL-based database applications. *The Practical SQL Handbook* covers topics that are usually neglected or given short shrift in user's manuals: database design, indexes, nulls, joins, subqueries, views, performance, and data integrity.

HOW TO LEARN SQL WITH THIS BOOK

Let's begin with a few expectations. First of all, we expect you to read large parts of this book while sitting at your terminal. Second, we expect you to study and reproduce the examples. Third, we expect you to practice, test, and explore. There's no substitute for interactive practice, even if your ultimate intention may be to program a highly sophisticated application.

From there, a lot is up to you. Learning styles differ: some people absorb new material through carefully considering prose explanations; others take in concepts just by looking at pictures. We expect this book to be equally helpful whether you choose to read every word of it or to briefly scan the text and rely mainly on the examples. Words and phrases in **boldface** indicate the first mention of an entry that is defined in the glossary.

Some of the hundreds of examples in *The Practical SQL Handbook* are deliberately simple in order to illustrate basic concepts. Others are more difficult. At the most complex end of the range you'll find SQL statements that may serve as models for your own applications. Wherever their complexity warrants it, examples are dissected and explained in detail.

The fact that every version of SQL is different from every other version, at least in some details, means that no general-purpose book on SQL can guarantee all of its examples to work exactly as presented. The good news is that our decision to base *The Practical SQL Handbook* on the industry SQLs rather than on the official SQL standard will make the "translation" process more straightforward. With the reference materials supplied with your SQL product, the lists of cross-system analogies in keywords and operators in Appendix B, and a little detective work, you'll be able to test most of our examples on whatever SQL or SQL-like system you're using.

All the examples in *The Practical SQL Handbook* are guaranteed to work in the language with which they were developed—Sybase SQL Server Transact-SQL—and the language of the relational database system shipped with the book: Sybase SQL Anywhere. We don't claim to represent in depth any implementation of SQL, or to cover any other dialect's strengths or limitations. We do cover (in broad strokes) the major areas of commonality among industry SQLs.

With very few exceptions, all examples are derived from our sample database, called the *bookbiz* database. Chapters 2 and 3 explain the sample database. You don't have to use the same sample data we do, but that's the best approach—it will help you see more quickly whether your results are correct.

The *bookbiz* database is very small. Its size and simplicity will allow you to become comfortable with the copy provided on the SQL Anywhere CD as you work through the examples in the book, and later re-create it on your own system. On the other hand, it is complex enough to illustrate important points about the significant relational issues.

The Structure of This Book

Each chapter of *The Practical SQL Handbook* presents one SQL feature or a cluster of related features. The discussion follows a pattern, beginning with the following:

- Definition—what does it do
- Minimal syntax—a simple "vanilla" version of the command (one that is stripped of most optional clauses and extensions, which tend to vary from SQL to SQL)
- A simple example

Following this initial description of syntax and usage, we elaborate on the role of this feature in the relational model, and its possible use in database applications.

If necessary, we then provide additional syntax—optional clauses offering additional functions or fine-tuning capabilities—and more-complex examples. In this way, each new feature has a complete description and example.

Where possible, each example builds on previous ones. However, the examples in each chapter stand alone, so that you can complete a chapter at one sitting. Learning SQL is like learning any other foreign language: the learning process begins with imitation, proceeds through comprehension, and should end with fluency. At each of these stages, the key to success is *practice*.

Interactive practice with SQL will be more pleasant and efficient if you follow some simple time-saving procedures:

Save your practice SQL statements in operating system files. (Your system should provide a method for doing this.) If you are not certain that a SQL query (data retrieval operation) is producing the desired results, save the results for off-line examination. Keep some log or record of what worked and what didn't, and save the error message, too, if you can.

Save your successes. Keep elegant SQL solutions on file: you may want to imitate them for other purposes later on.

Structure an application's queries into separate modules or subroutines. Like modern structured programming, good SQL applications should be made of many subroutines and be open to constant reapplication and recycling.

Make yourself a crib sheet. Even if your system has provided you with a quick reference card, make your own list and quick sketches of favorite commands. This will reinforce learning. You will soon find that you use some SQL commands much more often than others.

Improve on our solutions. In our experience, the more you work at expressing yourself in SQL, the simpler and more elegant your statements become.

The point of learning SQL and practicing it interactively is to be able to express any desired operation properly, so that you get the results you want. In order to achieve this level of proficiency, you'll have to explore and test-drive your relational system's SQL until you're sure you can trust it. You don't want to find out when you're running at fifty transactions per second that your results have been invalidated by a SQL error (or a logic error).

SQL requires practice because it's a foreign language, and the entity that speaks it best—your system's parser—isn't human. Although SQL has a limited number of keywords and operators and is relatively easy to read, there are areas that are tricky. Like many other high-level languages for computers, SQL has a definite grammar and structure and a fair number of specific syntax rules. SQL may be English-like, but it's still far from being a natural language. Sooner or later, you'll come across some operations that SQL simply cannot perform.

The Practical SQL Handbook will help you understand SQL's strengths and limits. It will assist in heading off potential disasters caused by poor database design or unwieldy and unmaintainable SQL-based applications, and make the learning of SQL as quick and painless as possible.

AN OVERVIEW OF THE BOOK

Chapter 1: SQL and Relational Database Management. This chapter briefly defines and informally illustrates the relational model, and presents the chief features of the SQL language as the voice of the relational model.

Chapter 2: Designing Databases. Database design is often an intimidating prospect. This chapter surveys the most helpful techniques, using the sample database to illustrate the analysis of data and the decision making involved in database design. It discusses primary and foreign keys, entity-relationship modeling, and the normalization rules, which can act as guidelines for good database design.

Chapter 3: Creating and Filling a Database. The design proposed in the previous chapter becomes a reality here, as the SQL commands for creating databases, tables, and indexes, and for adding, changing, and deleting data, are examined in detail. An explanation of our SQL syntax conventions accompanies this initiation into hands-on use of the SQL language.

Chapter 4: Selecting Data from the Database. This chapter, with which you can start using the SQL Anywhere CD to run examples, presents the basic elements of the SELECT command. It explains how to retrieve particular rows and columns from a single table, and covers computed values, comparison operators, and logical operators.

Chapter 5: Sorting Data and Other Selection Techniques. Other clauses in the SELECT statement allow you to sort your data, eliminate duplicates from the results, or use aggregate functions to report averages, sums, or counts.

Chapter 6: Grouping Data and Reporting from It. The SELECT statement also includes language for grouping data and reporting from it using the aggregate functions described in the previous chapter. This chapter covers these SQL features and also returns to the controversial topic of how a relational database management system should handle null values (missing information).

Chapter 7: Joining Tables for Comprehensive Data Analysis. The join operation is one of the hallmarks of the relational model. This chapter explains how to use the join operation to retrieve data from one or more tables. A complex variant on simple selection, joins confront users with significant issues in analyzing and verifying the results of data retrieval.

Chapter 8: Structuring Queries with Subqueries. This chapter deals with the proper use and application of nested queries, or subqueries. The correlated subquery (notorious for causing confusion) is explained, with many examples.

Chapter 9: Creating and Using Views. This chapter discusses views (virtual tables) and their use in providing customized access to data. Views can also provide data security, since you can grant other users access to specified portions of a table for specified operations. The thorny issue of updating views is described in some detail.

Chapter 10: Security, Transactions, Performance, and Integrity. This chapter is devoted to considerations encountered in real-world database management. It explains the SQL commands for specifying permissions, returns to the subject of indexing to discuss its use in boosting performance, and covers mechanisms for transaction management. It also describes extensions to the SQL language that provide database consistency and referential integrity. Some of the features discussed here are specific to Sybase's implementation of SQL.

Chapter 11: Solving Business Problems. Here's where you can practice the skills you learned in earlier chapters, with SQL code samples based on questions and answers found on the Internet, reproduced in terms of the *bookbiz* database. Here you'll find examples of real-world problems, including formatting results, finding data, working with multitable queries, using the GROUP BY clause, and creating sequential numbers. Chapter 11 is a code cookbook, full of recipes you can use (with your own modifications) on the job.

Chapter 12: Mistakes and How to Avoid Them.   This chapter also contains code recipes taken from the Internet and translated into *bookbiz* terms, but with a different flavor: they aren't solutions but examples of common errors. Look here for mistakes with GROUP BY, HAVING and WHERE interactions, DISTINCT, as well as for fundamental misunderstandings of what SQL can do. Used wisely, this chapter can help you avoid some classic wrong code.

Appendix A: Syntax Summary for the SQL Used in This Book.

Appendix B: Industry SQL Equivalents.

Appendix C: Glossary.

Appendix D: The* bookbiz *Sample Database.   (This appendix includes a chart of tables with data, data structure diagram, and CREATE and INSERT statements.)

Appendix E: Bibliography

Chapter 1

SQL and Relational Database Management

RELATIONAL DATABASE MANAGEMENT

SQL is the language in which one "speaks" relational database. But just what is a relational database management system?

All database management systems store and manipulate information. The relational approach to database management is based on a mathematical model that includes formidable-sounding components such as relational algebra and relational calculus. Most working definitions of relational database management, however, rely on descriptions and functional specifications rather than on theoretical precision.

C. J. Date gives this informal definition of a relational database management system, or DBMS:

- It represents all information in the database as tables.
- It supports the three relational operations known as **selection**, **projection**, and **join**, for specifying exactly what data you want to see (and it can carry out these operations without requiring the system to physically store its data in any particular form).

Dr. E. F. Codd, the inventor of the relational model, has developed a detailed list of criteria that implementations of the relational model must meet. A comprehensive explanation of this list, often called "Codd's rules," would introduce terminology and theoretical issues not really within the scope of this book. We do touch on many of these issues, however, in subsequent chapters. Here, we summarize the features of Codd's twelve-rule test for relational systems and use these, in combination with Date's more basic definition, to come up with a general definition. To be considered fully relational, a relational database management system must

- Represent all information in the database as tables
- Keep the logical representation of data independent from its physical storage characteristics
- Use one high-level language for structuring, querying, and changing the information in the database (theoretically, any number of database languages could fit this bill; in practice, SQL is *the* relational language)
- Support the main relational operations (selection, projection, join) and set operations such as union, intersection, difference, and division
- Support views, which allow the user to specify alternative ways of looking at data in tables
- Provide a method for differentiating between unknown values (**nulls**) and zero or blank
- Support mechanisms for integrity, authorization, transactions, and recovery

The rest of this chapter gives an overview of these points; most of them are discussed further in subsequent chapters. After reading the brief explanations here, you'll begin to understand the lay of the relational land.

The Relational Model: It's All Tables

Codd's very first rule says that all information in a relational database is represented by values in **tables**. In a relational system, tables have (horizontal) **rows** and (vertical) **columns** (see Figure 1-1). All data is represented in table format—there's no other way to see the information in the database.

A note on terminology: Because table, row, and column are the common terms used in commercial relational database management systems, they're the ones we'll use in this book. However, you may come across references to **relation**, **tuple**, and **attribute**. They are very nearly synonymous with table, row, and column, respectively; so are **file**, **record**, and **field**. The first three are academic terms; the last three stem from general data processing vocabulary.

A set of related tables forms a **database**. The tables in a relational database are separate but equal. There is no hierarchical ranking of tables and, in fact, no necessary physical relationship among them.

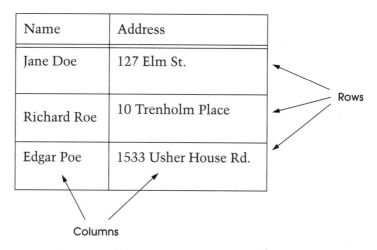

Name	Address
Jane Doe	127 Elm St.
Richard Roe	10 Trenholm Place
Edgar Poe	1533 Usher House Rd.

Rows

Columns

Figure 1–1. The *personnel* Table

Each table consists of a set of rows and columns. Each row describes one occurrence of an **entity**—a person, a company, a sale, or some other thing. Each column describes one characteristic of the entity—a person's name or address, a company's phone number or president, a sale's items sold or quantity or date.

Each data element, or **value**, can be identified as the intersection of a row (the horizontal element) and a column (the vertical element). To zero in on the exact data element you want, you need to know the name of its table and what column it's in, and the value of its row's **primary key**, or unique identifier. (As we'll discuss in Chapter 2, it is necessary that each row be uniquely identified by one of its values.)

For example, suppose you want to know Richard Roe's address. To instruct the system to show you that particular piece of information, you tell it to fetch Richard Roe's address from the table called *personnel*. The column name is *address* (or some such thing); the name *Richard Roe* is the primary key value identifying that row (see Figure 1-2).

There are two types of tables in a relational database: **user tables** and **system tables**. User tables contain the information that is the database management system's raison d'être—information on sales, orders, personnel schedules, and the like. The system tables, also known as the **system catalog** (or data dictionary), contain the database description. System tables are usually kept up-to-date by the DBMS itself, but they can be accessed just like any other table. Being able to access the system tables as if they were any other table is another of Codd's rules for relational systems.

Name	Address
Jane Doe	127 Elm St.
Richard Roe	10 Trenholm Place
Edgar Poe	1533 Usher House Rd.

The intersection of Richard's row and the address column is Richard's address.

Figure 1-2. Locating a Specific Piece of Data in a Table

To reiterate: all the information in the database, whether it's system data or user data, is represented as tables.

Independence Forever

In database management, as in so many other aspects of life, independence is something to strive for. Data independence is a crucial aspect of database management: it lets applications change without affecting database design, and it lets database design change without affecting applications. A database management system should not force you to make irrevocable decisions about what data you'll store, how you'll access it, or what your users will require. You don't want to be stuck with a system that's become obsolete because your work requirements have changed.

The relational model provides data independence on two important levels: *physical* and *logical*. **Physical data independence** means that the representation of the data—the user's eye view—is completely independent of how the data is physically stored. As a consequence, physical storage can be changed or rearranged without affecting either your view of the data or the logical database design.

Such changes can become necessary or desirable, especially in large multi-user systems. For example, when you run out of storage space, you'll need to add physical storage. When a storage device breaks down, you'll have to replace it—in a hurry. Usually less urgently, you may want to improve performance, efficiency, or ease of use by changing the method by which the system locates the physical data. (These methods are referred to generically as **access strategies**, which often make use of **indexes**.)

A second type of independence provided by relational systems, known as **logical independence**, means that relationships among tables, columns, and rows can change without impairing the function of application programs and ad hoc queries. You can split tables between rows, or between columns, without disrupting applications or queries. You can also get an answer to any ad hoc question that you ask the system about the database, even though the database's logical design has changed.

Physical and logical data independence account for two more of Codd's twelve rules.

A High-Level Language

The definition of a relational system, as well as Codd's rules, requires that a single language—sometimes called a **comprehensive data sublanguage**—be able to handle all communications with the database. In the commercial world of relational database management, that language is SQL.

SQL is used for **data manipulation** (retrieval and modification), **data definition**, and **data administration**. Every retrieval, modification, definition, or administrative operation is expressed as a SQL **statement** or **command**.

There are two varieties of data manipulation operations: **data retrieval** and **data modification**. Retrieval means finding the particular data you want; modification means adding, removing, or changing the data.

Data retrieval operations (often called **queries**) search the database, fetch information you've requested in the most efficient way possible, and display it. All SQL queries are expressed using the keyword SELECT.

The rest of this chapter includes some simple SQL queries. Don't worry about the syntax right now: it'll be fully explained in Chapter 3, before you're expected to sit down at a computer terminal and replicate anything you see here. For now, just glance at the examples and results to get the flavor of SQL and an impression of what the statement is doing.

Here's a SELECT statement that shows you all the data in the *publishers* table, which is part of the *bookbiz* database:

```
SQL:
select *
from publishers
```

The asterisk (*) is a shorthand device for asking for every column in the table. Here are the results the query would produce:

Results:

```
pub_id pub_name                address       city            state
------ --------------------    ------------  --------------  -----
0736   New Age Books           1 1st St      Boston          MA
0877   Binnet & Hardley        2 2nd Ave.    Washington      DC
1389   Algodata Infosystems    3 3rd Dr.     Berkeley        CA
(3 rows affected)
```

Data modification operations are accomplished using the INSERT, DE-LETE, and UPDATE keywords, respectively. You can add a row to the *publishers* table like this:

SQL:

```
insert into publishers
values ('0010', 'Pragmatics', '4 4th Ln.', 'Chicago', 'IL')
```

When you look at the data again with a SELECT statement, you see the new row:

SQL:

```
select *
from publishers
```

Results:

```
pub_id pub_name                address       city            state
------ --------------------    ------------  --------------  -----
0010   Pragmatics              4 4th Ln.     Chicago         IL
0736   New Age Books           1 1st St      Boston          MA
0877   Binnet & Hardley        2 2nd Ave.    Washington      DC
1389   Algodata Infosystems    3 3rd Dr.     Berkeley        CA
```

Other SQL commands perform data definition operations, such as creating or removing objects like tables, indexes, and views. This statement sets up a table called *test,* with two columns: one called *id* that holds integers, and another called *name* that holds up to fifteen characters.

SQL:

```
create table test
(id int,
name char(15))
```

You can SELECT from the *test* table, even before it has any data in it:

```
SQL:
select *
from test
```

Here's what the system shows you:

```
Results:
id      name
------ ---------------
(0 rows affected)
```

In the final category of SQL statements are data administration, or **data control,** commands. They allow you to coordinate the use of the database and maintain it in its most efficient state.

One important aspect of administration in a shared database system is the ability to control access to the data. The SQL keyword GRANT, controlling which users can access data, is a good example of an administrative command. Here's a GRANT statement that gives a user named *karen* permission to select data from the *test* table:

```
SQL:
grant select
on test
to karen
```

Before we go on to consider the relational operations, remember that these remarks are strictly introductory—don't try to learn the details of SQL syntax yet.

Relational Operations

Three specific data retrieval (or query) operations are part of the definition of a relational database management system. The relational operations—projection, selection (also called **restriction**), and join—allow you to tell the system exactly what data you want to see. Projection selects columns, selection selects rows, and join brings together data in related tables.

The physical and logical independence described earlier in this chapter mean that you don't have to worry about where the data is physically stored, or how to find it—that's the database management system's problem. SQL is considered a **nonprocedural language** because it allows you to express what you want without specifying any of the details about where it's located or how to get it.

All three of the data retrieval operations are expressed with the SQL keyword SELECT. This can be confusing: in SQL, you use SELECT not only for the selection operation, but also for projections and joins.

To give you a bit more of the flavor of the all-important SELECT statement, here's a simplified version of its syntax:

```
SQL:
SELECT select_list
FROM table_list
WHERE search_conditions
```

The next subsections explain how this deceptively simple-looking statement is used to express all three relational operations.

Projection.   The projection, or project, operation allows you to list (in the select list) which *columns* you want to see. For example, if you want to see all the rows in the table that contains information about publishers, but only the columns that contain the publishers' names and identification numbers, you'd write this data retrieval statement:

```
SQL:
select pub_id, pub_name
from publishers
```

Here are the results you would get:

```
Results:
pub_id pub_name
----- -----------------------
0010   Pragmatics
0736   New Age Books
0877   Binnet & Hardley
1389   Algodata Infosystems

(4 rows affected)
```

Once again, don't concern yourself with the SQL syntax at this point. Focus on understanding the conceptual point: *a projection specifies a subset of the columns in the table.* Note that the results of this projection (or any other relational operation) are displayed as a table. Result tables are sometimes called **derived tables** to distinguish them from the **base tables,** which contain the raw data.

Selection. The selection, or select, operation allows you to retrieve a subset of the rows in a table. To specify the rows you want, you put conditions in a WHERE clause. The SELECT statement's WHERE clause specifies the criteria that a row must meet in order to be included in the selection. For example, if you want information about publishers located in California only, here's what you'd type:

```
SQL:
select *
from publishers
where state = "CA"
```

Here are the results you would get:

```
Results:
pub_id pub_name                address    city       state
-----  --------------------    ---------- ---------  -----
1389   Algodata Infosystems 3 3rd Dr.  Berkeley   CA

(1 row affected)
```

You can combine projection and selection in many ways to zero in on just the columns and rows in a table you want to see.

Join. The join operation works on two or more tables at a time, combining the data so that you can compare and contrast information in your database. The join operation gives SQL and the relational model a good deal of their power and flexibility. You can find any relationship that exists among data elements, not just the relationships you anticipated when you designed your database.

When you "join" two tables, it's as if you're melding them together for the duration of the query. The join operation combines data by comparing values in specified columns and displaying the results.

The easiest way to understand the join operation is with an example. Let's suppose you want to know the names and publishers of all the books

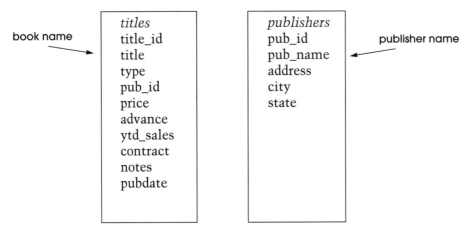

Figure 1-3. Columns in the *titles* and *publishers* Tables

in the database. The name of each book is stored in the *titles* table. So is a good deal of other information about each book, including the identification number of its publisher (see Figure 1-3). However, the publisher's name isn't in the *titles* table—that information is in the *publishers* table.

The problem can be solved because both the *publishers* table and the *titles* table contain the publishers' identification numbers: you can join the two tables in order to display the publisher's name along with the book's title (see Figure 1-4).

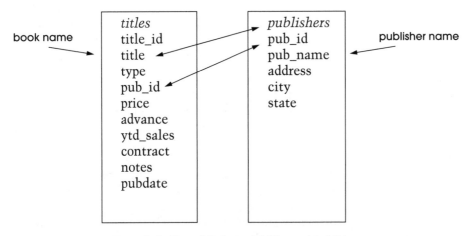

Figure 1-4. Shared Columns in *titles* and *publishers*

The system tests for every instance in which the two *pub_id* columns are the same; whenever there is a match, it creates a new row—containing columns from both tables—as the result of the join. Here's the query:

SQL:

```
select title, pub_name
from titles, publishers
where publishers.pub_id = titles.pub_id
```

The *title* column in the SELECT clause comes from the *titles* table, the *pub_name* column from the *publishers* table. Projection can specify columns from several tables in the select list. The FROM clause indicates the two tables that are to be joined; the WHERE clause says that rows in these tables are to be linked when the identification numbers in the two *pub_id* columns are the same.

Here are the results:

Results:

```
title                                   pub_name
-------------------------------------   -------------------
You Can Combat Computer Stress!         New Age Books
Computer Phobic and Non-Phobic
  Individuals: Behavior Variations      New Age Books
Is Anger the Enemy?                     New Age Books
Life Without Fear                       New Age Books
Prolonged Data Deprivation: Four
  Case Studies                          New Age Books
Emotional Security: A New Algorithm     New Age Books
Silicon Valley Gastronomic Treats       Binnet & Hardley
The Gourmet Microwave                   Binnet & Hardley
The Psychology of Computer Cooking      Binnet & Hardley
Onions, Leeks, and Garlic: Cooking
  Secrets of the Mediterranean          Binnet & Hardley
Fifty Years in Buckingham Palace
  Kitchens                              Binnet & Hardley
Sushi, Anyone?                          Binnet & Hardley
The Busy Executive's Database Guide     Algodata Infosystems
Cooking with Computers: Surreptitious
  Balance Sheets                        Algodata Infosystems
Straight Talk About Computers           Algodata Infosystems
But Is It User Friendly?                Algodata Infosystems
Secrets of Silicon Valley               Algodata Infosystems
```

```
Net Etiquette                        Algodata Infosystems

(18 rows affected)
```

At this point in the discussion, you might wonder if we're not overselling the importance of the join operation. Why not just put all those columns in the same table in the first place? If the table gets big and unwieldy, why not simply use the projection operation to limit the number of columns that are displayed at one time?

Those are reasonable questions; the answer is that the number of columns in a table must often be limited for reasons of both consistency and convenience. The discussion of database design in the next chapter sets out guidelines for deciding which columns to put into which tables.

Alternatives for Viewing Data

A **view** is an alternative way of looking at the data in one or more tables. Views are sometimes called **virtual tables** or derived tables. Another term for the table(s) on which a view is based is base table(s). It is a shiftable frame through which you can see only the particular data that concerns you. You can derive a view from one or more database tables (or, for that matter, from other views), using any desired selection, projection, and join operations. Views allow you to create customized tables tailored to special needs. In effect, you capture a cluster of selection, projection, and join operations to use as the foundation for future queries.

The data you see when you look at a view (or "through" a view, as it's often put) is not actually stored in the database the way data in "real" or base tables is. It's important to realize that a view is not a copy of the data in another table. When you change data through a view, you're changing the real thing. Like selection results, a view looks like an ordinary database table.

Views are set up with the SQL CREATE VIEW statement. You can make virtually any SELECT statement into a view simply by incorporating it into a CREATE VIEW command. To make the previous example into a view, you would use the CREATE VIEW command shown here:

```
SQL:
create view Books_and_Pubs
as
select title, pub_name
from titles, publishers
where publishers.pub_id = titles.pub_id
```

When you select from the view, it displays results from the query that you used to create it.

In the ideal relational system, you would be able to display a view and operate on it almost exactly as you could any other table. In the real world, different versions of SQL place limitations on view manipulation, in particular with respect to updates. One of Codd's rules explicitly addresses view updatability, stipulating that a true relational system should allow all updates that are "theoretically" possible. Most relational database management systems fall short of his standards on this one.

Chapter 9 is devoted to views, and includes a discussion of what a "theoretically updatable" view means.

Nulls

In the real world of information management, data is often missing or incomplete: you forgot to ask for a phone number, a respondent to a questionnaire refuses to divulge his age, a book has been contracted but the publication date has not been set. Such missing information leaves gaping holes in your set of tidy tables.

The unsightliness of these holes is not the real problem, of course. The danger is that they might introduce inconsistencies into your database. In order to preserve the integrity of your data, the relational model, as well as Codd's rules, use the concept of nulls to handle missing information.

"Null" does not mean zero or blank. Rather, it indicates that a value is unknown, unavailable, or inapplicable. Essentially, the use of nulls changes two-valued logic (yes/no or something/nothing) into three-valued logic (yes/no/maybe or something/nothing/not sure).

In the opinion of relational expert C. J. Date, nulls are not the perfect solution to the problem of missing information. However, they are an integral part of both the official SQL standard and the de facto industry standard. Nulls are such an important topic that they are covered in several chapters: Chapter 3 explains how to set up tables that allow nulls in certain columns; Chapter 4 touches on issues in selecting nulls; Chapter 5 considers nulls with ordering and aggregate functions; and Chapter 6 summarizes the issues regarding nulls in database management.

Security

The security issue can be summarized as the need to control who can use what data, and for what purpose. The SQL GRANT and REVOKE commands allow certain privileged users to choose who will be authorized to look at or change database information. In most SQL implementations, access and data modification **permissions** can be controlled on the levels of both tables and columns.

The privileged users who bestow these permissions are the **owners** of databases and database objects. A user owns a database or one of its objects by virtue of having created it with one of the SQL CREATE commands; some systems allow ownership to be transferred from the creator to another user.

Most multiuser systems designate another privileged user, even higher on the totem pole than owners, who is often called the **system administrator** or **database administrator**. The user in this role often possesses wide powers to grant and revoke permissions (and is also responsible for a variety of other maintenance and administrative tasks).

Views can be used as an additional security mechanism: users can be granted permission to access only the particular subset of data that's included in a view. Views are covered in Chapter 9; the GRANT and REVOKE commands are covered in Chapter 10.

Integrity

Integrity is a serious and complex issue in relational database management. In general, it means the consistency of the data in the database. Inconsistencies in data arise in several ways. One kind of inconsistency can be introduced by system failure—a hardware problem, a software bug, or a logical error in an application program. Relational database management systems that protect data from this type of inconsistency do so by guaranteeing that SQL commands either run to completion or are canceled. The processes by which this guarantee is enforced are often called **transaction management**. Transactions and SQL's method of handling them are discussed in Chapter 10.

Another kind of integrity, called **entity integrity**, is a design issue. Entity integrity requires that no primary key be allowed to have a null value.

A third variety of data integrity, called **referential integrity**, means consistency among pieces of information that are repeated in more than one table. For example, if you correct an employee's improperly entered Social Security number in one table, other tables that include employee information probably still reference the old number, so you have to update them, too. *It's vital that when information is changed in one place, it is also changed in every other place it appears.*

Codd's rules firmly state that relational database management systems should support not only entity and referential integrity, but also the ability "to specify additional integrity constraints reflecting either business policies or government regulations." Furthermore, Codd says, integrity constraints must be

- Definable in the same high-level language used by the rest of the system
- Stored in the data dictionary, not in application programs

In the early days, only a few implementations of SQL met Codd's integrity criteria, but this is changing. The 1992 ANSI SQL standard (often called "SQL2") provides for **constraints** in the CREATE TABLE statements that can enforce referential integrity and business rules. Most vendors have implemented these new features in some form. They are covered in Chapter 3.

BEGINNING DATABASE DESIGN

Now that you have a basic understanding of relational database systems, you may be impatient to get started. But before you can do any data retrieval or modification, you have to get data into the database. And before you can do that, you have to decide what the database should look like. We cover database design in Chapter 2.

Chapter 2

Designing Databases

DATABASE DESIGN

The process of deciding what the database will look like is called **database design.** Designing a database involves choosing

- The tables that belong in the database
- The columns that belong in each table
- How tables and columns interact with each other

Database design is concerned with the *logical* structure of the database. In the relational model, decisions about logical design are completely independent of the database's *physical* storage and structure. The logical structure is also independent of what the end user eventually sees: that can be customized with views created by the designer (see Chapter 9 for details) or with front-end application programs.

Database design using the relational model offers some important advantages over the design process used in other database models:

- The independence of the logical design from both the physical design and the end user's view
- The flexibility of the database design—design decisions don't limit the questions you can ask about the data in the future

Because the relational model does not require you to define access paths among your data, you can query about any kind of logical relationship the database contains, not just the relationships for which you originally planned. (In this chapter, we assume that "you" are the database designer.)

On the other hand, relational systems have no *built-in* protections against poor design decisions, no automatic way to distinguish a good design from a bad one. There is simply no set of automated tools that can substitute for your understanding of relational design principles and procedures.

Database design, like some of the other issues touched on in this book, is a very large subject. Professional careers have been devoted to it, and hundreds of articles and dozens of books have been written about it—some of them extremely technical and bristling with jargon and abstract terminology, others aimed at casual users of personal computers. (The ones we've found most helpful are listed in the bibliography.)

While the discussion in this chapter is brief, and decidedly practical rather than theoretical, it is meant to give you enough understanding to design a moderately complex database. It will acquaint you with the jargon and the issues so that you'll be able to tackle more technical discussions of database design if you need to do so. The basic principles are the same whether the database you're designing is simple or complex.

If you're working with a single-user system, the database is likely to be straightforward enough so that, with the help of this chapter, you can bootstrap yourself to design competence.

If you're working in a multiuser situation, on the other hand, the design and creation of the database is usually the job of a specialist. This is especially true if your application is critical to the mission of your organization and involves sharing data with other users. This specialist—whose role may be called system administrator, database administrator, or MIS specialist—is qualified by his or her experience in and understanding of the local computing environment, the organization's business policies, and the rules of relational database design. A database designer who is knowledgeable about all of these factors is more likely to provide a database that is easy to use and maintain, as well as conducive to efficiency and consistency.

Even if you'll be relying on an expert for database design, this chapter will help you become a better SQL user by showing you how to analyze the relationships among the data. A grasp of relational design issues is invaluable both in learning and practicing SQL and in maintaining, updating, or querying a database that someone else has set up. Furthermore, when it comes time to ask the design guru for help, knowledge of the ground rules will make your questions and requests more intelligent.

Like the rest of *The Practical SQL Handbook*, this chapter takes the *bookbiz* database as its main example. Once you've worked your way through this chapter and have come to understand how *bookbiz* is designed, you'll need to know how to put it online with the SQL CREATE commands—a process called data definition. We discuss data definition in Chapter 3.

Other issues connected to database design and data definition include customization (setting up views tailored to each end user's needs—see Chapter 9), security (deciding who to authorize for what options on what data—see Chapter 10), and integrity (guaranteeing the consistency of related data items—mentioned here and treated in more detail in Chapters 3 and 10).

How to Approach Database Design

Discussions of database design for relational systems—this one included— often seem schizophrenic. On the one hand, you're told that the relational model makes database design intuitive and easy; on the other hand, you're told that unless your database is "simple" (whatever that is), you'll have to either refer to other sources (which sounds ominous), or let the gurus do it for you (so why bother to wade through endless explanations?).

Recognizing this confusion, relational theorist C. J. Date postulates that "database design has the property that (in simple cases at least) it is often easier just to do it than to try and articulate exactly what it was you did." In our attempt to explain exactly what to do when you design a database, we will encourage and educate your intuitive impulses, as well as briefly discuss two design aids: **normalization** and **entity-relationship modeling**.

Educating the intuition is mostly a matter of demonstrating a few mistakes that beginning designers are likely to make. Once the flaws have been pointed out, the correct structures become obvious by comparison.

As for the formal design methodologies, most experts stress that they are guidelines rather than rigid rules. The best way to describe the existence of real-world objects and the relationships among them is to some degree a subjective matter—almost as much in database design as in natural language. Often there's more than one correct solution to a design problem, and there is sometimes good reason to violate even the most basic design rule.

But this doesn't mean that the theories of database design are not useful. Even as a beginner, it's important that you understand the basics. As your experience grows, you will probably rely on the formal methodologies more and more, but don't let them tyrannize you.

Getting Started. Many discussions of relational database design focus almost entirely on how to apply the normalization rules. Basically, normalization means protecting your data integrity by avoiding duplicate data. This often results in splitting a table that initially seems to "make sense" into two or more related tables that can be "put back together" with the join operation. The technical term for this process is **non-loss decomposition**, which simply means splitting a table into several smaller tables without losing information.

The normalization guidelines are most valuable as an ex post facto check on your work: once you have a pretty good idea which columns go into which tables, you can analyze them according to the normalization rules in order to make sure you haven't committed any database design faux pas. An understanding of normalization can also guide you as you build your design, but it's not a recipe for creating a database structure from scratch.

So how do you figure out what columns go where in the first place? What *is* the recipe? The answer is that there isn't a very precise one. But you can get a good deal of help from entity-relationship modeling—analyzing the data in terms of the entities (objects or things) it describes and the relationships (one-to-one, one-to-many, or many-to-many) between those entities.

In practice, designing a database requires combining a thorough understanding of the world you're trying to model with entity-relationship modeling and normalization. Then, you examine your results and do it again. Database design is usually an iterative process, in which you keep getting closer and closer to what you want, but often move back a step or two and redo earlier work as you refine your idea of what you need.

To give you a more concrete idea, here's an example of some steps you might follow when you design a database:

1. Investigate and think about the information environment you're modeling. Where will the information come from and in what form? How will it be entered into the system and by whom? How frequently will it change? What is most critical in terms of response time and availability?

   Examine all paper and on-line files and forms that are currently used to store and track the organization's data; consider also what kind of output is needed from the database—reports, purchase orders, statistical information—and for whom. In a shared database environment, you'll need to collect information by interviewing other people in the organization, either individually or in groups. Don't forget anyone who will be involved in any way with the data—generating it, handling it, changing it, querying it, making reports from it, and so on.

2. Make a list of the entities (things that are the subjects of the database), along with their properties or attributes. The entities are likely to wind up being tables (each row describing one thing, such as a person or company or book); the properties are likely to be columns in those tables (the person's salary, the company's address, the book's price). Of course, you can list all possible attributes first and then

group them into entities, rather than starting with entities. Whichever method you choose, keep reviewing your work. Do the attributes really belong where you put them, or would they make more sense attached to a different entity? Do you need additional entities? More or different attributes?

3. As you work, find a systematic way to record the design decisions you're making, either on paper or with a text editor. Designers generally start with lists and then move to sketches of the tables and the relationships among them, called **data structure** or **entity-relationship (E-R) diagrams**.

4. Once you have made preliminary decisions about the entities and their attributes, make sure that each entity has an attribute (or group of attributes) that you can use to uniquely identify any row in the future table. This unique identifier is often called the primary key. If no natural primary key emerges, you may have to add a column to serve as a surrogate key.

5. Next, consider the relationships between the entities. Are they one-to-many (one publisher has many titles but each title has only one publisher) or many-to-many (an author can write multiple books and a book can have multiple authors)? Do you have ways to join the data in one proposed table to that in other related tables? **Foreign keys** (columns that match a primary key in a related table) serve this function.

6. After you have a draft of the database design, look at it as a whole and analyze it according to the normalization guidelines (discussed later in this chapter) to find logical errors. Correct any violations of the normal forms—or make a conscious decision to override the normalization guidelines in the interests of ease of comprehension or performance. Document the reasons for such decisions.

7. Now you're ready to put the database online and add some prototype data, using SQL for both steps. Experiment with some of the queries and reports you think you'll need. You may want to make some benchmark tests (see Chapter 10) to try out a few variations on the design.

8. Reevaluate what you've done in the light of how satisfied you are with the results.

Most of the rest of this chapter is devoted to an explanation of how we approached the design of the *bookbiz* database. This detailed, step-by-step discussion should help you understand the database design process.

The Characteristics of a Good Design

What is a good database design—a "clean" design, as the jargon has it? Broadly speaking, a good design

- Makes your interactions with the database easier to understand
- Guarantees the consistency of the database
- Paves the way for the highest performance your system can deliver

Some factors that make a database easy to understand are not technically part of database design. However, wide tables are difficult to read and understand. On the other hand, splitting data into many small tables makes it hard to see relationships. Settling on the right number of columns is a compromise between ease of comprehension and adherence to the normalization guidelines.

A well-designed database helps prevent the introduction of inconsistent information and the unintentional deletion of information. It accomplishes these ends by minimizing the unnecessary duplication of data within tables and making it possible to support referential integrity among tables. The perils of data inconsistency are explained in more detail later in this chapter.

Finally, a well-designed database is a prerequisite for satisfactory performance. Again, the number of columns in a table is important: the retrieval of data can be slower if results have to come from many tables rather than one. On the other hand, huge tables can require the system to handle more data than may be absolutely necessary to answer a particular query. In other words, the number and size of tables affect performance. (Also crucial for performance purposes are appropriate choices about which columns to index, and what kind of indexes to put on them. Indexing is a matter of physical design rather than logical database design and is discussed in Chapters 3 and 10.)

Those are some of the benefits of good database design. A bad design, on the other hand, can

- Foster misunderstandings of query results
- Increase the risk of introducing inconsistencies in the data
- Force redundant data entry
- Make life difficult if you need to change the structure of the tables that you've built and filled with data

No single solution can fully satisfy all the objectives of good design. Frequently, you juggle trade-offs, making choices based on the needs and uses of the application for which the database is being designed.

Introducing the Sample Database

The first characteristic to note about the *bookbiz* database is that it is not a real-world database, but simply a learning tool. Its primary purpose is to provide you with a small collection of interesting data to manipulate as you study SQL syntax and semantics.

The *bookbiz* database is about a fictitious publishing company that has three subsidiary publishing lines. The database stores information that editors, administrators, and executives might want about books, their authors, their editors, and the company's financial arrangements. It can produce many kinds of reports summarizing current sales, comparing different book lines, discovering which editors work with which authors, and so on. In real life, the database would probably support many other kinds of uses and many more kinds of reports.

Users of the *bookbiz* database can pose many different questions, including these:

- Which authors live in California?
- Which business books cost more than $9.95?
- Who has written the greatest number of books?
- How much do we owe the author of *Life Without Fear*?
- What's the average advance paid for all the psychology books?
- How would increasing the price of all the cookbooks by 10 percent affect royalty payments?
- How are sales of the computer subsidiary doing?

As the database designer, don't try to just imagine what questions are most important to the future users of the database you're designing. You need to research their needs by reviewing current data collection and retrieval methods and by interviewing your users individually, in groups, or both.

One important area of investigation is the organization's business rules and policies that affect the data. The policies of the publisher for which *bookbiz* is being designed include these:

- An author may have written more than one book.
- A book may have been a collaborative project of more than one author.
- The order of the authors' names on the title page is critical information, as is the percentage of the royalties each will collect.
- An editor may be working on more than one book, and a single book may be assigned more than one editor.
- A sales order may be for one or many titles.

DATA ENTITIES AND RELATIONSHIPS

We begin the consideration of designing *bookbiz* with a somewhat simplified version of entity-relationship modeling. At the most basic level,
entity-relationship modeling (also called entity modeling) means identifying

- The things—entities—about which information will be stored in the
  database system
- The properties of these things
- The relationships among them

Entities: Things with an Independent Existence

Let's start by considering the entities that make up a subset of the *bookbiz*
database. If we ignore for the moment most of the financial information
that *bookbiz* tracks, a preliminary list of entities might look like this:

- The authors who have written books published by the company
- The books themselves
- The editors working for the company
- The subsidiary publishing houses owned by the company

Each item in this list is an entity with an independent existence in the
world under consideration—the world of the *bookbiz* database. Each is represented in the database by a table. (Other kinds of data elements are also
represented by tables, but that's jumping ahead of the story.)

Each of these entity types has certain properties that are to be recorded
in the database. Among the properties are

```
book's name
book's price
book's publication date
author's name
author's address
author's telephone number
editor's name
editor's address
editor's phone number
publisher's name
publisher's address
```

Each item in this list refers to one property or attribute of the entity in question (the author, book, editor, or publishing subsidiary); each is a potential column in the database. Column names should be selected for clarity (to describe the kinds of values the column names) and brevity (to minimize both typing and the width of displays).

The list of entities and their properties we've identified might be taken as a first tentative step in deciding on the tables and columns to be included in the database. You might sketch these decisions like this:

```
titles table
name                  price                      pubdate
---------------       ---------------------      -----------

authors table
name                  address          phone
---------------       --------------   -----------

editors table
name                  address          phone
---------------       --------------   -----------

publishers table
name                  address
---------------       --------------
```

Another way to view the information is in an entity-relationship diagram, as shown in Figure 2-1. The usual convention is to display each table as a box, with columns listed inside.

This sketch of four tables, each with several columns, is a first stab at the structure of the database; you can imagine that the tables will contain multiple rows of data. Each row in a table represents an **occurrence** (or **instance**) of the entity—a single book, author, editor, or publishing company.

One of the jobs of the database design is to provide a way to distinguish among entity occurrences, so that the system can retrieve a particular row. As you might have guessed, rows (representing occurrences of entities) are distinguished from each other by the values of the table's primary key. In fact, the (informal) definition of a primary key is the column or combination of columns that uniquely identifies the row.

Primary Keys. What is the primary key for each of these tables? Consider the *authors* table. Of the columns identified so far, *name* is the obvious

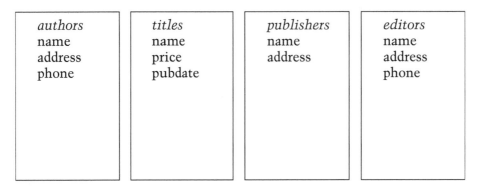

Figure 2–1. A Preliminary *bookbiz* Sketch

candidate for the primary key: an author's name distinguishes him or her from other authors. But the *name* column is problematic as a primary key for several reasons. First, the value in *name* is made up of the author's first name and last name. Combining first and last names is usually a bad idea, if only because it would be difficult (in many systems, impossible) to sort authors alphabetically by last name. So the first necessary change is to split the *name* column (in both *authors* and *editors*) into two columns (see Figure 2-2).

Now, getting back to the question of identifying the primary key of the *authors* table, it might seem as though the combination of the columns *au_lname* and *au_fname* is the right choice. In fact, that combination would work pretty well—until the table grew large enough to contain dupli-

authors	*titles*	*publishers*	*editors*
au_lname	name	name	**ed_lname**
au_fname	price	address	**ed_fname**
address	pubdate		address
phone			phone

Figure 2–2. Splitting the Authors' and Editors' Names into Two Columns

cate names. Once there are two Mary Smiths, for example, the *au_lname-au_fname* combination would no longer uniquely identify each author.

Another problem with using values like names as unique identifiers is the frequency with which they are entered incorrectly. It's easy to misspell names: imagine a data entry clerk on the phone entering a new record about Anne Ringer—or is it Ann Ringer? Other kinds of proper names, like names of companies or organizations, are even worse. How many variations might there be on the name of the phone company, for example: AT&T, A.T. and T., Ma Bell, and so on. To a computer, these are all different companies.

For these reasons, it's usually a good idea to create a separate column explicitly designed to serve as the primary key. Real-world examples of such unique identifiers are common: Social Security numbers, employee identification numbers, license plate numbers, purchase order numbers, student identification numbers, airline flight numbers, and so on.

In the *authors* and *editors* tables, we'll use Social Security numbers. For the *titles* and *publishers* tables, we'll arbitrarily assign some identifying codes. As a recordkeeping convention, we'll underline these columns to show they are primary keys (see Figure 2-3).

Choosing and setting up the column(s) for a table's primary key is one of the crucial steps in database design. Despite the importance of primary keys, early versions of SQL had no syntax for designating them. The 1992 ANSI standard for SQL, now adopted by most vendors, supports the PRIMARY KEY clause in the CREATE TABLE statement (see Chapter 3 for details). Vendors have also developed their own implementation-specific methods of dealing with this important concept.

authors	*titles*	*publishers*	*editors*
au_id	**title_id**	**pub_id**	**ed_id**
au_lname	name	name	ed_lname
au_fname	price	address	ed_fname
address	pubdate		address
phone			phone

Figure 2–3. Defining Primary Keys

One-to-Many Relationships

At this point we have structures for four tables in the *bookbiz* database: *authors*, *titles*, *editors*, and *publishers*. Some of the properties of each of the entities described by the tables have been specified, and a primary key has been identified for each table.

However, you may have noticed that certain important relationships among the data are not yet represented in the proposed design. For example, there's nothing in these four tables that tells you about the connection between a particular publisher and the books it puts out.

The relationship between publishers and books can be described as **one-to-many**: each book has only one publisher, while each publisher can produce many books. One-to-many relationships among data are often written as *1-to-N* or *1:N*.

How can you represent this one-to-many relationship? In the *bookbiz* database, a first impulse might be to add a column for *title_id* in the *publishers* table, as shown in Figure 2-4.

The *title_id* column in the *publishers* table is a foreign key. You can use it to point to specific rows in the *titles* table and join title and publisher information. Unfortunately, this proposed solution sends your database design off in the wrong direction. Remember the data relationship we're modeling—one publisher, many books—and consider what happens whenever a new book is published. You'll add a new row to *titles*, with book name, price, and so on.

```
title_id title                                price  date
-------- ----------------------------------   -----  -------
BU2075   You Can Combat Computer Stress!      2.99   6/30/85
```

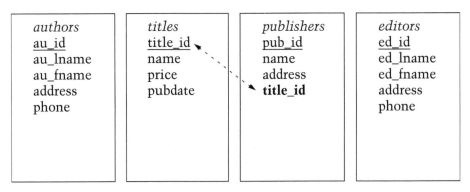

Figure 2-4. Adding a Foreign Key

For each row in *titles*, you'll have to add a row to *publishers*. The *publishers* row will repeat three columns of existing information (publisher number, name, and address) and add one column of new information (*title_id*) to point to the fuller description in the *titles* table.

```
pub_id pub_name          address               title_id
------ ----------------  --------------------- --------
0736   New Age Books     1 1st St Boston MA     BU2075
```

Recall that one of the goals of database design is to control redundancy, because redundancy introduces opportunities for error. A better solution is to add a *publishers* foreign key to the *titles* table (see Figure 2-5).

When a new book comes out, you add a row (with a *pub_id* column) to the *titles* table—you don't need to do anything to the *publishers* table unless the company takes on a new subsidiary.

```
title_id title                             price date    pub_id
-------- -------------------------------   ----- ------- ------
BU2075   You Can Combat Computer Stress! 2.99  6/30/85 0736
```

With these changes a structure begins to emerge:

- The *publishers* table has one row for each publisher.
- The *titles* table has one row for each book.
- Publisher ID numbers are repeated in the *titles* table because there are many books for each publisher—but that's far less redundancy than would occur with other options.

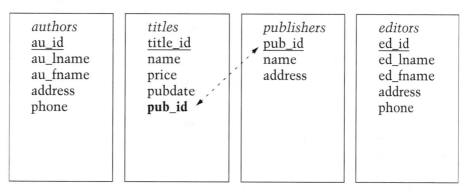

Figure 2-5. Changing the Foreign Key

You can use the logical connection between the *pub_id* columns in *titles* and *publishers* for joining the two tables. *In other words, this design is planned with the join operation in mind, to allow users to retrieve information about publishers and titles in one query.*

In the *publishers* table, *pub_id* is the primary key. In the *titles* table, the *pub_id* column is a foreign key. The relational model requires that one-to-many relationships be represented by means of primary key–foreign key pairings.

Foreign Keys. Like the concept of primary key, the concept of foreign key is crucial in database design. Informally, a foreign key is a column (or combination of columns) in one table whose values match those of the primary key in some other table.

A consideration of the logical relationship between the information in the primary and foreign key columns introduces some further questions. What happens in the *pub_id* column of the *titles* table if the row describing the publisher is deleted from or changed in the *publishers* table? Should the description of a book be allowed to refer to a publisher ID number if that publisher no longer exists in the database? It doesn't make sense logically, and it violates the definition of a foreign key, which requires the value in a foreign key column(s) to match the value in a primary key column somewhere in the database.

A complete database design should include planning for primary key/ foreign key consistency (or referential integrity). For example:

- When a publisher's ID number is updated in or deleted from the *publishers* table, the system should automatically reproduce the change in the *titles* table, either by updating all corresponding values in the *titles* table *pub_id* column or by cascading (propagating) the *publishers* delete to *titles* rows with matching *pub_id*s.
- When a new title is added, the system should have a way of verifying that the associated *pub_id* is valid (that is, that it exists in the *publishers* table).

At this point, just make a note of these issues. The next chapter gives hints on how to handle some primary key–foreign key issues with the REFERENCES constraints in the CREATE TABLE statement. Vendors also have introduced implementation-specific ways to control integrity, such as SQL extensions for procedural code that can be executed in the database (often called procedures or triggers; discussed in Chapter 10).

Many-to-Many Relationships

After identifying all the one-to-many relationships in the *bookbiz* database, and associating them with primary key–foreign key pairings, the next step is to consider other kinds of data relationships. For example, how are authors and books related?

Some books are written by more than one author, and some authors have written more than one book. In other words, authors and books have a **many-to-many** relationship (often written as *N-to-N*, or *N:N*, and sometimes called an **association**). According to entity-relationship theory, associations in relational databases are represented as tables of their own. In other words, the *bookbiz* database needs a table for authors, a table for titles, and a table to represent the association between them, as shown in Figure 2-6.

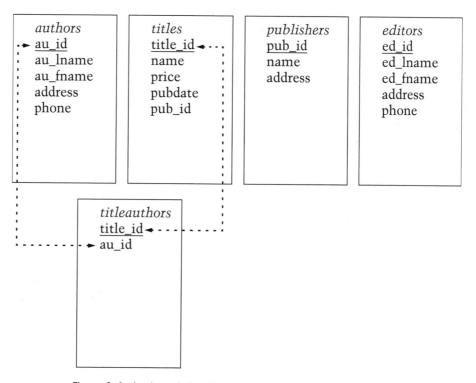

Figure 2–6. An Associating Table in a Many-to-Many Relationship

The *titleauthors* table represents the many-to-many relationship between authors and books. It is a base table just like *titles* and *authors*, but it is an association rather than an independent entity. When a user of the *bookbiz* database wants information about who wrote which books, he or she writes a join query that uses the *titleauthors* table as a connecting table between *titles* and *authors*.

The *titleauthors* and *titles* tables join on their respective *title_id* columns; *titleauthors* and *authors* join on each table's *au_id* column. In other words, *title_id* in *titleauthors* is a foreign key whose matching primary key is *title_id* in *titles*; *au_id* in *titleauthors* is the foreign key whose matching primary key is *au_id* in *authors*. The general principle, as stated by C. J. Date, is that "in the relational model, participants in an association are identified by foreign keys with the table representing that association."

What is the primary key in *titleauthors*? Neither the author ID nor the title ID uniquely identifies rows in *titleauthors*: the IDs of titles with more than one author are repeated, as are the IDs of authors who have written more than one book. However, each title ID–author ID combination *is* unique. As Date puts it, "For a given association, it will often be the case that the combination of all foreign keys for participants in that association will have the uniqueness property." The primary key of *titleauthors*, then, is the combination of *title_id* and *au_id*.

The *editors* and *titles* tables have a similar relationship. An editor can work on more than one book, and a book can have multiple editors. This many-to-many relationship also calls for a connecting table.

One-to-One Relationships

Take a final look at the entities. If you find a one-to-one (1:1) relationship between two tables, you might be better off collapsing them into one table. The main reason for 1:1 relationships is speed in queries. For example, if you have information about titles that you seldom use (notes on copyright information, lists of change pages), you might want to keep it in a separate table so that you don't have to access the information when running common queries. Generally speaking, you should avoid 1:1 structures when you first design a database unless you know your data very well.

The Entity-Relationship Approach Summarized

Entity-relationship modeling is much larger, more precise, and more detailed than the procedures discussed so briefly here indicate. However, the approach just outlined can help you design a good database that checks out against the next design methodology to be considered, the normalization rules. Before we turn to that topic, here is a review list of the basic steps discussed so far:

1. Represent each independent entity (book, author, publisher, editor, employee, department, student, course, company, and so on) as a base table.

2. Represent each property of an entity (author's address, book's price, and so on) as a column of the entity's table.

3. Make sure each table has a primary key. The key may be an existing property (a name) or an artificial one that you add (a Social Security number, an order number), or a combination of two or more properties. At any rate, it must uniquely describe each row.

4. Locate one-to-many relationships between tables. Check that there is a foreign key column(s) in the "many" table pointing to the primary key column(s) in the "one" table. Consider the referential integrity constraints associated with each foreign key.

5. Represent each many-to-many relationship (or association) as a "connecting table" between the two tables that participate in the association. Include in this connecting table foreign keys that point to the entity tables. The primary key of the connecting table is often the combination of those foreign keys.

After each pass, look at your needs again. Have you incorporated the business rules? Can you get the information you need? Such a check against the *bookbiz* requirements reveals a few shortcomings: There's no way to record author order or royalty split. There's also no notation for contracts, and you need to keep track of advances. Sales are another topic not covered in this design. With these points in mind, you might modify the E-R diagram as in Figure 2-7, using arrows to show the relationships between tables:

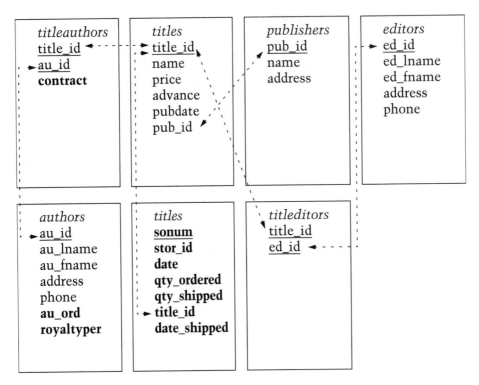

Figure 2–7. A Fuller E-R Diagram

THE NORMALIZATION GUIDELINES

Basically, the normalization guidelines are a set of data design standards called the **normal forms**. Five normal forms are widely accepted, although many more than that have been proposed. Making your tables match these standards is called normalization.

The normal forms progress in order from first through fifth. Each form implies that the requirements of the previous forms have been met. If you follow normalization rule number one, your data will be in first normal form. If you follow normalization rule number three, your data will be in third normal form (and also in first and second normal form).

Following the normalization guidelines usually means splitting tables into two or more tables with fewer columns, designing primary key–foreign key relationships into the new, smaller tables so that they can be reconnected with the join operation.

One of the main advantages of splitting tables according to the normalization guidelines is the reduction of data redundancy within tables. This may seem confusing when the existence of matching primary key–foreign key hooks means that these columns are duplicated. But *intentional duplication* is not the same thing as redundancy. In fact, the maintenance of intentional duplication (that is, consistency) between primary and foreign keys is a major point of referential integrity.

The normalization guidelines, like entity-relationship modeling, were developed as part of the academic work on database theory. While they are extremely useful, they can be followed too slavishly. Most database designers find that putting their data in third or fourth normal form is usually as far as they need to go.

First Normal Form

First normal form requires that at each row-and-column intersection, there must be one and only one value, and that value must be atomic: there can be no repeating groups in a table that satisfies first normal form.

This reveals a problem with the new *sales* table. How will you handle a single sales order that includes multiple books, as shown in Figure 2-8?

```
                    Bookbiz Sales Order Form

   Order # 14   Store 7131   Date: 5/29/87

   Item #  Title   # Ordered  # Shipped   Ship date
   -------------------------------------------------------
   1.      PS1372      20         20       May 29 1987
   2.      PS2106      25         25       Apr 29 1987
   3.      PS3333      15         10       May 29 1987
   4.      PS7777      25         25       Jun 13 1987
   5.
   6.
```

Figure 2–8. A Bookbiz Sales Order Form

sonum	stor_id	date	title_id			
13	7066	5/24/87	PC8888			
14	7131	5/29/87	PS1372	PS2106	PS3333	PS7777
15	7067	6/15/87	TC3218	TC4203	TC7777	

Not a rectangle-shaped table

Figure 2-9. Tables Must Be Rectangular

You can't record multiple *title_id*s in one field—that would violate first normal form. Adding columns like *title1*, *title2* is just a disguise for repeating groups, and leaves you with the same problems. It's not a great solution practically speaking, either; as soon as a sales order includes a third book, you'll have to restructure the table again, adding a *title3* column. Since all data must be represented in regular rectangular tables, multiple entries just don't fit the model, as shown in Figure 2-9.

Where there are repeating columns, the correct design involves a **master table** (*sales*) for the sales order as a whole and a **detail table** (*salesdetails*) to hold information for individual order lines in the sales order (Figure 2-10). Notice that entity-relationship principles would have led to the same conclusion, since this is a one-to-many structure (one sales order, many lines).

While you're looking at repeating fields, make a note to break up any compound columns into their elements: *address* needs to have separate columns for *city* and *state*, for example.

Second Normal Form

The second normalization rule states that *every nonkey column must depend on the entire primary key*. Therefore, a table must not contain a nonkey column that pertains to only part of a composite primary key. Putting a table into second normal form requires making sure that all the non–primary key columns (the columns that give information about the subject but do not uniquely define it) relate to the entire primary key and not just to one of its components.

To illustrate, look at the *contract* column in the *titleauthors* table. Does it apply to each author-title combination? If each author on a book has a separate contract, it does, but if the company signs contracts only when all authors are in agreement, it doesn't.

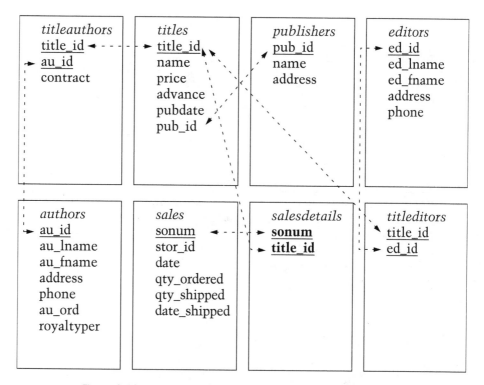

Figure 2-10. Breaking the *sales* Table into *sales* and *salesdetails*

In this case, your legal division informs you that a contract is about a book, not about each individual author, and you move the column to the *titles* table (Figure 2-11). This illustrates why database design is tricky: your decisions often depend on the particular business model your company uses.

In sum, second normal form requires that *no nonkey column be a fact about a subset of the primary key*. It applies when the primary key is made up of more than one column, and is irrelevant when the primary key is one column only.

Third Normal Form

Third normal form applies the principle addressed by second normal form in a more general way: it's not limited to *composite* primary keys. Third normal form requires that *no nonkey column depend on another nonkey column*. Each nonkey column must be a fact about the primary key column.

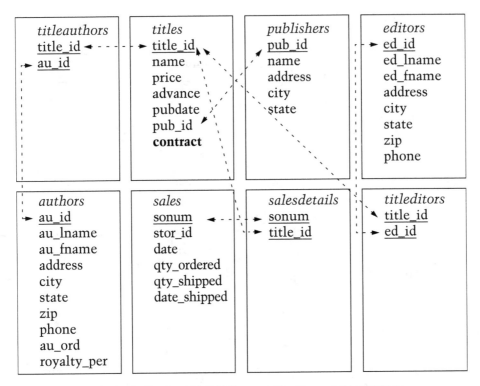

Figure 2–11. The *bookbiz* E-R Diagram after Second Normal Form

In the *authors* table, the primary key is *au_id*. When you check each column, you find that *au_ord* (the position of an author's name on a multi-author book) is not about an individual author (*au_id*), because an author may have several books and occupy a different position on each (first, second, or third author). Author order really concerns each author-title relationship. The same is true of *royaltyper*. Both of these columns belong in the *titleauthors* table.

The *qty_ordered* and *qty_shipped* columns in the *sales* table also illustrate this principle. They concern individual line items, not the whole sales order, and should be moved to the *salesdetails* table. The *date_shipped* column is more of a puzzle:

- If orders are shipped only when all line items are ready, *date_shipped* applies to the order as a whole, and should go in the *sales* table.
- If items are shipped as they become available, the column belongs in the *salesdetails* table.

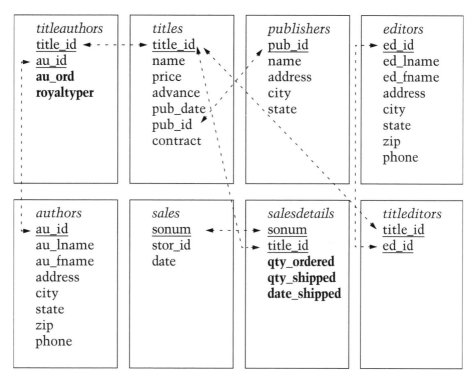

Figure 2–12. The *bookbiz* E-R Diagram after Third Normal Form

Since books are often out of print or otherwise unavailable, we'll assume the second model. The revised diagram is shown in Figure 2-12.

Analyzing the structures of these tables, you'll see that they satisfy both second and third normal forms. They satisfy second normal form because every nonkey column is a fact about the entire primary key. They satisfy third normal form because no nonkey column is a fact about another non-key column. To summarize, in William Kent's memorable phrase: Every nonkey column provides a fact about the key, the whole key, and nothing but the key.

Fourth and Fifth Normal Forms

Fourth normal form forbids independent one-to-many relationships between primary key columns and nonkey columns. We'll use a rather unlikely example as an illustration: one author can have many cars and many pets, but there is no connection between cars and pets even though each is legitimately related to a particular author.

```
au_lname    car                          pet
----------  ---------------------------  --------
Ringer      1987 Chevy Nova              Rover
Ringer      1994 Volvo Station Wagon
Bennet      1990 VW Rabbit               Spot
Green                                    Valiant
Green       1989 Toyota Corolla          Fluffy
Green                                    Sam
```

Putting these two different kinds of information in the same table can lead to unsightly blanks where there are more pets than cars (as in Green's case) or more cars than pets (as in Ringer's case). Deleting a car or a pet (if a car dies or a pet moves to another home) could also cause blanks in rows.

The problem here is with the spurious relationship that seems to exist between cars and pets by virtue of their positional association in the row. It is better to put each of these entities in a separate table and to record their relationship to an author by using the author ID as a foreign key column. For example:

```
car                          au_id
---------------------------  -----------
1987 Chevy Nova              998-72-3567
1994 Volvo Station Wagon     998-72-3567
1990 VW Rabbit               409-56-7008
1989 Toyota Corolla          213-46-8915


pet      au_id
-------  --------------------
Rover    998-72-3567
Spot     409-56-7008
Valiant  213-46-8915
Fluffy   213-46-8915
Sam      213-46-8915
```

Fifth normal form takes the process to its logical end, *breaking tables into the smallest possible pieces in order to eliminate all redundancy within a table*. Tables normalized to this extent consist of little more than the primary key. Here's an example:

```
titles table
title_id    title

authors table
au_id       au_lname    au_fname

authors&titles table
au_id       title_id

prices table
title_id    price

advances table
title_id    advance

pets table
pet         au_id
```

One advantage of putting a database into fifth normal form is control of database integrity. Since you are assured that each piece of nonkey data (data that is not a primary key or a foreign key) is likely to occur only once in the database, it's relatively easy to update that kind of data without worrying about keeping all the duplicates up-to-date. If a book's price changes, for example, you make an entry in the *prices* table only. You don't have to scan the other tables to see if the price appears there.

However, since each table has so few columns, you have to repeat the same keys over and over in order to be able to join the tables and get meaningful information out of them. Changing the value of a single key (a particular *title_id*, for example) is a consistency problem of a different order. You still have to identify every place where that value exists and make sure it gets updated. Fortunately, the values in primary key columns tend to change much less frequently than those in nonkey, dependent columns.

The moral is moderation: strive to reach a balance between redundant data and redundant keys.

REVIEWING THE DATABASE

Let's review the process by which the design of the *bookbiz* database was developed. We started by proposing four tables: *authors*, *titles*, *publishers*, and *editors*. It seems intuitive to design a table for each of these things; the entity-relationship approach states explicitly that each independent entity be represented by a base table. Entity-relationship theory also called for two more base tables—one to model the association among *titles* and *authors* (*titleauthors*), and one for the association among *titles* and *editors* (*title-ditors*). We later added the *sales* and *salesdetails* tables.

That leaves only one *bookbiz* table undescribed: the *roysched* table, which lists the royalty rate to which authors are entitled as a function of the starting rate and the number of books sold. The *roysched* table is a **lookup table** used primarily for reference purposes. Its data will not change unless the royalty schedule itself changes—which would happen only if an author's contract were to be renegotiated or a new title added.

That makes nine tables in all.

Before we go into more detail about the full *bookbiz* database, take a look at the final data structure diagram (Figure 2-13). Each box in the diagram represents a table, with its name and the names of its columns inside it. The lines connecting the boxes represent relationships among the tables, showing the anticipated joins between them. (Other joins are also possible—these are just the explicitly planned ones.)

The *N* and *1* on either end of the line between *titles* and *publishers* indicate a many-to-one relationship between the tables. There can be many titles to one publisher but there can't be many publishers to one title.

Summarizing the *bookbiz* Database

Now let's take a closer look at the nine tables in the *bookbiz* database, to better familiarize you with the material on which the examples in the rest of *The Practical SQL Handbook* are based.

The *bookbiz* database keeps track of the activities of three subsidiary publishing companies. Since the fiscal arrangements of the subsidiaries are not independent, the parent publisher has chosen to maintain a single database.

The *publishers* table contains information about the three publishing lines: their identification numbers, names, and addresses.

For each author under contract with any of the publishers, the *authors* table contains an identification number (Social Security number), first and last name, and address information. The *editors* table contains similar information about each editor, with the addition of a position column that describes the type of work the editor does (acquisitions or project management).

For each book that has been or is about to be published, the *titles* table contains an identification number, name, type, publisher identification number, price, advance, year-to-date sales, contract status, comments, and

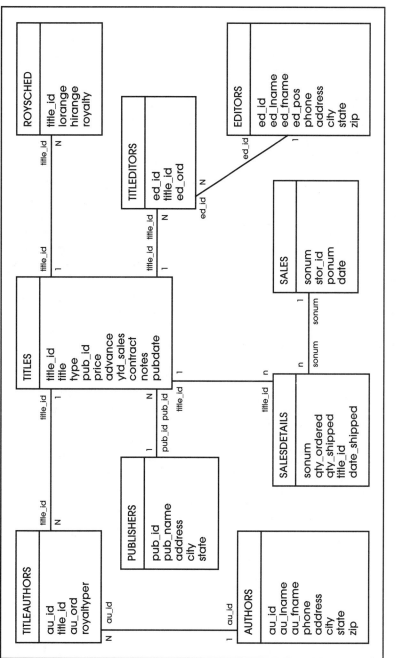

Figure 2-13. The Data Structure Diagram for the Sample Database *bookbiz*

publication date. The numbers in the *ytd_sales* column, which will change as more books are sold, might be kept current in one of several ways:

- By making periodic entries using the data modification commands
- By coding logic into an application program that automatically updates *ytd_sales* whenever a sale is entered into the *salesdetails* table
- By using SQL to define a **trigger** that accomplishes the same automatic updating (Triggers, not covered in the 1992 ISO-ANSI SQL standard, are provided as extensions by a number of relational database management systems. See Chapter 10.)

The titles and authors are represented in separate tables that can be linked with a third table, the *titleauthors* table. For each book, *titleauthors* contains a row for every author involved, with information on the title ID, the author ID, the author cover credit order (which name comes first), and the royalty split among the authors of a book. The *titleditors* table similarly links the titles and their editors. Instead of cover credit order, it lists editing order, so that it's possible to find who was the first or last editor.

The *roysched* table lists the unit sales ranges and the royalty connected with each range. The royalty is some percentage of the net receipts from sales. The percentage is used to calculate the amount due each author based on sales of his or her book.

The *sales* table has top-level information about each purchase order received from bookstores: sales order number (assigned by the publisher), store identification, purchase order number (assigned by the store), and date. The *salesdetails* table contains information about each line in the purchase order (assuming any purchase order may involve more than one book): title, quantity ordered, quantity shipped, and date shipped.

Of course, a real publisher's database would be much more complex, with tables for stores, employees, distributors, production costs, vendors, subcontractors, and the like. (As an exercise, you might try sketching some of these tables and deciding how they would relate to the tables already in *bookbiz*.) However, these nine tables do present enough material to work with for learning SQL, and they are used throughout this book.

Testing Your Database Design

Once you've come up with a proposed design for your database, you should create the tables and insert some data. (The next chapter gives detailed information on these procedures.) Then you should test your design by running queries and updating the data. Your tests may reveal oversights in the design.

Database designs are seldom satisfactory when based entirely on theory. It's essential to play with your design interactively before undertaking serious production efforts—especially if you plan to use it in an application that will involve thousands of lines of programming code and tens of thousands of rows of data. Don't wait until you've invested hundreds of hours in a flawed design. You can avoid problems by working interactively with a prototype of the database.

Other Database Definition Considerations

If you were about to put a real-world database online, you'd have several additional critical issues to consider before proceeding: indexing, security, and integrity.

Deciding which columns to index, and what kind of index is best for each column, is an important part of database implementation, and is covered in Chapter 3.

Security is discussed in Chapter 10.

Planning for data integrity is a major part of database design. It involves setting up a system to make sure changes to one piece of data apply to all copies of that data anywhere in the database, so that you won't end up with orphans or inaccuracies. An example using *bookbiz* might be discovering that an author's ID number was incorrect. If you changed it in the *authors* table only, you'd never again be able to find out what books that author had written, because that author's ID number in *titleauthors* would no longer match the ID number in *authors*. In order to access the information in *titleauthors*, you'd have to make sure that when the author ID changed in *authors*, it also changed in *titleauthors*.

We'll assume you've considered these issues as you developed your design and made some mental notes. You'll learn how to implement SQL 92 referential constraints in the next chapter. Other integrity issues, not yet supported by all vendors, are deferred to Chapter 10.

IMPLEMENTING THE DESIGN

Now that you understand the logical design of the *bookbiz* database, you're ready to see how the normalized E-R diagram gets translated in SQL commands.

Chapter 3

Creating and Filling a Database

CREATING DATABASES AND OBJECTS WITH SQL

Once you've designed your database on paper, as discussed in the previous chapter, you're ready to put it on line. Using the SQL CREATE commands, you can tell your relational database management system the name, structure, and other characteristics of your database and database objects. You add data to the database with the INSERT command.

If you use the runtime Sybase SQL Anywhere compact disc distributed with this book, you won't need to type the CREATE or INSERT commands: The *bookbiz* database has already been set up for you. Just load the program on your PC. The SQL Anywhere software on the CD gives you full query capabilities. The only limitations are on creating new objects or changing existing data (it's essentially a read-only version).

The CD also contains the script (set of SQL commands) used to create the *bookbiz* database and its data. You can use this script if you prefer to put the *bookbiz* database on your own database management system or on a full-strength version of SQL Anywhere. You may have to edit the script to conform to the rules of your particular SQL dialect.

The complete structure of *bookbiz* and statements for entering all of its data are in Appendix D.

SQL SYNTAX

This is the first chapter for which you'll actually be sitting at a terminal and typing commands, so now is the time to get familiar with the conventions used in this book to represent SQL examples and syntax.

An example is a SQL command that you might actually type, just as it appears (Figure 3-1).

```
select pub_id, pub_name, address, city, state
from publishers
where pub_id = '0736'
```

All words are in
lowercase letters.

Figure 3–1. An Example of an Example

A syntax statement is more like a template that tells you exactly what is required (and what's permitted) for the command in question (Figure 3-2).

Because a lot of information is packed into each syntax statement, it often helps to compare syntax statements to associated SQL examples.

Here are the conventions we use in this book for SQL syntax:

- Although SQL is a **free-form language**, meaning that there are no requirements for how many words you put on a line or where you break a line, the examples and syntax in this book are usually formatted so that each clause of a statement begins on a new line. Long or complex clauses extend to additional lines; these lines are indented.
- For syntax statements, words or phrases the user should supply are always in lowercase letters. In Figure 3-2, select_list, table_list, and WHERE conditions are placeholders for values (constants, expressions, and **identifiers**—names of databases, tables, or other database objects) you supply when you submit a command to SQL. Check your system documentation for rules on identifiers: minimum and maximum length, characters that cannot be used (often blanks and periods), and whether case is significant (the *AUTHORS* table is usually not the same as the *authors* table).
- SQL keywords in syntax statements are always shown in uppercase letters, though in most versions of SQL, you may type them (unlike

Keywords (words with special meaning to SQL) are in uppercase letters.

```
SELECT select_list
FROM table_list
WHERE conditions
```

Placeholders for words you
supply are in lowercase letters.

Figure 3–2. An Example of a Syntax Statement

identifiers) in any case. The keywords in the syntax example (Figure 3-2) are SELECT, FROM, and WHERE; the ability to type them in any case means that "SELECT" is the same as "select" is the same as "SeLeCt".

- Curly braces ({}) around words or phrases mean that you *must* choose at least one of the enclosed options. If the options are separated by vertical bars (|), you must pick only one, but if they are separated by commas (,), you must pick one and you may pick more.
- Square brackets ([]) mean using an option is . . . optional. If the options are separated by vertical bars (|), you can pick none or one, but if they are separated by commas (,), you can pick none, one, or more. Figure 3-3 shows how braces, brackets, bars, and commas work together.

The braces and brackets are not part of the statement, so don't type them when you enter a SQL command. If you choose more than one option, separate your choices with commas. Ellipses (...) mean that you can repeat the last unit as many times as you like.

Here's a (non-SQL!) example of how these elements might be used in syntax:

```
BUY thing_name = price AS {cash | check | credit}
    [, thing_name = price AS {cash | check | credit} ]...
```

In this invented syntax statement, "BUY" and "AS" are required keywords. The items inside braces and separated by vertical bars indicate that you must choose one (and only one) of the methods of payment. You may also choose to buy additional things—as many of them as you like. For each thing you buy, give its name, its price, and a method of payment. Here's

`{early_lunch	no_lunch}`	You **must** choose **one**
`{soup , salad , sandwich}`	You **must** choose **one or more**
`[dessert]`	You **don't have to** choose it
`[coffee	soda	wine]`	You **may** choose **none or one**
`[tomato , pickle , onion]`	You **may** choose **none, one, or several**

Figure 3–3. The Meaning of Brackets, Braces, Vertical Bars, and Commas in Syntax Statements

how you'd translate the syntax into a real-life example involving lunch and a book:

```
buy lunch = 4.95 as cash, book = 34.95 as check
```

When you see parentheses (( )) in syntax, they are actually part of what you type (unlike brackets and braces). Don't forget them.

A SQL statement generally requires a **terminator**, which sends the SQL command to the database management system for processing. Different SQL dialects use different terminators; common terminators include the semicolon (;) and the word "go." Database systems with graphical user interfaces (or GUIs, pronounced "gooeys") allow you to click a button or choose a menu option. Since the possibilities vary, we generally have not included terminators in the examples or syntax.

Coping with Failure

Errors in SQL statements occur for many reasons. Among the most common are typing mistakes, syntax errors, failing to include character data in quotes, and using an incorrect object name. Figure 3-4 illustrates these mistakes.

```
slect name                          Type select, not slect;
from authers                        authors, not authers.


select name, phone
where state = 'CA'                  The FROM clause should
from authors                        precede the WHERE clause.


select name
from authors
where state = CA                    'CA' should be in quotes.


select title
from documents                      The name of the table is titles.
```

Figure 3–4. Common Errors in SQL Statements

When you type a statement that your version of SQL does not understand, the command will not be executed. Instead, the system will display some sort of error message on your screen, the helpfulness of which varies a great deal from system to system (and even within systems). A good error message tells you as much as possible about where you went wrong, including the type of error that has been detected and the line on which the mistake is located.

Here are a couple of examples from SQL Anywhere:

```
SQL:
select *
from pulbihsers

Results:
table pulbihsers not found

SQL:
slect *
from publishers

Results:
syntax error near '*'
```

After looking at the message, you can correct the error and resubmit your SQL statement. (Error messages in other versions of SQL may look quite different.)

CREATING DATABASES

A database is a named allocation of storage space that will contain tables, views, indexes, and other database objects. You begin by creating the database; then you create each of the objects in it.

Since a significant amount of storage space may have to be set aside for each new database (even if the database will never contain much data), permission to create databases is often jealously guarded in multiuser environments. If this is the case in your situation, you won't have to learn about the SQL command to create a database—you can go on to the sections that discuss creating database objects. However, you will have to ask your system administrator to issue the command to create a database for you. Let the system administrator know that your database will be a small one used for learning purposes, and won't require much storage space.

In a single-user system, it's up to you to be aware of your storage needs and capacities. You'll usually have to rely on operating system facilities for determining them.

In most multiuser versions of SQL, each database is controlled or owned by a specified user, charged with certain responsibilities and bestowed certain rights. These rights and responsibilities vary widely among database management systems, but often include

- Setting up permissions for other users within the database
- Making backup copies of the database on a regular basis and running the recovery procedures in case of system failure
- Enlarging the database if more space becomes necessary
- Owning most of the production database objects
- Understanding the kind of data that is in the database and how it is used

Typically, a database is owned by the user who created it. But since the system administrator often maintains a monopoly on database creation, some relational database management systems provide a facility that allows the system administrator to transfer ownership to other users.

Depending on both the database software and the hardware you're using, databases may be physically stored on disks, on disk partitions, or in operating system files. We use the generic term **database device** for all of these possibilities.

In most database system installations, only the system administrator worries about physical storage. Users who will be issuing the SQL commands to create databases often do so according to instructions from the system administrator.

The 1992 SQL ANSI standard (often called SQL-92) does not include a CREATE DATABASE statement. Instead, it provides a CREATE SCHEMA command for defining the portion of a database that a specific user owns. Typically, a database consists of more than one **schema**.

Commercial versions of SQL, however, generally have a CREATE DATABASE command. In its most vanilla form (that is, without any optional clauses and extensions), its syntax looks like this:

```
CREATE DATABASE database_name
```

To create the *bookbiz* database on a system that supports the comma, type this command:

```
SQL:
create database bookbiz
```

(SQL Anywhere uses an initialization utility rather than the *Create Database* command.)

Depending on the implementation, the syntax may include other clauses that let you (or the system administrator) control the location of the database (the database device on which the database will be physically stored) and its size (how much device space the database can use before the system stops it), and other options. The full syntax for the Sybase System 11 SQL Server CREATE DATABASE command, for example, looks like this:

```
CREATE DATABASE database_name
[ON {DEFAULT | device_name } [= SIZE]
  [, device_name [= SIZE]]...]
[LOG ON database_device [= SIZE]
[, database_device [= SIZE]]...]
[WITH OVERRIDE]
[FOR LOAD]
```

To get an idea of the range of possibilities among commercial systems, check Appendix B. It lists, by vendor, syntax statements for many of the commands in this book.

Choosing a Database

Creating a database does not usually imply using it. Depending on the version of SQL you're using, you may have to type a command like one of the following after you create a database (but before you create any of its objects):

```
USE database_name
```

or

```
DATABASE database_name
```

You may also be able to use a CONNECT command or a graphical user interface to choose the database you want to use. Check your system documentation for specifics.

CREATING TABLES

Once you've created a database and moved to it, you can begin creating tables.

Tables are the basic building blocks of any database. They hold the rows and columns of your data. With SQL's data definition commands, you can create tables, drop tables, and alter them (add, remove, rearrange, or change the characteristics of columns).

In most SQL implementations, the user who creates a table is its owner, and is responsible for granting permissions for its use to other users. When you create a table with SQL, you do at least the following:

- Name it
- Name the columns it contains
- Specify the datatype of each column
- Specify (or accept the default) null status of each column—whether that column permits or forbids null values

The *bookbiz* database, for maximum flexibility, uses only these basic elements in table definitions. However, many vendors have accepted additional possibilities for the CREATE TABLE statement supported in SQL-92, including

- Defaults (values assumed when you don't explicitly enter anything, like today's date on a sales order)
- Constraints that check (limit) the possible values you can enter for a column (for example, *pub_id*s can be 0736, 0877, or 1389 only)
- Constraints defining a column as a primary key, unique, or both
- Constraints setting up reference checks among primary and foreign keys

We'll start with simplified CREATE TABLE syntax (column name, datatype, and null status) and discuss the constraints later in this chapter.

The SQL command for setting up a table is called CREATE TABLE. (Make sure you're using the correct database before you enter a CREATE TABLE statement.) A simplified form of the CREATE TABLE syntax is

```
CREATE TABLE table_name
(column_name datatype [NULL | NOT NULL]
[, column_name datatype [NULL| NOT NULL] ]...)
```

An example is the **CREATE TABLE** statement for the *authors* table:

SQL:
```
create table authors
  (au_id char(11) not null,
  au_lname varchar(40) not null,
  au_fname varchar(20) not null,
  phone char(12) null,
  address varchar(40) null,
  city varchar(20) null,
  state char(2) null,
  zip char(5) null)
```

Let's examine this syntax, since it's more complicated than any introduced so far.

- The first clause, the CREATE TABLE clause, is straightforward—just make sure the table names you choose follow your system's rules for identifiers.
- The second line of the syntax begins with an opening parenthesis, which you must be sure to type.
- Then give the name of the first column, followed by a space and the name of its datatype. (For some datatypes, you must specify a length, scale, or precision—usually by putting an integer in parentheses immediately following the datatype.)
- The keywords NULL and NOT NULL inside square brackets indicate that they are optional. The vertical bar between them means you can use only one or the other, not both. The system makes the choice if the user doesn't. The SQL-92 default is to permit nulls, but not all commercial systems follow it. Get in the habit of explicitly spelling out the options you choose, even if you are accepting defaults. It'll make your work much easier to follow.
- The third line of the syntax, also enclosed in square brackets, repeats the definition of a column and is followed by an ellipsis. The brackets mean that defining a second column is optional; the ellipsis means that you can define as many columns as you like (within the limitations of your system—check your reference guide). Note that each

column definition is separated from the next by a comma; and don't forget the parenthesis at the end of the list of columns.

In addition to system-specific limits on the number of columns that you may include in a single table, check restrictions on row length (the total bytes that all the columns use). Usually, the limit is large enough so that you won't have to think about it. But if you're defining a table with lots of columns or with very large columns, you may have to compute exactly how long each row will be. To figure this out, add together the lengths of the longest data value each column can hold—determined by the column's assigned length (if it has one) or by the length that applies to its datatype.

Choosing a Datatype

The datatype of a column specifies what kind of information the column will hold (characters, numbers, dates, and so on), so that the system will know how the data is to be physically stored, and how it can be manipulated. For example, a character datatype holds letters, numbers, and special characters, while an integer datatype holds whole numbers only. Data in integer columns can be manipulated with arithmetic operators, while character data cannot.

Relational systems can handle a wide variety of datatypes. But be careful in making assumptions—even when two systems use the same datatype name, their meanings may be different. You'll want to check your system's reference manuals to find out what datatypes are available to you, and when and how to use them.

Choosing the proper datatypes is more binding than many other design decisions, since in many versions of SQL it is difficult to change a column's datatype identity. However, most SQLs provide datatype conversion functions, so that data stored as one type can be treated as if it were another type. For example, even if you have stored only numbers in a character column, it may be difficult or impossible to change the datatype of the column. But you may be able, with the help of a data conversion function, to perform arithmetic operations on those numbers, even though those operations are incompatible with character columns.

Here's a summary of some possible datatypes, along with hints on the kind of data for which each typically is used:

- **Character datatypes** hold letters, numbers, and special characters. The two general types are fixed-length character (*character* or *char*) and variable-length character (*variable character* or *varchar*). Fixed-

or variable-length national character (*national character, nchar, national character varying, nvarchar*) are also available for specific character sets. Some systems make special character datatypes available for storing large pieces of text; they are often called *long* or *text*. Most character datatypes have a length parameter specifying the maximun size of the column (a number in parentheses after the datatype).

Character datatypes are the best choice in some situations that may seem surprising at first—such as zip codes and phone numbers. Zip codes are best stored in character columns because they often need to be sorted—and codes that begin with zero may not sort properly if they are stored as numbers. Some systems, in fact, simply strip leading zeroes off all numbers. (Sort order varies from implementation to implementation.)

Special characters often used in phone numbers (hyphens and parentheses) are rejected unless a column is stored as characters.

- **Whole-number datatypes** hold integers only (no fractions or decimals). They are often known by such names as *number, integer, int, smallint,* and *tinyint.* All commercial versions of SQL provide arithmetic operations for use with whole numbers and aggregate functions that allow you to find the maximum, minimum, average, total, and count of the values in a column of whole numbers. Some SQLs provide other functions, such as statistical operations.

- **Decimal datatypes** hold numbers with fractions. Exact decimal numbers are known as *decimal* or *numeric.* You can usually define their precision (the total number of digits on both sides of the decimal point) and scale (the number of digits after the decimal point). Approximate decimal numbers have names like *real, double, double precision, float* and *smallfloat.* Their precision and number of significant digits vary among database management systems, sometimes depending on the particular hardware you're using.

- **Money datatypes** hold currency values. If your system does not have a specific money datatype, use an exact decimal type.

- **Date** and **time datatypes** record date, time, and combinations of date and time. Special date functions for determining the interval between two dates, and for adding or subtracting a given amount of time to a date, are sometimes provided.

- **Binary datatypes** hold code, images, and hexadecimal data. Like character data, they come in fixed and variable lengths, and may have long versions.

- **Serial datatypes** maintain a sequentially increasing number. In some cases this feature is treated as a distinct datatype. In others, it may be available as a property or function you apply to one of the basic datatypes.

Become familiar with the characteristics of your system's datatypes so that you can use them effectively.

Choosing a Datatype Length.   Be sure to check on how your system handles the physical storage of datatypes. Find out which datatypes are **fixed length**—in other words, those for which the amount of storage space specified in the CREATE TABLE statement is allocated for each value in the column, no matter how much data is actually entered. For example, a column defined as *char(10)* would be allocated ten bytes or characters of storage space, no matter what value you enter in the column. Longer values may be truncated; values shorter than ten characters may be padded with blanks at the end, like this:

```
name
- - - - - - - - - -
Greenjeans
Kangaroo__
Ho_____
Rumpelstil
```

Datatypes that don't take length specifications are often fixed length. If your implementation allocates eight bytes of storage for integer columns, for example, all eight bytes will be used whether the value you enter in the column is "3" or "300000".

The data in variable-length datatypes is stored as its actual length, not as its defined length. Say your system supplies a variable-length character datatype and you've defined a column like the one shown earlier as *varchar(10)* instead of *char(10)*. The "10" still represents the maximum length, but shorter values are not blank-padded. The first value (Greenjeans) would take ten bytes of storage, but the second (Kangaroo) would take only eight, the third (Ho) would take two, and so on.

Using fixed-length datatypes when much of the actual data is a great deal shorter than the length specified can waste storage space.

Choosing Precision and Scale.   Exact decimal datatypes may allow you to choose precision and scale. For example, if you expect an exact decimal number to have a total of six places, including three to the right of the decimal point, you'd describe it as something like *decimal (6, 3)*.

Assigning Null Status

Most systems allow you to assign null or not null status to each column when you create a table. A few systems do not support null values at all— they always insert some default value other than null (such as zero or blank) when a column has no entered value.

Assigning null status to a column instructs the system to insert a null in that column if the user does not enter a value. As we've explained, a null represents some unknown, unavailable, or inapplicable value—it's not the same as blank or zero.

Assigning not null status to a column means that nonentries in that column are not allowed. If you don't specify a value for that column, the system will reject the entry and display an error message. (In systems that provide the capability of specifying default values for a column, the default is automatically entered if you don't specify a value for a not null column.) In many systems, null is the default. But don't rely on the default: spell out what you want so that others will know what you had in mind.

How do you decide the null status of columns when you're designing a table? You should not permit nulls in columns in which known values are essential to the utility of the database. Primary key columns should never allow nulls because they uniquely identify the row. For example, without the *au_id* column, you'd have no way to find a book's author(s) in the *book-biz* database. The database was designed so that the *authors* table can be linked to *titles* by joins on the *au_id* and *title_id* columns.

You may decide that other columns should forbid null entries, too: perhaps you should disallow nulls in the *au_lname* and *au_fname* columns, on the grounds that it doesn't make sense to enter an author's address or phone number without entering his or her name.

However, when you know or suspect that a column will contain some unknown or inapplicable data, it should permit nulls. Missing addresses and phone numbers are common, so these columns should allow nulls. And, the first name column in an authors table might permit nulls, because an author's nom de plume could consist of a single name (such as Colette).

In the *titles* table, the *title_id* and *title* columns do not allow nulls; most of the other columns do. Nulls are forbidden because *title_id* is the primary key—each title identification number indicates a unique book. On the other hand, the *advance* column does permit null values. While an advance with a null title ID would make no sense at all, a title ID with a null advance might simply mean that the publisher and author haven't agreed on the exact amount yet or that the clerk hasn't entered it.

While null would mean "not yet known" in the case of an advance not yet decided upon, it can have slightly different meanings in other situations.

Null can mean that the value will never be known. For example, if you added a *phone* field to the *authors* table and some authors' telephone numbers were unlisted, you'd have to reconcile yourself to a permanent null. Then again, null might mean something like "not applicable"—for example, if the author didn't have a telephone.

Unlike primary keys, foreign keys sometimes can have null values. In the case of books and publishers, the *titles.pub_id* column allows null. This is because, in the *bookbiz* business model, books are sometimes acquired by the mother publishing company and assigned to one of the subsidiary lines later on. For a short time, a book might lack a publisher.

Note that the decision about whether to allow nulls in a foreign key depends not on theoretical considerations, but on the logical meaning of the relationship between the information in the primary and foreign key columns—and that depends on the real-world situation: a company policy, an organization's rule, and so on.

The Table Creation Process

Creating a table, like creating a database, involves a series of steps that begins with design and ends with issuing a SQL command. Here's an outline of the process for tables without any SQL-92 constraints. It assumes you've already designed and normalized your database, and therefore know which columns will be in each table.

- Decide on the datatype (and length, precision, and scale, if required) of each column.
- Decide which columns should accept null values, and which should not.
- Decide which columns need to be unique. (In a system that doesn't use constraints, you'll enforce uniqueness with indexes, discussed in this chapter and in Chapter 10. Information on PRIMARY KEY and UNIQUE constraints is covered later in this chapter.)
- Make a note of primary key–foreign key pairings. The simple syntax used in the CREATE TABLE statements for *bookbiz* doesn't allow you to do anything with the pairs, except make sure that they have compatible datatypes, sizes, and null status. In the more complex syntax we'll explore later on, you'll be able to use constraints to enforce some referential integrity.
- If you're in a multiuser environment, make sure you have permission to create tables and indexes. If not, see your system administrator or the owner of the database in which you're working.

- Create the table (and any indexes it needs) with the CREATE TABLE and CREATE INDEX statements.

Figure 3-5 shows the structure of the *titles* table: column names, datatypes, null status, columns that must be unique, and primary and foreign keys.

Column	Datatype	Null?	Unique?	Keys
title_id	varchar(11)	not null	yes—titleidind	primary
title	varchar(80)	not null	no—titleind	
type	char(12)	null		
pub_id	char(4)	null		foreign (*publishers* table)
price	money	null		
advance	money	null		
ytd_sale	int	null		
contract	bit	not null		
notes	varchar(200)	null		
pubdate	datetime	null		

Figure 3–5. Charting the *titles* Table Structure

Defining the Tables in the Sample Database. Now you are ready to apply these syntax rules to real tables. Here's a CREATE TABLE command for the *titles* table:

```
SQL:
create table titles
(title_id char(6) not null,
title varchar(80) not null,
```

```
    type char(12) null,
    pub_id char(4) null,
    price money null,
    advance money null,
    ytd_sales int null,
    contract bit not null,
    notes varchar(200) null,
    pubdate datetime null)
```

If your system does not supply a *bit* datatype, you may create the *con-tract* column with a character datatype. Such a column could allow nulls.

The CREATE TABLE statements for the eight remaining tables in the *bookbiz* database are contained in Appendix D and on the CD.

CREATING INDEXES

In a relational database management system, an index is a mechanism for boosting performance. Just as an index in a book helps you quickly find the pages you want to read, an index on a column speeds data retrieval. When you're looking for a particular subject in a book, you don't want to read every page to find the topic of interest. Similarly, when you're searching for a given piece of data, an index can serve as a logical pointer to its physical location.

There are several important differences, however, between an index in a book and an index in a relational database management system. The reader of a book decides whether or not to consult the index. The user of a relational database management system decides whether or not to create an index, and the system itself determines if and how the index is used for each query the user submits. Indexes, once they are set up, are transparent to database users (except where vendors have added SQL extensions to give expert users or database administrators some control over system use of indexes—a topic beyond the scope of this book).

While each edition of a book and its index are printed once, the data in a relational system and its indexes may change frequently. Each time the data in a table is modified, one or more of the table's indexes may have to change to reflect those modifications. Again, users have nothing to do with keeping the indexes up to date; the system handles this task on its own.

One more characteristic that distinguishes indexes on database tables from most book indexes is that it's very common for a table to have more than one index (just as some books are indexed by subject and by author). It's also possible for a table (and for a book) to have no index at all.

This section explains the syntax of the CREATE INDEX and DROP INDEX statements, describes the varieties of indexes typically available in relational systems, and gives some pointers about how to decide which columns to index. Chapter 10 discusses in more detail how indexes affect performance.

The CREATE INDEX Statement

Most systems have a command with syntax similar to this:

```
CREATE [UNIQUE] INDEX index_name
ON table_name (column_name)
```

The column and table names specify the column you want indexed and the table that contains it.

To create an index on the *au_id* column of the *authors* table, the command is

```
SQL:
create index auidind
on authors (au_id)
```

It's a good idea to plan and create your indexes when you create your table. However, SQL also allows you to create indexes after there's data in a table.

Most systems also allow **composite indexes** (indexes involving more than one column) and **unique indexes** (indexes that prevent duplication of data). Another indexing option provided in some systems is a **clustered index** (one that is sorted not only logically but physically). Check your system's reference manuals to see which type of indexes are allowed.

Composite Indexes. Composite indexes are used when two or more columns are best searched as a unit because of their logical relationship. For example, the *authors* table has a composite index on *au_fname* and *au_lname*.

The syntax for creating a composite index must specify all the columns in it. A command to create a composite index on the *authors* table might look something like this:

```
SQL:
create index aunameind
on authors (au_lname, au_fname)
```

In most SQL dialects, the composite index columns don't have to be in the same order as the columns in the CREATE TABLE statement. For example, the order of *au_lname* and *au_fname* could be reversed in the preceding index creation statement. For performance reasons, it's generally a good idea to start with the name of the column you use most often in searches.

Unique Indexes.   A unique index is one in which no two rows are permitted to have the same index value. The system checks for duplicate values when the index is created (if data already exists) and each time data is added. Unique indexes are usually created on the primary key column(s) in order to enforce their function as unique identifiers of the row.

Specifying a unique index makes sense only when uniqueness is a characteristic of the data itself. For example, you would not want a unique index on a *last_name* column, since there is likely to be more than one *Smith* or *Wong* in tables of even a few hundred rows. On the other hand, a unique index on a column holding Social Security numbers would be a good idea. Uniqueness is a characteristic of the data: each person has a different Social Security number. Furthermore, a unique index serves as an integrity check. A duplicate Social Security number reflects some kind of error in data entry or on the part of the government.

SQL implementations that support unique indexes must have some way of enforcing that uniqueness. Usually, the system guarantees uniqueness by rejecting commands that would

- Create a unique index on existing data that includes duplicate values
- Change data on which there is a unique index in such a way that duplicates would be introduced

You can use the UNIQUE keyword on composite indexes as well as on single-column indexes.

Clustered Indexes.   Some relational database management systems offer you the choice of a clustered or nonclustered index. When a clustered index is created, it means that the system will sort and re-sort the rows of a table on an ongoing basis, so that their physical order on the database device is always the same as their logical (indexed) order.

Since a clustered index controls the physical location of data, there can be only one clustered index per table. It is often created on the primary key, but it makes more sense to put it on the column that you most often retrieve in order.

With a nonclustered index, the physical order of the rows is not the same as their indexed order. Each of the nonclustered indexes on a table can provide access to the data in a different sorted order.

Finding data using a clustered index is almost always faster than using a nonclustered index. A clustered index is especially advantageous when many rows with contiguous **key values** (indexed values) are being retrieved—that is, on columns that are often searched for ranges of values. Once the row with the first key value is found, rows with subsequent indexed values are guaranteed to be physically adjacent, and no further accesses are necessary. However, the presence of a clustered index may slow down data modification statements, since the system must take the time to rejuggle the index when key values are changed.

How, What, and Why to Index

Indexes speed the retrieval of data. An index on a column can often make the difference between a nearly immediate response to a query and a long wait.

So why not index every column? The most significant reason is that building and maintaining an index takes time and storage space on the database device.

A second reason is that inserting, deleting, or updating data in indexed columns takes a little longer than in unindexed columns, because of the time it takes the system to maintain the index when key values are changed. But this cost is usually outweighed by the extent to which indexes improve retrieval performance.

In general, it's usually appropriate to put indexes on columns you frequently use in retrievals, especially primary key columns and columns used in joins and sorts. Here are some more precise guidelines:

- The column or columns that store the table's primary key should almost always be indexed, especially if the primary key is frequently joined to columns in other tables. A unique index on the primary key prevents duplicates and guarantees that every value in the primary key column will in fact *uniquely* identify the row.
- A column that is often accessed in sorted order probably should be indexed, so that the system can take advantage of the indexed order.

- Columns that are regularly used in joins should be indexed, since the system can perform the join faster.
- A column that is often searched for ranges of values might be a good choice for indexing if your system provides clustered indexes. Once the row with the first value in the range is found, rows with subsequent values are guaranteed to be physically adjacent. A clustered index does not offer as much of an advantage for searches on single values.

These are some cases in which indexes are not useful:

- Columns that are rarely referenced in queries don't benefit from indexes in terms of performance, since the system seldom or never has to search for rows on the basis of values in these columns. However, you may still want to use an index to enforce uniqueness.
- Columns that can have only two or three values (for example, male, female, unknown) gain no real advantage from being indexed.
- Small tables with few rows don't get a performance boost from indexes: the system will generally choose a **table scan** (examining the table rows one by one) instead of using an index. The length of time it takes to perform a scan is directly proportional to the number of rows in the table.

Indexes are a very complex issue. To use them well, you need to understand how your system's query optimizer works, and what performance issues your application has—topics not covered here. Generally speaking, you should start out by picking what seem to be reasonable indexes, and then look for performance problems during your prototyping, benchmarking, and testing phases. When you have a clear idea of your needs, you can adjust the indexes to meet them.

CREATING TABLES WITH SQL-92 CONSTRAINTS

Many commercial systems have adopted the SQL-92 CREATE TABLE options for PRIMARY KEY, UNIQUE, DEFAULT, CHECK, REFERENCES, and FOREIGN KEY. These elements provide some important data integrity protections.

- PRIMARY KEY marks the column (which cannot allow nulls) as the primary key of the table. Every value entered must be unique or else the input is rejected. The handling of this constraint internally varies from system to system, but it is often equivalent to an index. If the primary key includes multiple columns, PRIMARY KEY is defined on the table level.

- UNIQUE also guarantees the distinctness of every value in the column, but it allows the column to be defined as NULL (note that only *one* null entry is allowed per UNIQUE column).
- DEFAULT defines a value that the system automatically supplies when the user entering data doesn't give one explicitly. For example, you might define a default for the *type* column of the *titles* table. If a book hasn't yet been categorized, and the data entry clerk therefore can't make an entry in the *type* column, the system would automatically insert whatever default value you've chosen—perhaps the word "unclassified." (If no default is defined and the *type* column permits null values, the system will automatically insert the value "NULL".)
- CHECK specifies what data may be entered in a particular column: it is a way of defining the domain of the column. For example, you might want to make sure that a *title_id* is always two letters followed by four numerals, or a *type* is one of a list of six acceptable terms. If a user attempts to make an entry that violates a check constraint, the system rejects the data modification command. Check constraints are sometimes called **rules** or **validation rules**, since they allow the system to check whether a value being entered in a column falls within the column's domain. Check constraints that involve more than one column are defined on the table level.
- REFERENCES and FOREIGN KEY tie primary and foreign keys together. When you enter a value in a foreign key column defined with REFERENCES, it must exist in the table and column referenced, or else the entry is rejected.

Before you create a table with defaults and constraints, sketch your requirements. Figure 3-6 shows defaults and constraints you might use for the *titles* table.

Syntax for these features varies from vendor to vendor, so check your system manuals for specifics. Usually, it looks something like the following syntax summary, with column-level constraints optionally following each column definition. The constraint clauses always include the constraint keyword (DEFAULT, CHECK, PRIMARY KEY, UNIQUE, FOREIGN KEY, REFERENCES) and optionally the word CONSTRAINT and a name for the constraint. (Naming constraints may simplify the process of dropping or changing them. Although most systems generate constraint labels you can

Column	Datatype	Null?	Key	Default	Check Constraint	References
title_id	char(6)	not null	primary, unique		2 letters followed by 4 digits	
title	varchar(80)	not null	unique			
type	char(12)			unclassified	business, mod_cook, trad_cook, psychology, popular_comp, unclassified	
pub_id	char(4)	null				publishers. pub_id
price	money	null				
advance	money	null				
ytd_sale	int	null				
contract	bit	not null				
notes	varchar(200)	null				
pubdate	datetime	null		today		

Figure 3–6. Using Constraints in Creating the *titles* Table

use, they are often cumbersome.) We've put table-level constraints at the end of the list of elements, but that's not required. Notice that a column can have more than one constraint, and that constraints are *not* separated with commas, though columns are:

```
CREATE TABLE table_name
(column_name datatype [NULL | NOT NULL] [DEFAULT default_value]
   [column_constraint_clause]...
[, column_name datatype [NULL | NOT NULL][DEFAULT default_value]
   [column_constraint_clause]...]...
   [table_constraint_clause]...)
```

Here's a SQL Anywhere version of the *titles* table (called *titlescnstr*) using the defaults and constraints (all column-level, and printed in bold for easy visibility) shown in Figure 3-6. (You'll find an explanation of LIKE and IN in the next chapter. For the *pubdate* default, CURRENT DATE is a SQL Anywhere DEFAULT option that supplies today's date. Other systems provide similar functions.)

```
create table titlescnstr
(title_id char(6) not null
  primary key
  check (title_id like '[A-Z][A-Z][0-9][0-9][0-9][0-9]'),
title varchar(80) not null
  unique,
type char(12)
 default 'unclassified' null
  check (type in ('business', 'mod_cook', 'trad_cook',
    'psychology', 'popular_comp', 'unclassified')),
pub_id char(4) null
  references publishers (pub_id),
price money null,
advance money null,
ytd_sales int null,
contract bit not null,
notes varchar(200) null,
pubdate datetime null
  default current date)
```

The Sybase SQL Server code for the same table differs in a few areas:

SQL:
```
create table titlescnstr
(title_id char(6) not null
```

```
   constraint tididx primary key
   constraint tidcheck check
     (title_id like '[A-Z] [A-Z] [0-9] [0-9] [0-9] [0-9]'),
title varchar(80) not null
   constraint titleidx unique,
type char(12)
   default 'unclassified' null
   constraint typecheck check
     (type in ('business', 'mod_cook', 'trad_cook',
       'psychology', 'popular_comp', 'unclassified')),
pub_id char(4) null
   references publishers (pub_id),
price money null,
advance money null,
ytd_sales int null,
contract bit not null,
notes varchar(200) null,
pubdate datetime
   default getdate() null)
```

Check your system manuals for details on the implementation you use.

Table-level constraints involve more than one column. Figure 3-7 shows constraints required for the *titleauthors* table.

The following example shows how you'd use SQL Anywhere to implement the references and primary key requirements in the *titleauthors* table (called *titleauthorscnstr* to avoid confusion). The primary key constraint is a table-level constraint because it includes more than one column.

Column	Datatype	Null?	Key	Default	Check Constraint	References
au_id	char(11)	not null	primary key			authors.au_id
title_id	char(6)	not null				titles.title_id
au_ord	tinyint	null				
royaltyshare	float	null				

Figure 3-7. Using Constraints in Creating the *titleauthors* Table

SQL:

```
create table titleauthorscnstr
(au_id char(11) not null references authors (au_id),
title_id char(6) not null references titles (title_id),
au_ord tinyint null,
royaltyshare float null,
primary key (au_id, title_id))
```

Check constraints can also be on the table level, when they involve more than one column (but they must be from the same table). In the *salesdetails* table, there are columns for the quantity ordered and the quantity shipped. You could use a table-level check constraint to make sure the quantity shipped is never larger than the quantity ordered. Figure 3-8 charts the table requirements, including two references, the check on quantity, and a table-level (compound) primary key.

SQL:

```
create table salesdetailscnstr
  (sonum int not null references sales (sonum),
  qty_ordered smallint not null,
  qty_shipped smallint null,
  title_id char(6) not null references titles (title_id),
  date_shipped datetime null,
  check (qty_shipped <= qty_ordered),
  primary key (sonum, title_id))
```

Column	Datatype	Null?	Key	Default	Check Constraint	References
sonum	int	not null	primary key			sales.sonum
title_id	char(6)	not null				titles.title_id
qty_shipped	smallint	null			qty_shipped not > than qty_ordered	
qty_ordered	smallint	not null				
date_shipped	datetime	null				

Figure 3–8. Using Constraints in Creating the *salesdetails* Table

This SQL Anywhere CREATE TABLE command requires a primary key or unique index on the *sonum* column in the *sales* table, in order for the first REFERENCES clause to work. Don't forget to add it before you try to run this command.

A number of systems provide commands outside the CREATE TABLE context to handle defaults, rules, and integrity constraints. These are discussed in Chapter 10. Early systems sometimes considered defaults and integrity constraints an application-by-application decision and did not support them through SQL.

CHANGING AND DELETING DATABASES AND OBJECTS

By now you've noticed a pattern: you build databases and database objects with a CREATE command of some sort. Most systems have corresponding DROP commands to remove databases and objects. (Strangely enough, not until its 1988 draft did the ANSI standard include such a command.) ALTER commands are also common for changing objects.

Changing Databases

Some SQL versions include a command that allows you to change the size of a database (usually to make it bigger). The ability to add database device space for a database is extremely important for any application that will grow over time. Also important (and less frequently implemented) is the ability to shrink a database in order to reclaim unused database device space.

Changing Table Definitions

After you've designed and created your database and worked with it for a while, you may find that it isn't quite right or that the application requirements have changed. Some systems allow you to change the structure of a table (even after it has data in it) with a command such as ALTER TABLE. Syntax may include keywords to add and drop columns, and to change a column's name, datatype, length, null status, and constraints.

For example, to add a column to the *authors* table, your system might allow you to type something like this:

```
SQL:
alter table authors
add birth_date datetime null
```

Usually, columns added with the ALTER TABLE statement must allow nulls. That's because when the new column is added to all the existing rows, it must contain some value, and "null" (unknown) is the obvious choice.

Many relational systems don't provide commands for making structural changes besides the addition of columns—for removing columns, renaming columns, or changing a column's datatype or null status. But often there's a way around such limitations. If you can't physically drop a column, for example, you can create a view that excludes it, and do all your data retrieval and modification commands through that view. You can also use a view to create the illusion of a permanent change in

- The name of a column, simply by giving the column a new heading in the SELECT clause of the CREATE VIEW statement
- The datatype of a column, assuming your system has some sort of data conversion function

Another possible work-around for restructuring is to create a new table with the structure you want, dump the data from the old table into an operating system file, and then reload it into the new table. In some systems, you can use a command (in Sybase SQL Server called SELECT INTO) to pull data from one table into a new table that may have a different structure. See Chapter 9 for details.

Removing a Database

Removing a database or a database object deletes both the structure and any data associated with it. For that reason, most systems allow you to issue a DROP command only if you own the object or have special permission to delete it.

The syntax of the DROP DATABASE command is usually something like this:

```
DROP DATABASE database_name
```

The DROP DATABASE command is very dangerous, since removing a database obliterates all of its contents.

Removing a Table

The command to remove a table from a database is DROP TABLE. In most SQL dialects, its syntax is this:

```
DROP TABLE table_name
```

When you issue this command, you remove the specified table from the database, together with its contents.

If you want to keep the table structure but remove all of its data, use the DELETE command (more about it later in this chapter).

Removing an Index

There are two situations in which you might want to drop an index:

- You or someone else has created an index on a column, but the index is not used for most or all queries.
- You are about to issue a large number of data modification statements that will change key values. Since the system may have to do a lot of work to keep the index up-to-date, it might be more efficient to drop the index and then re-create it (with the CREATE INDEX statement) after changing the data.

It may still take some time to rebuild the index later, but you may prefer to postpone the lag time, rather than to endure a degradation in the system's performance during the data modifications.

In most systems, the command to remove an index has syntax something like this:

```
DROP INDEX table_name.index_name
```

When you issue this command, the system removes the specified index from the database. To drop the index *auidind* in the *authors* table, the command is this:

```
SQL:
drop index authors.auidind
```

ADDING, CHANGING, AND REMOVING DATA

Once you've designed and created a database, its tables, and (optionally) its indexes, you'll want to put data into the tables and start to work—adding, changing, and removing data as necessary. You've got the structure. Now you need some contents.

SQL provides three basic commands for changing data, collectively called data modification statements.

- The INSERT statement adds new rows to the database.
- The UPDATE statement changes existing rows in the database.
- The DELETE statement removes rows from the database.

This section discusses the SQL data modification commands. The next section gives samples of the INSERT statements that load the sample data from the *bookbiz* database.

Another method of adding data to a table is to load it from an operating system file with some kind of bulk copy or bulk insert command. This method is especially appropriate when you are transferring data that was used with one database management system to another system.

Many relational database systems also have a graphical user interface **form** system (like a paper form with blanks where you can type data) for data modification. A form is often more convenient than a data modification statement because it gives you a context in which to work. However, all data modification actions in a relational database system are based on SQL commands, so it's a good idea to look at their syntax even if you don't plan to use them.

Data modification statements are not necessarily available to everyone. The database owner and the owners of database objects can use the GRANT and REVOKE commands to decide which users are allowed to issue which data modification statements.

You can modify (INSERT, UPDATE, or DELETE) data in only one table per statement. However, in some systems, the modifications you make can be based on data in other tables, even data in other databases. You can actually pull values from one table into another, using a SQL SELECT statement within a data modification command. Instructions on this variation on data modification are given later in this chapter.

The data modification statements work on views as well as on tables, with some restrictions. See Chapter 9 for details.

Adding New Rows

The INSERT statement allows you to add rows to the database in two ways: with the VALUES keyword or with a SELECT statement. The first INSERT syntax we'll explain uses the VALUES keyword.

The VALUES keyword specifies data values for some or all of the columns in a new row. A generalized version of the syntax for the INSERT command using the VALUES keyword is the following:

```
INSERT INTO table_name [(column1 [, column2]...)]
VALUES (constant1 [, constant2]...)
```

This INSERT statement adds a new row to the *publishers* table, giving a value for every column in the row:

```
SQL:
insert into publishers
values ('1622', 'Jardin, Inc.', '5 5th Ave.', 'Camden', 'NJ')
```

Notice that you have to type the data values in the same order as the column names in the original CREATE TABLE statement (that is, first the ID number, then the name, the address, the city, and finally the state). The VALUES data is surrounded by parentheses. Most systems require single or double quotes around character and date data, and commas to separate the values.

Use a separate INSERT statement for each row you add.

Inserting Data into Some Columns.   When you add data in some, but not all, of the columns in a row, you need to specify those columns. The columns that you don't put data into need to have defaults or be defined as null to prevent failure. For example, adding data in only two columns (say, *pub_id* and *pub_name*) requires a command like this:

```
SQL:
insert into publishers (pub_id, pub_name)
values ('1756', 'HealthText')
```

The order in which you list the column names has no effect on the INSERT statement as long as the order in which you list the data values matches it. The following example (which reverses the order of *pub_name* and *pub_id*) has exactly the same effect as the previous example:

```
SQL:
insert into publishers (pub_name, pub_id)
values ('HealthText', '1756')
```

Both INSERT statements put "1756" in the identification number column and "HealthText" in the publisher name column. What happened in the *address*, *city*, and *state* columns? The following SELECT statement shows the row that was added to *publishers*:

```
SQL:
select pub_id, pub_name, address, city, state
from publishers
where pub_name = 'HealthText'
```

```
Results:
pub_id      pub_name              address    city     state
---------   ------------------    ---------  -------  -------
1756        HealthText            NULL       NULL     NULL
```

The system enters null values in the *address*, *city*, and *state* columns because there were no values for these columns in the INSERT statement, and the *publishers* table allows null values in these columns. If your system doesn't permit null values, you'll probably see some default such as blanks or zeroes in those columns.

If you had defined *city* and *state* as not null in the CREATE TABLE statement, the insert wouldn't have worked, because columns that don't permit null values won't accept a nonentry. Here's what happens with Transact-SQL when you try an INSERT statement that doesn't specify a value for the *pub_id* column, which was assigned not null status when the *publishers* table was created:

```
SQL:
insert into publishers (pub_name, address, city, state)
values ('Tweedledum Books', '1 23rd St.', 'New York', 'NY')
```

```
Results:
column 'pub_id' in table 'publishers' cannot be NULL
```

SELECT in an INSERT Statement

You can use a SELECT statement in an INSERT statement to get values from one or more other tables. A simple version of the syntax for the INSERT command using a SELECT statement is this:

```
INSERT INTO table_name [(insert_column_list)]
SELECT column_list
   FROM table_list
   WHERE search_conditions
```

SELECT in an INSERT statement lets you pull data from all or some of the columns from one table into another. If you insert values for a subset of the columns, you can use UPDATE at another time to add the values for the other columns.

When you insert rows from one table into another, the two tables must have compatible structures—that is, the matching columns must be the same datatypes, or datatypes between which the system automatically converts.

If all the columns of the two tables are compatible in the same order that they appeared in their CREATE TABLE statements, you don't need to specify column names in either table. Suppose a table called *newauthors* contains some rows of author information in the same format as *authors*. To add to *authors* all the rows in *newauthors*, type a command like either of the following:

```
SQL:
insert into authors
select au_id, au_lname, au_fname, phone, address, city,
   state, zip
from newauthors

insert into authors
select *
from newauthors
```

If the columns in the two tables (the one you're inserting into and the one you're getting data from) are not in the same order in their respective CREATE TABLE statements, you can use either the INSERT or the SELECT clause to reorder the columns so that they match.

For example, say the CREATE TABLE statement for the *authors* table contains the columns *au_id*, *au_fname*, *au_lname*, and *address* in that order, while *newauthors* contains *au_id*, *address*, *au_lname*, and *au_fname*. You'd have to make the column sequence match in the INSERT statement. You could do this by listing the columns of *authors* in the INSERT clause:

```
SQL:

insert into authors (au_id, address, au_lname, au_fname)
   select * from newauthors
```

You could also do it by listing the columns of *newauthors* in the SELECT clause:

```
SQL:

insert into authors
   select au_id, au_fname, au_lname, address
   from newauthors
```

If the column sequence in the two tables fails to match, the system cannot complete the INSERT operation, or completes it incorrectly, putting data in the wrong columns. For example, you might get truncated address data in the *au_lname* column, probably not what you wanted.

Expressions.   One of the beneficial side effects of using a SELECT statement inside an INSERT statement is that it allows you to include **expressions** (strings of characters, mathematical calculations, and functions, alone or in combination with columns or each other) to change the data that you're pulling in. (See Chapters 4, 5, 6, 7, and 8 for a full range of possibilities.)

Here's an example of a SELECT clause with an expression involving a column and a mathematical computation: Imagine that one of the publishing subsidiaries has purchased a series of books from another publishing company that conveniently uses a table with exactly the same structure as the *titles* table. The newly purchased books are in a table named *Books*, and you want to load this data into *titles*. However, the company from which the books were purchased underpriced its wares, and you want to increase the price of all the new books by 50 percent. A statement to increase the prices and insert the rows from *Books* into *titles* looks like this:

```
SQL:
insert into titles
select title_id, title, type, pub_id, price * 1.5,
  advance, royalty, ytd_sales, contract, notes, pubdate
  from Books
```

Inserting Data into Some Columns. You can use the SELECT statement to add data to some, but not all, of the columns in a row, just as you do with the VALUES clause. Simply specify the columns to which you want to add data in the INSERT clause.

For example, if there are books in the *titles* table that do not yet have contracts and hence do not have entries in the *titleauthors* table, you might try to use this statement to pull their *title_id* numbers out of the *titles* table and insert them into the *titleauthors* table as placeholders:

```
SQL:
insert into titleauthors (title_id)
select title_id
  from titles
  where contract = 0
```

However, this statement is not legal, because a value is required for the *au_id* column of *titleauthors* (the table definition doesn't permit nulls and there is no default value). You can put in *xxxxxx* as a **dummy value** for *au_id* like this, using it as a constant:

```
SQL:
insert into titleauthors (title_id, au_id)
select title_id, 'xxxxxx'
  from titles
  where contract = 0
```

The *titleauthors* table now contains two new rows with entries for the *title_id* column, dummy entries for the *au_id* column, and null values for the other two columns. If you have a unique index or UNIQUE or PRIMARY KEY constraint on the column, however, this maneuver won't work.

Most versions of SQL forbid listing the INSERT table in the FROM clause:

```
SQL:
insert into test
  select *
  from test
```

Sybase SQL Server is one system that allows this syntax.

CHANGING EXISTING DATA: UPDATE

While the INSERT statement adds new rows to a table, the UPDATE statement changes existing rows. Use it to change values in single rows, groups of rows, or all the rows in a table.

The UPDATE statement specifies the row or rows you want to change, and the new data. The new data can be a constant or expression that you specify, or it can be data pulled from other tables.

Here's a simplified version of the UPDATE syntax for updating specified rows with an expression:

```
UPDATE table_name
SET column_name = expression
[WHERE search_conditions]
```

The UPDATE Statement

The UPDATE keyword is followed by the name of a table or view. As in all the data modification statements, you can change the data in only one table or view at a time.

If an UPDATE statement violates an integrity constraint (one of the values being added is the wrong datatype, for example), the system does not perform the update and usually displays an error message. See Chapter 8 for restrictions on updating views.

The SET Clause

The SET clause specifies the column(s) and the changed value(s). The WHERE clause determines which row or rows will be updated. Note that if you don't have a WHERE clause, you'll update the specified columns of *all* the rows with the values in the SET clause.

For example, here's what the *publishers* table looks like:

```
SQL:
select *
from publishers

Results:
pub_id  pub_name               address       city         state
-------  ---------------------  ------------  -----------  -----
0736    New Age Books          1 1st St      Boston       MA
0877    Binnet & Hardley       2 2nd Ave.    Washington   DC
1389    Algodata Infosystems   3 3rd Dr.     Berkeley     CA
1622    Jardin, Inc.           5 5th Ave.    Camden       NJ
1756    HealthText             NULL          NULL         NULL

(5 rows affected)
```

If all the publishing houses in the *publishers* table move their head offices to Atlanta, Georgia, this is how you update the city and state entries in the table:

```
update publishers
set city = 'Atlanta', state = 'GA'
```

Here's what the table looks like now:

```
SQL:
select *
from publishers

Results:
pub_id  pub_name               address       city         state
-------  ---------------------  ------------  -----------  -----
0736    New Age Books          1 1st St      Atlanta      GA
0877    Binnet & Hardley       2 2nd Ave.    Atlanta      GA
1389    Algodata Infosystems   3 3rd Dr.     Atlanta      GA
1622    Jardin, Inc.           5 5th Ave.    Atlanta      GA
1756    HealthText             NULL          Atlanta      GA

(5 rows affected)
```

(You'd probably want to change the street addresses, too.) In the same way, you can change the names of all the publishers to "ZIPP!" with this statement:

```
SQL:

update publishers
set pub_name = "ZIPP!"
```

Now the table looks like this:

```
SQL:
select *
from publishers
```

```
Results:
pub_id  pub_name                  address        city          state
-------  ----------------------    -----------    -----------   -----
0736     ZIPP!                     1 1st St       Atlanta       GA
0877     ZIPP!                     2 2nd Ave.     Atlanta       GA
1389     ZIPP!                     3 3rd Dr.      Atlanta       GA
1622     ZIPP!                     5 5th Ave.     Atlanta       GA
1756     ZIPP!                     NULL           Atlanta       GA
```

(5 rows affected)

You can also use computed column values in an update.
To double all the prices in the *titles* table, use this statement:

```
SQL:
update titles
set price = price * 2
```

Since there is no **WHERE** clause, the change in prices is applied to every row in the table.

The WHERE Clause

The WHERE clause in an UPDATE statement specifies which rows to change. (It is similar to the WHERE clause in a SELECT statement, which is discussed in Chapters 4, 5, 6, 7, and 8.) For example, in the unlikely event that northern California becomes a new state called Pacifica (abbreviated PC) and the people of Oakland vote to change the name of their city to something exciting (like Big Bad Bay City), here is how you can update the *authors* table for all residents of the former Oakland, whose addresses would now be out of date:

SQL:
```
update authors
set state = 'PC', city = 'Big Bad Bay City'
where state = 'CA' and city = 'Oakland'
```

Here's the new look of the *authors* table:

SQL:
```
select au_fname, au_lname, city, state
from authors
```

Results:

au_fname	au_lname	city	state
Johnson	White	Menlo Park	CA
Marjorie	Green	Big Bad Bay City	PC
Cheryl	Carson	Berkeley	CA
Michael	O'Leary	San Jose	CA
Dick	Straight	Big Bad Bay City	PC
Meander	Smith	Lawrence	KS
Abraham	Bennet	Berkeley	CA
Ann	Dull	Palo Alto	CA
Burt	Gringlesby	Covelo	CA
Chastity	Locksley	San Francisco	CA
Morningstar	Greene	Nashville	TN
Reginald	Blotchet-Halls	Corvallis	OR
Akiko	Yokomoto	Walnut Creek	CA
Innes	del Castillo	Ann Arbor	MI
Michel	DeFrance	Gary	IN

Dirk	Stringer	Big Bad Bay City	PC
Stearns	MacFeather	Big Bad Bay City	PC
Livia	Karsen	Big Bad Bay City	PC
Sylvia	Panteley	Rockville	MD
Sheryl	Hunter	Palo Alto	CA
Heather	McBadden	Vacaville	CA
Anne	Ringer	Salt Lake City	UT
Albert	Ringer	Salt Lake City	UT

```
(23 rows affected)
```

You'd need to run additional UPDATE statements for the addresses of Pacifica residents in other cities.

The WHERE clause of an UPDATE statement can also contain a subquery that refers to one or more other tables. For information on subqueries, see Chapter 8.

REMOVING DATA: DELETE

It's just as important to be able to remove rows as it is to be able to add or change them. Like INSERT and UPDATE, DELETE works for single-row operations as well as multiple-row operations. Also like the other data modification statements, you can delete rows based on data in other tables.

The DELETE syntax looks like this:

```
DELETE FROM table_name
WHERE search_conditions
```

The WHERE clause specifies which rows to remove. If you decide to remove one row from *publishers*—the row added for publisher identification number 1622—type this:

```
SQL:
delete from publishers
where pub_id = '1622'
```

Note that once you delete the row that describes this publisher, you can no longer find the books the company publishes by joining the *publishers* and *titles* tables on publisher identification numbers.

If there is no WHERE clause in the DELETE statement, *all* rows in the table are removed.

BEGINNING DATA RETRIEVAL

Now you are ready to begin putting the sample database tables online. The CD distributed with this edition of *The Practical SQL Handbook* contains everything you need.

- If you will be using the runtime SQL Anywhere, just follow the directions in the *readme* file to install the software and the *bookbiz* database.
- To run the database on your own relational database management system, check the *bookbiz.sql* file. It contains the CREATE and INSERT statements for the *bookbiz* database. You may need to edit the file to reflect your system's syntax. For example, datatype names vary from SQL to SQL. You may need to substitute the datatype definition in your system that seems most similar to the one used in the file. You may also need to change the command terminator (GO in the file).

Chapter 4

Selecting Data from the Database

AMONG THE SELECT?

In many ways, the SELECT statement is the real heart of SQL. It lets you find and view your data in a variety of ways. You use it to answer questions based on your data: how many, where, what kind of, even what if. Once you become comfortable with its sometimes dauntingly complex syntax, you'll be amazed at what the SELECT statement can do.

Since SELECT is so important, five chapters focus on it. This one starts out with the bare bones: the SELECT, FROM, and WHERE clauses, search conditions, and expressions. Chapter 5 delves into some SELECT refinements: ORDER BY, the DISTINCT keyword, and aggregates. Chapter 6 covers the GROUP BY clause, the HAVING clause, and making reports from grouped data. Chapter 6 also summarizes the issues regarding null values in database management. Chapter 7 introduces multiple-table queries with a comprehensive discussion of joining tables. Chapter 8 moves on to **nested queries**, also known as subqueries.

Queries in this chapter use single tables so that you can focus on manipulating the syntax in a simple environment.

SELECT Syntax

The most complicated SELECT statement begins with this skeleton:

```
SELECT list_of_columns
FROM table[s]
[WHERE search_conditions]
```

SQL:

```
select address
from personnel
where name = 'Richard Roe'
```

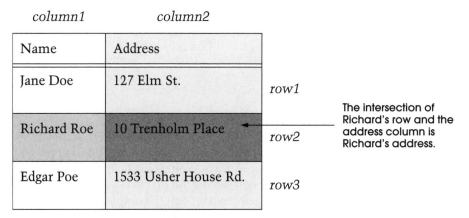

Figure 4-1. Selecting Data from the *personnel* Table

The select list identifies the *columns* you want to retrieve. The table list specifies the *tables* those columns are in. The WHERE clause qualifies the *rows*—it chooses the ones you want to see. Both the SELECT and WHERE clauses can include calculations, constants, and other expressions. Artful combinations of the SELECT, FROM, and WHERE clauses produce meaningful answers to your questions and keep you from drowning in a sea of data.

You can think of the SELECT and WHERE clauses as horizontal and vertical axes on a matrix, as illustrated in Figure 4-1.

The data you get from the SELECT statement is at the intersection of the SELECT (column) and WHERE (row) clauses (here *row2, column2*). Let's look at a SELECT statement with one of the sample tables, *authors*.

The *authors* table stores information about authors: their ID numbers, names, addresses, and phone numbers. If you want to know just the names of authors who live in California (not their addresses and phone numbers), you use the select list and the WHERE clause to limit the data that the SELECT statement returns.

Here's a query that uses the SELECT clause's select list to limit the columns you see. It shows just the first and last names for each author, ignoring their ID numbers, addresses, and phone numbers.

SQL:

```
select au_lname, au_fname
from authors
```

Results:

```
au_lname                           au_fname
-----------------------------      -------------
White                              Johnson
Green                              Marjorie
Carson                             Cheryl
O'Leary                            Michael
Straight                           Dick
Smith                              Meander
Bennet                             Abraham
Dull                               Ann
Gringlesby                         Burt
Locksley                           Chastity
Greene                             Morningstar
Blotchet-Halls                     Reginald
Yokomoto                           Akiko
del Castillo                       Innes
DeFrance                           Michel
Stringer                           Dirk
MacFeather                         Stearns
Karsen                             Livia
Panteley                           Sylvia
Hunter                             Sheryl
McBadden                           Heather
Ringer                             Anne
Ringer                             Albert
```

```
(23 rows affected)
```

Notice that this display still doesn't provide exactly what you want, since it lists all authors regardless of the state they live in. You need to refine the data retrieval statement further with the WHERE clause.

SQL:

```
select au_lname, au_fname
from authors
where state = 'CA'
```

Results:

au_lname	au_fname
White	Johnson
Green	Marjorie
Carson	Cheryl
O'Leary	Michael
Straight	Dick
Bennet	Abraham
Dull	Ann
Gringlesby	Burt
Locksley	Chastity
Yokomoto	Akiko
Stringer	Dirk
MacFeather	Stearns
Karsen	Livia
Hunter	Sheryl
McBadden	Heather

(15 rows affected)

Now you're looking at just the names of authors having a California address. The rows for the eight authors living elsewhere are not included in the display.

In practice, SELECT syntax can be either simpler or more complex than the example just shown. It can be simpler in that the SELECT and (usually) FROM clauses are the only required ones in a SELECT statement. The WHERE clause (and all other clauses) are optional. On the other hand, the full syntax of the SELECT statement includes all of these phrases and keywords:

```
SELECT [ALL | DISTINCT] select_list
  FROM {table_name | view_name}
    [, {table_name | view_name}]...
  [WHERE search_conditions]
  [GROUP BY column_name [, column_name]...]
   [HAVING search_conditions]
  [ORDER BY {column_name | select_list_number}  [ASC | DESC]
     [, {column_name | select_list_number}  [ASC | DESC]]...]
```

Although SQL is a free-form language, you do have to keep the clauses in a SELECT statement in syntactical order (for example, a GROUP BY clause must come before an ORDER BY clause). Otherwise, you'll get syntax errors.

You may also need to qualify the names of database objects (according to the customs of your SQL dialect) if there is any ambiguity about which object you mean. For example, if there are several columns called *notes* in a database, you may have to specify which *notes* column you're talking about by including the database name, the table or view name, and the owner name—something like this:

```
database.owner.table_name.notes
database.owner.view_name.notes
```

The examples in this chapter involve queries on a single table, so qualification is not an important issue here. Qualifiers are also omitted in most books, articles, and reference manuals on SQL because the short forms make the SELECT statements more readable. However, it's never wrong to include them.

CHOOSING COLUMNS: THE SELECT LIST

The first clause of the SELECT statement—the one that begins with the keyword SELECT—is required in all SELECT statements. The keywords ALL and DISTINCT, which specify whether duplicate rows are to be included in the results, are optional. DISTINCT and ALL are discussed in the next chapter.

The **select list** specifies the column or columns that are to be included in the results. It can consist of one or more column names, or of an asterisk, which is shorthand for all the columns. You can also use expressions—constants, column names, functions, or any combination of these connected by arithmetic operators and parentheses. Here are some examples of expressions:

```
ytd_sales * price
price * 1.2
(12000 - 500) / 13
avg(advance)
```

Make sure to separate each element in a select list from the following element with a comma.

Choosing All Columns: SELECT *

The asterisk (*) has a special meaning in the select list. It stands for *all the column names* in *all the tables* in the table list. The columns are displayed in the order in which they appeared in the CREATE TABLE statement(s). Most people read a SELECT * statement as "select star." Use it when you want to see all the columns in a table.

The general syntax for selecting all the columns in a table is this:

```
SELECT *
FROM table_list
```

Because SELECT * finds all the columns currently in a table, changes in the structure of a table (adding, removing, or renaming columns) automatically modify the results of a SELECT *. Listing the columns individually gives you more precise control over the results, but SELECT * saves typing (and the frustration of typographical errors). SELECT * is most useful for tables with few columns, since displays of many columns can be confusing. It also comes in handy when you want to get a quick look at a table's structure (what columns it has, and in what order).

The following statement retrieves all columns in the *publishers* table and displays them in the order in which they were defined when the *publishers* table was created. Since no WHERE clause is included, this statement retrieves every row.

```
SQL:
select *
from publishers

Results:
pub_id pub_name                 address      city         state
------ ---------------------    -----------  -----------  -----
0736   New Age Books            1 1st St     Boston       MA
0877   Binnet & Hardley         2 2nd Ave.   Washington   DC
1389   Algodata Infosystems     3 3rd Dr.    Berkeley     CA

(3 rows affected)
```

You get exactly the same results by listing all the column names in the table in order after the SELECT keyword:

```
SQL:
select pub_id, pub_name, address, city, state
from publishers
```

An asterisk in the select list of a multiple-table query will cause SQL to display all the columns in all the tables in the table list. Some systems also let you use both an asterisk and column names in the select list. This is most useful in multiple-table queries, when you qualify the asterisk with a table name. Here's a data retrieval statement that finds *publishers* information for each *title_id* in the *titles* table. You see all the columns from the *publishers* table (because of *publisher.** in the select list) and only one column from the *titles* table (because of *title_id* in the select list).

```
SQL:
select title_id, publishers.*
from titles, publishers
where titles.pub_id = publishers.pub_id
```

Results:

title_id	pub_id	pub_name	address	city	state
BU2075	0736	New Age Books	1 1st St	Boston	MA
PS1372	0736	New Age Books	1 1st St	Boston	MA
PS2091	0736	New Age Books	1 1st St	Boston	MA
PS2106	0736	New Age Books	1 1st St	Boston	MA
PS3333	0736	New Age Books	1 1st St	Boston	MA
PS7777	0736	New Age Books	1 1st St	Boston	MA
MC2222	0877	Binnet & Hardley	2 2nd Ave.	Washington	DC
MC3021	0877	Binnet & Hardley	2 2nd Ave.	Washington	DC
MC3026	0877	Binnet & Hardley	2 2nd Ave.	Washington	DC
TC3218	0877	Binnet & Hardley	2 2nd Ave.	Washington	DC
TC4203	0877	Binnet & Hardley	2 2nd Ave.	Washington	DC
TC7777	0877	Binnet & Hardley	2 2nd Ave.	Washington	DC
BU1032	1389	Algodata Infosystems	3 3rd Dr.	Berkeley	CA
BU1111	1389	Algodata Infosystems	3 3rd Dr.	Berkeley	CA
BU7832	1389	Algodata Infosystems	3 3rd Dr.	Berkeley	CA
PC1035	1389	Algodata Infosystems	3 3rd Dr.	Berkeley	CA
PC8888	1389	Algodata Infosystems	3 3rd Dr.	Berkeley	CA
PC9999	1389	Algodata Infosystems	3 3rd Dr.	Berkeley	CA

```
(18 rows affected)
```

If you didn't use the qualified *, you'd have to write the query this way:

```
SQL:
select title_id, publishers.pub_id, pub_name, address,
   city, state
from titles, publishers
where titles.pub_id = publishers.pub_id
```

(Chapter 7 explains the intricacies of the join operation. Don't worry about the syntax for this query now.)

Choosing Specific Columns

To select a subset of the columns in a table, as some of the previous examples have demonstrated, simply list the columns you want to see in the select list:

```
SELECT column_name[, column_name]...
FROM table_name
```

Separate each column name from the following column name with a comma.

Rearranging Result Columns. The order in which columns appear in a display is completely up to you: use the select list to order them in any way that makes sense.

Here are two examples. Both of them find and display the publisher names and identification numbers from all three of the rows in the *publishers* table. The first one prints *pub_id* first, followed by *pub_name*. The second reverses that order. The information is exactly the same; only the organization changes.

```
SQL:
select pub_id, pub_name
from publishers
```

```
Results:
pub_id    pub_name
------    ---------------
0736      New Age Books
0877      Binnet & Hardley
1389      Algodata Infosystems

(3 rows affected)

SQL:
select pub_name, pub_id
from publishers

Results:
pub_name                 pub_id
--------------------     ------
New Age Books            0736
Binnet & Hardley         0877
Algodata Infosystems     1389

(3 rows affected)
```

Expressions: More than Column Names

The SELECT statements you've seen so far show exactly what's stored in a table. This is useful, but often not useful enough. SQL lets you add to and manipulate these results to make them easier to read or to do "what if" queries. You can also use strings of characters, mathematical calculations, and functions provided by your system in the select list, with or without column names.

Renaming Columns and Naming Expressions.   When the results of a query are displayed, each column has a default heading, its name as defined in the database. Column names in databases are often cryptic (so they'll be easy to type) or have no meaning to users unfamiliar with departmental acronyms, nicknames, or project jargon.

You can solve this problem by specifying column headings to make query results easier to read and understand. To get the heading you want, simply type `column_name column_heading` or `column_name as column_heading` in the select list in place of the column name. (Some systems allow an alternate syntax like `column_heading` = `column_name`.)

For example, to change *pub_name* to *Publisher*, try one of the following statements:

```
SQL:
select pub_name Publisher, pub_id
from publishers
```

```
SQL:
select pub_name as Publisher, pub_id
from publishers
```

The results now show a new column heading:

```
Results:
Publisher                                 pub_id
---------------------------------------   ------
New Age Books                             0736
Binnet & Hardley                          0877
Algodata Infosystems                      1389

(3 rows affected)
```

A column heading is usually not limited to the size of the current column. The *pub_id* column, for example, can take a column heading longer than its defined length of four characters. Look what happens in the display when you change the column heading to a string such as "Identification#."

```
SQL:
select pub_name as Publisher, pub_id as Identification#
from publishers
```

```
Results:
Publisher                                 Identification#
---------------------------------------   ---------------
New Age Books                             0736
Binnet & Hardley                          0877
Algodata Infosystems                      1389

(3 rows affected)
```

In most systems, the display size stretches to accommodate the longer heading; if you use a smaller heading, however, it doesn't shrink the display size below its datatype-defined size.

Most SQL dialects that allow you to add column headings have some restrictions (check your reference guide for details). Ordinarily, you can't put quotes around or spaces in a column heading: "Identification #" (with a blank between the word and the pound sign) probably won't work.

You can use the same technique to create headings for columns based on strings, calculations, and other expressions: *New_price*, *Double_Advance*, and so on:

```
SQL:
select title, advance * 2 as Double_Advance
from titles
```

Character Strings in Query Results. Sometimes a little text can make query results easier to understand. That's where **strings** (of characters) come in handy.

Let's say you want a listing of publishers with something like "The publisher's name is" in front of each item. All you have to do is insert the string in the correct position in the select list. Be sure to enclose the entire string in single or double quotes so your system can tell it's not a column name, and separate it from other elements in the select list with commas.

Follow your system's rules for protecting embedded apostrophes and quotes if any appear in the string. Here, double single quotes do the trick and prevent the apostrophe from being interpreted as a close quote.

```
SQL:
select 'The publisher''s name is', pub_name as Publisher
from publishers

Results:

                             Publisher
-----------------------      ---------------
The publisher's name is      New Age Books
The publisher's name is      Binnet & Hardley
The publisher's name is      Algodata Infosystems

(3 rows affected)
```

The constants create a new column in the display only—what you see doesn't affect anything that's physically in the database.

You could also break each word in the string into a separate field, like this:

```
SQL:
select 'The', 'publisher', 'name', 'is', pub_name
from publishers


Results:

                              pub_name
--- ------------ ---- -- ------------------------------
The publisher    name is New Age Books
The publisher    name is Binnet & Hardley
The publisher    name is Algodata Infosystems

(3 rows affected)
```

This technique makes it easy to combine columns and text. Here's an example of doing just that:

```
SQL:
select 'The name for publisher #', pub_id, 'is', pub_name
from publishers


Results:

                         pub_id    pub_name
--------------------- ------ -- ----------------------
The name for publisher # 0736 is New Age Books
The name for publisher # 0877 is Binnet & Hardley
The name for publisher # 1389 is Algodata Infosystems

(3 rows affected)
```

Computations with Constants. The select list is the place where you indicate computations you want to perform on numeric data or constants.

Here are the available arithmetic operators:

Symbol	Operation
+	addition
–	subtraction
/	division
*	multiplication

The arithmetic operators—addition, subtraction, division, and multiplication—can be used on any numeric column. (Some systems add **modulo**, represented as %. A modulo is the whole-number remainder after division of one whole number by another. For example, 21 % 9 = 3, because 21 divided by 9 equals 2, with a remainder of 3.)

Certain arithmetic operations can also be performed on date columns, if your system provides date functions.

You can use all of these operators in the select list with column names and numeric constants in any combination. For example, to see what a projected sales increase of 100 percent for all the books in the *titles* table looks like, type this:

```
SQL:
select title_id, ytd_sales, ytd_sales * 2
from titles
```

Here are the results:

```
Results:
title_id ytd_sales
-------- ------------ -----------
BU1032       4095         8190
BU1111       3876         7752
BU2075      18722        37444
BU7832       4095         8190
MC2222       2032         4064
MC3021      22246        44492
MC3026       NULL         NULL
PC1035       8780        17560
PC8888       4095         8190
PC9999       NULL         NULL
PS1372        375          750
PS2091       2045         4090
PS2106        111          222
PS3333       4072         8144
```

```
PS7777              3336              6672
TC3218               375               750
TC4203             15096             30192
TC7777              4095              8190
```

```
(18 rows affected)
```

Notice the null values in the *ytd_sales* column and the computed column. When you perform any arithmetic operation on a null value, the result is NULL.

You can give the computed column a heading (say, *Projected_Sales*) by typing this:

SQL:
```
select title_id, ytd_sales, ytd_sales * 2 as Projected_Sales
from titles
```

For a fancier display yet, try adding character strings such as "Current sales =" and "Projected sales are" to the SELECT statement.

Sometimes, as in the previous example, you'll want both the original data and the computed data in your results. But you don't have to include the column on which the computation takes place in the select list. To see just the computed values, type this:

SQL:
```
select title_id, ytd_sales * 2
from titles
```

Results:
```
title_id
--------  -----------
BU1032              8190
BU1111              7752
BU2075             37444
BU7832              8190
MC2222              4064
MC3021             44492
MC3026              NULL
PC1035             17560
PC8888              8190
```

```
PC9999              NULL
PS1372               750
PS2091              4090
PS2106               222
PS3333              8144
PS7777              6672
TC3218               750
TC4203             30192
TC7777              8190

(18 rows affected)
```

Computations with Column Names. You can also use arithmetic operators for computations on the data in two or more columns, with no constants involved. Here's an example:

SQL:
```
select title_id, ytd_sales * price
from titles
```

Results:
```
title_id
-------- -----------------------
BU1032              81,859.05
BU1111              46,318.20
BU2075              55,978.78
BU7832              81,859.05
MC2222              40,619.68
MC3021              66,515.54
MC3026                   NULL
PC1035             201,501.00
PC8888              81,900.00
PC9999                   NULL
PS1372               8,096.25
PS2091              22,392.75
PS2106                 777.00
PS3333              81,399.28
PS7777              26,654.64
TC3218               7,856.25
TC4203             180,397.20
```

```
TC7777                      61,384.05
```

(18 rows affected)

Finally, you can compute new values on the basis of columns from more than one table. (The chapters on joining and subqueries give information on how to work with multiple-table queries, so check them for syntax details.)

Arithmetic Operator Precedence.   When there is more than one arithmetic operator in an expression, the system follows rules that determine the order in which the operations are carried out (Figure 4-2). According to commonly used precedence rules, multiplication and division are calculated first, followed by subtraction and addition. When more than one arithmetic operator in an expression has the same level of precedence, the order of execution is left to right. Expressions within parentheses take precedence over all other operations.

Here's an example. The following SELECT statement subtracts the advance on each book from the gross revenues realized on its sales (*price* multiplied by *ytd_sales*). The product of *ytd_sales* and *price* is calculated first because the operator is multiplication.

SQL:
```
select title_id, ytd_sales * price - advance
from titles
```

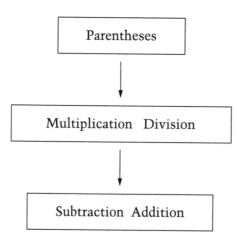

Figure 4-2. Precedence Hierarchy for Arithmetic Operators

To avoid misunderstandings, use parentheses. The following query has the same meaning and gives the same results as the previous one, but some may find it easier to understand:

```
SQL:
select title_id, (ytd_sales * price) - advance
from titles

Results:
title_id
-------- ------------------------
BU1032                 76,859.05
BU1111                 41,318.20
BU2075                 45,853.78
BU7832                 76,859.05
MC2222                 40,619.68
MC3021                 51,515.54
MC3026                      NULL
PC1035                194,501.00
PC8888                 73,900.00
PC9999                      NULL
PS1372                  1,096.25
PS2091                 20,117.75
PS2106                 -5,223.00
PS3333                 79,399.28
PS7777                 22,654.64
TC3218                    856.25
TC4203                176,397.20
TC7777                 53,384.05

(18 rows affected)
```

Another important use of parentheses is changing the order of execution: calculations inside parentheses are handled first. If parentheses are nested (one set of parentheses inside another), the most deeply nested calculation has precedence. For example, the result and meaning of the query just shown can be changed if you use parentheses to force evaluation of the subtraction before the multiplication:

```
SQL:
select title_id, ytd_sales * (price - advance)
from titles

Results:
title_id
-------- -------------------------
BU1032             -20,393,140.95
BU1111             -19,333,681.80
BU2075            -189,504,271.22
BU7832             -20,393,140.95
MC2222                  40,619.68
MC3021            -333,623,484.46
MC3026                       NULL
PC1035             -61,258,499.00
PC8888             -32,678,100.00
PC9999                       NULL
PS1372              -2,616,903.75
PS2091              -4,629,982.25
PS2106                -665,223.00
PS3333              -8,062,600.72
PS7777             -13,317,345.36
TC3218              -2,617,143.75
TC4203             -60,203,602.80
TC7777             -32,698,615.95

(18 rows affected)
```

SPECIFYING TABLES: THE TABLE LIST

The **table list** names the table(s), the view(s), or both, that contain columns included in the select list and in the WHERE clause. Separate table names in the table list with commas. The FROM syntax looks like this:

```
SELECT select_list
FROM [qualifier]{table_name | view_name}
  [, [qualifier]{table_name | view_name}]...
```

The full naming syntax for tables and views, with qualifying database and owner names, is always permitted in the table list. It's only necessary, however, when there might be some confusion about the name.

In many SQL dialects, you can give table names **aliases** to save typing. Assign an alias in the table list by giving the alias after the table name, like this:

```
SQL:
select p.pub_id, p.pub_name
from publishers p
```

The *p* in front of each of the column names in the select list acts as a substitute for the full table name (*publishers*). This query is equivalent:

```
SQL:
select publishers.pub_id, publishers.pub_name
from publishers
```

Since only one table is involved in these queries, there is no ambiguity about which *pub_id* column you're referencing, so using the table name—either its alias or its full name—as a qualifier is optional. Aliases are really useful only in multiple-table queries, where you need to qualify columns from different tables. You'll see examples of their use in Chapters 7 and 8.

SELECTING ROWS: THE WHERE CLAUSE

The WHERE clause is the part of the SELECT statement that specifies the search conditions. These conditions determine exactly which rows are retrieved. The general format is this:

```
SELECT select_list
FROM table_list
WHERE search_conditions
```

When you run a SELECT statement with a WHERE clause, your system searches for the rows in the table that meet your conditions (also called **qualifications**).

SQL provides a variety of operators and keywords for expressing the search conditions, including these:

- Comparison operators (=, <, >, and so on)

```
where advance * 2 > ytd_sales * price
```

- Combinations or logical negations of conditions (AND, OR, NOT)

```
where advance < 5000 or ytd_sales
> 2000
```

- Ranges (BETWEEN and NOT BETWEEN)

```
where ytd_sales between 4095 and 12000
```

- Lists (IN, NOT IN)

```
where state in ('CA', 'IN', 'MD')
```

- Unknown values (IS NULL and IS NOT NULL)

```
where advance is null
```

- Character matches (LIKE and NOT LIKE)

```
where phone not like '415%'
```

Each of these keywords and operators is explained and illustrated in this chapter.

In addition, the WHERE clause can include join conditions (see Chapter 7) and subqueries (see Chapter 8).

Comparison Operators

You often want to look at values in relation to one another, to find out which is "larger" or "smaller," or "lower" in the alphabet sort, or "equal" to some other database value or to a constant. SQL provides a set of comparison operators for these purposes. In most dialects, the comparison operators are these:

Operator	Meaning
=	equal to
>	greater than
<	less than
>=	greater than or equal to
<=	less than or equal to
!=	not equal to (or)
< >	not equal to

The operators are used in the syntax:

```
WHERE expression comparison_operator expression
```

An expression can be a constant, column name, function, subquery, or any combination of them connected by arithmetic operators.

In contexts other than SQL, the comparison operators are usually used with numeric values. In SQL, they are also used with *char* and *varchar* data (< means earlier in the dictionary order and > means later) and with dates (< means earlier in chronological order and > means later). When you use character and date values in a SQL statement, be sure to put quotes around them.

The order in which upper- and lowercase characters and special characters are evaluated depends on the character-sorting sequence you are using, imposed by your database system or by the machine you are using. In most systems, trailing blanks are ignored for the purposes of comparison. So, for example, "Dirk" would be considered the same as "Dirk " by the system.

The following SELECT statements and their results should give you a good sense of how the comparison operators are used. The first query finds the books that cost more than $15.00 dollars:

```
SQL:
select title, price
from titles
where price > $15.00

Results:
title                                            price
------------------------------------------------ -----
The Busy Executive's Database Guide              19.99
Straight Talk About Computers                    19.99
```

```
Silicon Valley Gastronomic Treats            19.99
But Is It User Friendly?                     22.95
Secrets of Silicon Valley                    20.00
Computer Phobic and Non-Phobic
    Individuals: Behavior Variations         21.59
Prolonged Data Deprivation:
    Four Case Studies                        19.99
Onions, Leeks, and Garlic: Cooking
    Secrets of the Mediterranean             20.95
```

(8 rows affected)

The next SELECT statement finds the authors whose last names follow McBadden's in the alphabet:

SQL:

```
select au_lname, au_fname
from authors
where au_lname >'McBadden'
```

Results:

```
au_lname                                     au_fname
------------------------------------------   --------------

White                                        Johnson
O'Leary                                      Michael
Straight                                     Dick
Smith                                        Meander
Yokomoto                                     Akiko
Stringer                                     Dirk
Panteley                                     Sylvia
Ringer                                       Anne
Ringer                                       Albert
```

(9 rows affected)

(Your results may differ, depending on the sort order your system uses. See Chapter 5 for more on this issue.) The next query displays hypothetical information—it doubles the price of all books for which advances over $10,000 were paid, and displays the title identification numbers and doubled prices:

```
SQL:
select title_id, price * 2
from titles
where advance > $10000
```

```
Results:
title_id
-------- -------------------------
BU2075                      5.98
MC3021                      5.98
```

```
(2 rows affected)
```

Here's a query that finds the telephone numbers of authors who don't live in California, using the not equal comparison operator (in different versions of SQL, the not equal operator can be != or < >):

```
SQL:
select au_id, phone
from authors
where state != 'CA'
```

```
Results:
au_id        phone
----------- ------------
341-22-1782 913 843-0462
527-72-3246 615 297-2723
648-92-1872 503 745-6402
712-45-1867 615 996-8275
722-51-5454 219 547-9982
807-91-6654 301 946-8853
899-46-2035 801 826-0752
998-72-3567 801 826-0752
```

```
(8 rows affected)
```

Connecting Conditions with Logical Operators

Use the **logical operators** AND, OR, and NOT when you're dealing with more than one condition in a WHERE clause. The logical operators are also called **Boolean operators**.

AND joins two or more conditions and returns results only when all of the conditions are true. For example, the query below will find only the rows in which the author's last name is Ringer and the author's first name is Anne. It will not find the row for Albert Ringer.

```
SQL:
select *
from authors
where au_lname = 'Ringer'
  and au_fname = 'Anne'
```

This example finds business books with a price higher than $10.00 and for which an advance of less than $20,000 was paid:

```
SQL:
select title, type, price, advance
from titles
where type = 'business'
  and price > $10.00
  and advance < $20000
```

```
Results:
title
   type                                  price              advance
-------------------------------------- -------------------- ------
The Busy Executive's Database Guide
   business                             19.99               5,000.00
Cooking with Computers: Surreptitious Balance Sheets
   business                             11.95               5,000.00
Straight Talk About Computers
   business                             19.99               5,000.00

(3 rows affected)
```

OR also connects two or more conditions, but it returns results when any of the conditions is true. The following query searches for rows containing Anne or Ann in the *au_fname* column:

SQL:
```
select au_id, au_lname, au_fname
from authors
where au_fname = 'Anne'
  or au_fname = 'Ann'
```

Results:

au_id	au_lname	au_fname
427-17-2319	Dull	Ann
899-46-2035	Ringer	Anne

(2 rows affected)

The following query searches for books with a price higher than $20.00 *or* an advance less than $5,000.

SQL:
```
select title, type, price, advance
from titles
where price > $20.00
  or advance < $5000
```

Results:

title			
type		price	advance
Silicon Valley Gastronomic Treats			
mod_cook		19.99	0.00
But Is It User Friendly?			
popular_comp		22.95	7,000.00
Computer Phobic and Non-Phobic Individuals: Behavior Variations			
psychology		21.59	7,000.00
Is Anger the Enemy?			
psychology		10.95	2,275.00

```
Prolonged Data Deprivation: Four Case Studies
   psychology                  19.99                    2,000.00
Emotional Security: A New Algorithm
   psychology                   7.99                    4,000.00
Onions, Leeks, and Garlic: Cooking Secrets of the Mediterranean
   trad_cook                   20.95                    7,000.00
Fifty Years in Buckingham Palace Kitchens
   trad_cook                   11.95                    4,000.00

(8 rows affected)
```

One more example using OR will demonstrate a potential for confusion.
Let's say you want to find all the business books, as well as any books with
a price higher than $10, as well as any with an advance less than $20,000.
The English phrasing of this problem suggests the use of the operator AND,
but the logical meaning dictates the use of OR because you want to find all
the books in all three categories, not just books that meet all three characteristics at once. Here's the SQL statement that finds what you're looking
for:

SQL:
```
select title, type, price, advance
from titles
where type = 'business'
  or price > $10.00
  or advance < $20000
```

Results:
```
title
   type                           price              advance
- - - - - - - - - - - - - - - - - - - - -  - - - - - - - - - - - - - - -  - - - - - - -
The Busy Executive's Database Guide
   business                       19.99               5,000.00
Cooking with Computers: Surreptitious Balance Sheets
   business                       11.95               5,000.00
You Can Combat Computer Stress!
   business                        2.99              10,125.00
Straight Talk About Computers
   business                       19.99               5,000.00
Silicon Valley Gastronomic Treats
   mod_cook                       19.99                   0.00
```

```
The Gourmet Microwave
    mod_cook                        2.99                    15,000.00
But Is It User Friendly?
    popular_comp                   22.95                     7,000.00
Secrets of Silicon Valley
    popular_comp                   20.00                     8,000.00
Computer Phobic and Non-Phobic Individuals: Behavior Variations
    psychology                     21.59                     7,000.00
Is Anger the Enemy?
    psychology                     10.95                     2,275.00
Life Without Fear
    psychology                      7.00                     6,000.00
Prolonged Data Deprivation: Four Case Studies
    psychology                     19.99                     2,000.00
Emotional Security: A New Algorithm
    psychology                      7.99                     4,000.00
Onions, Leeks, and Garlic: Cooking Secrets of the Mediterranean
    trad_cook                      20.95                     7,000.00
Fifty Years in Buckingham Palace Kitchens
    trad_cook                      11.95                     4,000.00
Sushi, Anyone?
    trad_cook                      14.99                     8,000.00

(16 rows affected)
```

Compare this query, and its results, to the earlier example that is identical except for the use of AND instead of OR.

The logical operator NOT negates an expression. When you use it with comparison operators, put it before the expression rather than before the comparison operator. The following two queries are equivalent:

SQL:

```
select au_lname, au_fname
from authors
where state != 'CA'
```

SQL:

```
select au_lname, au_fname, state
from authors
where not state = 'CA'
```

Here are the results:

```
Results:
au_lname                au_fname                 state
----------------        --------------------     -----
Smith                   Meander                  KS
Greene                  Morningstar              TN
Blotchet-Halls          Reginald                 OR
del Castillo            Innes                    MI
DeFrance                Michel                   IN
Panteley                Sylvia                   MD
Ringer                  Anne                     UT
Ringer                  Albert                   UT

(8 rows affected)
```

Logical Operator Precedence.   Like the arithmetic operators, logical operators are handled according to precedence rules. When both kinds of operators occur in the same statement, arithmetic operators are handled before logical operators. When more than one logical operator is used in a statement, NOT is evaluated first, then AND, and finally OR. Figure 4-3 shows the hierarchy.

Some examples will clarify the situation. The following query finds all the business books in the *titles* table, no matter what their advances are, as well as all psychology books that have an advance greater than $5,500. The advance condition pertains to psychology books and not to business books because the AND is handled before the OR.

```
SQL:
select title_id, type, advance
from titles
where type = 'business'
  or type = 'psychology'
  and advance > 5500

Results:
title_id  type        advance
--------  ----------  ----------
BU1032    business    5,000.00
BU1111    business    5,000.00
```

```
BU2075     business     10,125.00
BU7832     business      5,000.00
PS1372     psychology    7,000.00
PS2106     psychology    6,000.00

(6 rows affected)
```

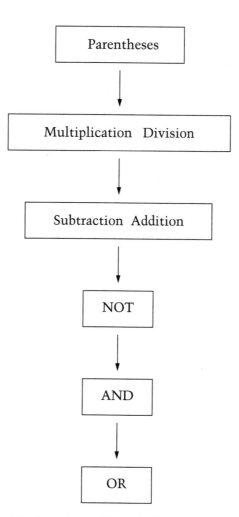

Figure 4-3. Precedence Hierarchy for Logical Operators

The results include three business books with advances less than $5,500 because the query was evaluated according to the precedence rules: first, all psychology books with advances greater than $5,500 were found; then, all business books were found.

You can change the meaning of the previous query by adding parentheses to force evaluation of the OR first. With parentheses added, the query finds all business and psychology books that have advances over $5,500:

```
SQL:
select title_id, type, advance
from titles
where (type = 'business'
  or type = 'psychology')
  and advance > 5500
```

```
Results:
title_id   type          advance
--------   ----------    ---------
BU2075     business      10,125.00
PS1372     psychology     7,000.00
PS2106     psychology     6,000.00

(3 rows affected)
```

The parentheses cause SQL to find all business and psychology books and, from among those, to find those with advances greater than $5,500.

Here's a query that includes arithmetic operators, comparison operators, and logical operators. It searches for books that are not bringing in enough money to offset their advances. Specifically, the query searches for any books with gross revenues (that is, *ytd_sales* times *price*) less than twice the advance paid to the author(s). The user who constructed this query has tacked on another condition: she wants to include in the results only books published before October 15, 1985, on the grounds that those books have had long enough to establish a sales pattern. The last condition is connected with the logical operator AND; according to the rules of precedence, it is evaluated after the arithmetic operations.

```
SQL:
select title_id, type, price, advance, ytd_sales
from titles
```

```
where price * ytd_sales <  2 * advance
and pubdate < '10/15/85'
```

Results:

title_id	type	price	advance	ytd_sales
PS2106	psychology	7.00	6,000.00	111

(1 row affected)

Ranges (BETWEEN and NOT BETWEEN)

Another common search condition is a range. There are two different ways to specify ranges:

- With the comparison operators > and <
- With the keyword BETWEEN

Use BETWEEN to specify an **inclusive range**, in which you search for the lower value and the upper value as well as the values they bracket. For example, to find all the books with sales between (and including) 4,095 and 12,000, you could write this query:

SQL:
```
select title_id, ytd_sales
from titles
where ytd_sales between 4095 and 12000
```

Results:

title_id	ytd_sales
BU1032	4095
BU7832	4095
PC1035	8780
PC8888	4095
TC7777	4095

(5 rows affected)

Notice that books with sales of 4,095 are included in the results. If there were any with sales of 12,000, they would be included too. In this way, the BETWEEN range is different from the greater than – less than (> <) range. The same query using the greater-than and less-than operators returns different results, because the range is not inclusive:

SQL:
```
select title_id, ytd_sales
from titles
where ytd_sales > 4095 and ytd_sales < 12000
```

Results:
```
title_id  ytd_sales
------    -------
PC1035    8780
```

```
(1 row affected)
```

The phrase NOT BETWEEN finds all the rows that are not inside the range. To find all the books with sales outside the range of 4,095 to 12,000, type this:

SQL:
```
select title_id, ytd_sales
from titles
where ytd_sales not between 4095 and 12000
```

Results:
```
title_id     ytd_sales
--------     ---------
BU1111        3876
BU2075       18722
MC2222        2032
MC3021       22246
PS1372         375
PS2091        2045
PS2106         111
PS3333        4072
PS7777        3336
```

```
TC3218              375
TC4203            15096
```

```
(11 rows affected)
```

You can get the same results with comparison operators, but notice in this query that you use OR between the two *ytd_sales* comparisons, rather than AND.

SQL:
```
select title_id, ytd_sales
from titles
where ytd_sales < 4095 or ytd_sales > 12000
```

Results:

```
title_id   ytd_sales
--------   ----------
BU1111         3876
BU2075        18722
MC2222         2032
MC3021        22246
PS1372          375
PS2091         2045
PS2106          111
PS3333         4072
PS7777         3336
TC3218          375
TC4203        15096
```

```
(11 rows affected)
```

This is another case where it's easy to get confused because of the way the question can be phrased in English. You might well ask to see all books whose sales are less than 4,095 *and* all books whose sales are greater than 12,000. The logical meaning, however, calls for the use of the Boolean operator OR. If you substitute AND, you'll get no results at all, since no book can have sales that are simultaneously less than 4,095 and greater than 12,000.

Lists (IN and NOT IN)

The IN keyword allows you to select values that match any one of a list of values. For example, without IN, if you want a list of the names and states of all the authors who live in California, Indiana, or Maryland, you can type this query:

```
SQL:
select au_lname, state
from authors
where state = 'CA' or state = 'IN' or state = 'MD'
```

However, you get the same results with less typing if you use IN. The items following the IN keyword must be separated by commas and enclosed in parentheses.

```
SQL:
select au_lname, state
from authors
where state in ('CA', 'IN', 'MD')
```

This is what results from either query:

```
Results:
au_lname           state
-------------      -----
White              CA
Green              CA
Carson             CA
O'Leary            CA
Straight           CA
Bennet             CA
Dull               CA
Gringlesby         CA
Locksley           CA
Yokomoto           CA
DeFrance           IN
Stringer           CA
MacFeather         CA
Karsen             CA
```

```
Panteley            MD
Hunter              CA
McBadden            CA
```

```
(17 rows affected)
```

The more items in the list, the greater the savings in typing by using IN rather than specifying each condition separately.

Perhaps the most important use for the IN keyword is in nested queries, also referred to as subqueries. For a full discussion of subqueries, see Chapter 8. However, the following example gives some idea of what you can do with nested queries and the IN keyword.

Suppose you want to know the names of the authors who receive less than 50 percent of the total royalties on the books they coauthor. The *authors* table gives author names, and the *titleauthors* table gives royalty information. By putting the two together using IN (but without listing the two tables in the same table list), you can extract the information you need.

The following query translates as "Find all the *au_id*s in the *titleauthors* table in which the authors make less than 50 percent of the royalty on any one book. Then select from the *authors* table all the author names with *au_id*s that match the results from the *titleauthors* query."

```
SQL:
select au_lname, au_fname
from authors
where au_id in
  (select au_id
   from titleauthors
   where royaltyshare < .50)
```

```
Results:
au_lname                au_fname
----------------        -----------
Green                   Marjorie
O'Leary                 Michael
Gringlesby              Burt
Yokomoto                Akiko
MacFeather              Stearns
Ringer                  Anne

(6 rows affected)
```

The six authors receive royalty shares of less than 50 percent on at least one book.

NOT IN finds the authors that do not match the items in the list. The following query finds the names of authors who do not make less than 50 percent of the royalties on at least one book.

SQL:

```
select au_lname, au_fname
from authors
where au_id not in
  (select au_id
    from titleauthors
    where royaltyshare < .50)
```

Results:

au_lname	au_fname
White	Johnson
Carson	Cheryl
Straight	Dick
Smith	Meander
Bennet	Abraham
Dull	Ann
Locksley	Chastity
Greene	Morningstar
Blotchet-Halls	Reginald
del Castillo	Innes
DeFrance	Michel
Stringer	Dirk
Karsen	Livia
Panteley	Sylvia
Hunter	Sheryl
McBadden	Heather
Ringer	Albert

(17 rows affected)

Selecting Null Values

From earlier chapters, you may recall that NULL is a placeholder for unknown information. It does not mean zero or blank.

To clarify this NULL–zero difference, take a look at the following listing showing title and advance amount for books belonging to one particular publisher.

SQL:

```
select title, advance
from titles
where pub_id = '0877'
```

Results:

```
title                                           advance
------------------------------------------- ----------
Silicon Valley Gastronomic Treats                  0.00
The Gourmet Microwave                         15,000.00
The Psychology of Computer Cooking                 NULL
Onions, Leeks, and Garlic: Cooking
   Secrets of the Mediterranean                 7,000.00
Fifty Years in Buckingham Palace Kitchens       4,000.00
Sushi, Anyone?                                  8,000.00
```

(6 rows affected)

A cursory perusal shows that one book (*Silicon Valley Gastronomic Treats*) has an advance of $0.00, probably due to extremely poor negotiating skills on the author's part. This author will receive no money until the royalties start coming in. Another book (*The Psychology of Computer Cooking*) has a null advance: perhaps the author and the publisher are still working out the details of their deal, or perhaps the data entry clerk hasn't made the entry yet. Eventually, in this case, an amount will be known and recorded. Maybe it will be zero, maybe millions, maybe a couple of thousand dollars. The point is that right now the data does not disclose what the advance for this book is, so the advance value in the table is NULL.

What happens in the case of comparisons involving nulls? Since a null represents the unknown, it doesn't match anything, even another null. For example, a query that finds all the title identification numbers and advances for books with moderate advances (under $5,000) will not find the row for MC3026, *The Psychology of Computer Cooking*.

SQL:
```
select title_id, advance
from titles
where advance < $5000
```

Results:
```
title_id  advance
--------  ----------
MC2222          0.00
PS2091      2,275.00
PS3333      2,000.00
PS7777      4,000.00
TC4203      4,000.00
```

(5 rows affected)

Neither will a query for all books with an advance over $5,000:

SQL:
```
select title_id, advance
from titles
where advance > $5000
```

Results:
```
title_id  advance
--------  ----------
BU2075     10,125.00
MC3021     15,000.00
PC1035      7,000.00
PC8888      8,000.00
PS1372      7,000.00
PS2106      6,000.00
TC3218      7,000.00
TC7777      8,000.00
```

(8 rows affected)

NULL is neither above nor below (nor equal to) $5,000 because NULL is unknown. But don't despair! You can retrieve rows on the basis of their NULL/NOT NULL status with a special pattern:

```
WHERE column_name IS [NOT] NULL
```

Use it to find the row for books with null advances like this:

SQL:
```
select title_id, advance
from titles
where advance is null
```

Results:
```
title_id  advance
--------  ----------
MC3026         NULL
PC9999         NULL
```

You can use the same pattern in combination with other comparison operators. Here's how a query for books with an advance under $5,000 *or* a null advance would look:

SQL:
```
select title_id, advance
from titles
where advance < $5000
   or advance is null
```

Results:
```
title_id  advance
--------  ----------
MC2222          0.00
MC3026          NULL
PC9999          NULL
PS2091      2,275.00
PS3333      2,000.00
PS7777      4,000.00
TC4203      4,000.00

(7 rows affected)
```

Matching Character Strings: LIKE

Some problems can't be solved with comparisons. Here are a few examples:

- "His name begins with 'Mc' or 'Mac'—I can't remember the rest."
- "We need a list of all the 415 area code phone numbers."
- "I forget the name of the book, but it has a mention of exercise in the notes."
- "Well, it's Carson, or maybe Karsen—something like that."
- "His first name is 'Dirk' or 'Dick.' Four letters, starts with a *D* and ends with a *k*."

In each of these cases, you know a pattern embedded somewhere in a column, and you need to use it to retrieve all or part of the row. The LIKE keyword is designed to solve this problem. You can use it with character fields (and on some systems, with date fields). It doesn't work with numeric fields defined as integer, money, and decimal or float. The syntax is this:

```
WHERE column_name [NOT] LIKE 'pattern' [ESCAPE escape_char]
```

The pattern must be enclosed in quotes and include one or more **wild-cards** (symbols that take the place of missing letters or strings in the pattern). You use the ESCAPE keyword when your pattern includes one of the wildcards and you need to treat it as a literal.

ANSI SQL provides two wildcard characters for use with LIKE, the percent sign (%) and the underscore (_).

Wildcard	Meaning
%	any string of zero or more characters
_	any single character

Many systems offer variations (notations for single characters that fall within a range or set, for example). Check your system's reference guide to see what's available.

Here are answers to the questions just posed and the queries that generated them. First, the search for Scottish surnames:

```
SQL:
select au_lname, city
from authors
where au_lname like 'Mc%' or au_lname like 'Mac%'
```

```
Results:
au_lname                                  city
- - - - - - - - - - - - - - - - - - - - - - - - - - - - -   - - - - - - - - - - - - - - - - - - - -

MacFeather                                Oakland
McBadden                                  Vacaville

(2 rows affected)
```

The LIKE pattern instructs the system to search for a name that begins with "Mc" and is followed by a string of any number of characters (%) or that begins with "Mac" and is followed by any number of characters. Notice that the wildcard is inside the quotes.

Now the 415 area code list:

```
SQL:

select au_lname, phone
from authors
where phone like '415%'


Results:
au_lname                                  phone
- - - - - - - - - - - - - - - - - - - - - - - - - - - - - - - - - - -   - - - - - - - - - - -

Green                                     415 986-7020
Carson                                    415 548-7723
Straight                                  415 834-2919
Bennet                                    415 658-9932
Dull                                      415 836-7128
Locksley                                  415 585-4620
Yokomoto                                  415 935-4228
Stringer                                  415 843-2991
MacFeather                                415 354-7128
Karsen                                    415 534-9219
Hunter                                    415 836-7128

(11 rows affected)
```

Here again, you're looking for some known initial characters followed by a string of unknown characters.

The book with "exercise" somewhere in its notes is a little more tricky. You don't know if it's at the beginning or end of the column, and you don't know whether or not the first letter of the word is capitalized. You can cover all these possibilities by leaving the first letter out of the pattern and using the same "string of zero or more characters" wildcard at the beginning and end of the pattern.

SQL:
```
select title_id, notes
from titles
where notes like '%xercise%'
```

Results:
```
title_id notes
-------- -----------------------------------------------------------
PS2106   New exercise, meditation, and nutritional techniques
         that can reduce the shock of daily interactions.
         Popular audience.  Sample menus included, exercise
         video available separately.
```

(1 row affected)

When you know the number of characters missing, you can use the single-character wildcard, the underbar (_). Here the first letter is either *K* or *C* and the next to the last is either *e* or *o*.

SQL:
```
select au_lname, city
from authors
where au_lname like '_ars_n'
```

Results:
```
au_lname                                   city
------------------------------------------ --------------------
Carson                                     Berkeley
Karsen                                     Oakland
```

(2 rows affected)

The next example is similar to the previous one. It looks for four-letter first names starting with *D* and ending with *k*.

SQL:
```
select au_lname, au_fname, city
from authors
where au_fname like 'D__k'
```

Results:

au_lname	au_fname	city
Straight	Dick	Oakland
Stringer	Dirk	Oakland

```
(2 rows affected)
```

You can also use NOT LIKE with wildcards. To find all the phone numbers in the *authors* table that do *not* have 415 as the area code, you could use either of these queries (they are equivalent):

SQL:
```
select phone
from authors
where phone not like '415%'

select phone
from authors
where not phone like '415%'
```

Wildcard characters are almost always used together with the LIKE keyword. Without LIKE, they are interpreted literally and represent exactly their own values. The query below finds any phone numbers that consist of the four characters "415%" only. It will not find phone numbers that start with 415:

SQL:
```
select phone
from authors
where phone = '415%'
```

What if you want to search for a value that contains one of the wildcard characters? For example, in one row in the *titles* table , the *notes* column contains a claim to increase readers' friends by some percentage. You can search for the percent mark by using ESCAPE to appoint a character to strip the percent sign of its magic meaning and convert it to an ordinary character. A wildcard directly after the escape character has only its literal meaning. Other wildcards continue to have their special significance. In the following LIKE expression, you are looking for a literal percent sign somewhere in the *notes* column. Since it's probably not the first or last character, you use wildcard percent signs at the beginning and end of the expression and a percent sign preceded by the escape character in the middle.

```
SQL:
select title_id, notes
from titles
where notes like '%@%%' escape '@'

Results:
title_id notes
-------- --------------------------------------------------------
TC7777   Detailed instructions on improving your position in
         life by learning how to make authentic Japanese sushi
         in your spare time. 5-10% increase in number of
         friends per recipe reported from beta test.

(1 row affected)
```

Here are some examples of LIKE with escaped and unescaped wildcard character searches. (The @ sign is the escape character.)

Symbol	Meaning
LIKE '27%'	27 followed by any string of 0 or more characters
LIKE '27@%'	27%
LIKE '_n'	an, in, on, etc.
LIKE '@_n'	_n

AND THERE'S MORE

The next chapter covers some refinements on selection: ordering results with ORDER BY, eliminating duplicates in results with DISTINCT, and aggregate functions.

Chapter 5

Sorting Data and Other
Selection Techniques

A NEW BATCH OF SELECT STATEMENT CLAUSES

Now that you're familiar with the fundamentals of the SELECT statement—SELECT, FROM, and WHERE—it's time to go on to some additional features. These include ORDER BY (for sorting query results), DISTINCT (for eliminating duplicate rows), and **aggregate functions** (for calculating group totals, sums, minimums, maximums, and counts). The next chapter covers GROUP BY (for creating groups), aggregate functions with groups, and HAVING (for putting conditions on groups).

SORTING QUERY RESULTS: ORDER BY

The ORDER BY clause can make your results more readable. It allows you to sort by any column or expression in the select list. Each sort can be in ascending or descending order.

Sort Order

"A" comes before " B," right? How about "A" and "a"? Or "A" and "À"? The answer depends on the **character set** and **sort order**.

- A character set is a list (or **repertoire**) of letters and special characters and its internal mapping to computer codes (**form-of-use**). Character sets may include non-English characters, and may use different combinations of these characters; consider the cedilla in Spanish, accents in French, and the non-Roman symbols of Hebrew and Chinese.

- The sort order (also called the **collating sequence** or the **collation**) determines the order of the characters. A sort order may handle uppercase letters before lowercase letters, or may consider them equivalent, for example.

Repertoire, form-of-use, and sort order are not defined in terms of SQL commands, but most database systems allow you to load or choose which character set you want to use and decide among possible sort orders for that character set. However, neither of these is an on-the-fly decision. You generally specify character set and sort order when you set the database system up. SQL-92 provides some commands relevant to picking among available character sets and sort orders (CREATE CHARACTER SET, DROP CHARACTER SET, CREATE COLLATION, DROP COLLATION, COLLATE, and COLLATION FROM), but they are not widely implemented. Check your system manuals for specifics.

The examples in this book use code page 850, a multilingual character set, and binary sort order. A listing of the characters in the set looks like this (the display comes from Sybase SQL Server *sp_helpsort* output):

```
    Binary Sort Order for Code Page 850 (cp850).
Characters, in Order

- - - - - - - - - - - - - - - - - - - - - - - - - - - - - - - - - - - -
!  "  #  $  %  &  '  (  )  *  +  ,  -  .  /  0  1  2  3  4  5  6  7  8  9  :  ;  <  =  >  ?
@  A  B  C  D  E  F  G  H  I  J  K  L  M  N  O  P  Q  R  S  T  U  V  W  X  Y  Z  [  \  ]  ^  _
`  a  b  c  d  e  f  g  h  i  j  k  l  m  n  o  p  q  r  s  t  u  v  w  x  y  z  {  |  }  ~  ‾
_  _  ‚  ƒ  „  …  †  ‡  ˆ  ‰  Š  ‹  Œ  _  _  _  _  ‘  ’  “  ”  •  –  —  ˜  ™  š  ›  œ  _  _  Ÿ
¡  ¢  £  ¤  ¥  ¦  §  ¨  ©  ª  «  ¬  -  ®  ¯  °  ±  ²  ³  ´  µ  ¶  ·  ¸  ¹  º  »  ¼  ½  ¾  ¿
À  Á  Â  Ã  Ä  Å  Æ  Ç  È  É  Ê  Ë  Ì  Í  Î  Ï  Ð  Ñ  Ò  Ó  Ô  Õ  Ö  ×  Ø  Ù  Ú  Û  Ü  Ý  Þ  ß
à  á  â  ã  ä  å  æ  ç  è  é  ê  ë  ì  í  î  ï  ð  ñ  ò  ó  ô  õ  ö  ÷  ø  ù  ú  û  ü  ý  þ  ÿ
```

How Sort Order Works

Let's say you want a listing of prices, title identification numbers, and publisher numbers from the *titles* table. You might write a query like this:

```
SQL:
select price, title_id, pub_id
from titles
```

```
Results:
price                       title_id pub_id
- - - - - - - - - - - - - - - - - - - - - -  - - - - - - - -  - - - - - -
                     19.99 BU1032   1389
                     11.95 BU1111   1389
                      2.99 BU2075   0736
                     19.99 BU7832   1389
                     19.99 MC2222   0877
                      2.99 MC3021   0877
                      NULL MC3026   0877
                     22.95 PC1035   1389
                     20.00 PC8888   1389
                      NULL PC9999   1389
                     21.59 PS1372   0877
                     10.95 PS2091   0736
                      7.00 PS2106   0736
                     19.99 PS3333   0736
                      7.99 PS7777   0736
                     20.95 TC3218   0877
                     11.95 TC4203   0877
                     14.99 TC7777   0877
```

```
(18 rows affected)
```

The information you asked for is all there, but it's a little hard to see what you've got because there is no meaningful order in the results. Books are listed in *title_id* order—that's where the clustered index is—but in this particular case, that organization doesn't help you understand the results. The information would probably be more useful if it were arranged by price. This is how you'd do it:

```
SQL:
select price, title_id, pub_id
from titles
order by price
```

Results:

```
price                    title_id pub_id
------------------------ -------- ------
                NULL MC3026    0877
                NULL PC9999    1389
                2.99 BU2075    0736
                2.99 MC3021    0877
                7.00 PS2106    0736
                7.99 PS7777    0736
               10.95 PS2091    0736
               11.95 BU1111    1389
               11.95 TC4203    0877
               14.99 TC7777    0877
               19.99 BU1032    1389
               19.99 BU7832    1389
               19.99 MC2222    0877
               19.99 PS3333    0736
               20.00 PC8888    1389
               20.95 TC3218    0877
               21.59 PS1372    0877
               22.95 PC1035    1389
```

(18 rows affected)

Now the rows are listed in price order.

ORDER BY Syntax

The general syntax for the SELECT statement ORDER BY clause looks
something like this:

```
SELECT select_list
FROM table_list
[WHERE conditions]
[ORDER BY {expression [ASC | DESC] | position [ASC | DESC]}
  [, {expression [ASC | DESC] | position [ASC | DESC] }]...]
```

Most (but not all) systems require that each sort element (column or
expression) appear in the select list. For expressions, you have three possible options: use an integer to represent the expression's position in the

select list, use a column heading you assigned in the select list (price *
ytd_sales as income), or (less commonly) use the whole expression.
Appendix B shows syntax for five systems. Check your reference manuals
for details on precisely how your system handles this useful clause.

Sorts within Sorts

Now that you have the results sorted by price, you might also want to
make sure that books within each price category by the same publisher are
listed together. Adding *pub_id* to the ORDER BY list is the way to do it:

```
SQL:
select price, title_id, pub_id
from titles
order by price, pub_id
```

```
Results:
price                        title_id  pub_id
---------------------------  --------  ------
                 NULL MC3026           0877
                 NULL PC9999           1389
                 2.99 BU2075           0736
                 2.99 MC3021           0877
                 7.00 PS2106           0736
                 7.99 PS7777           0736
                10.95 PS2091           0736
                11.95 TC4203           0877
                11.95 BU1111           1389
                14.99 TC7777           0877
                19.99 PS3333           0736
                19.99 MC2222           0877
                19.99 BU1032           1389
                19.99 BU7832           1389
                20.00 PC8888           1389
                20.95 TC3218           0877
                21.59 PS1372           0877
                22.95 PC1035           1389

(18 rows affected)
```

When you use more than one column in the ORDER BY clause, sorts are **nested** (that is, ordered by *price* first and then by *pub_id* within each price category).

You can have as many levels of sorts as you like. Many systems require that each sort element appear in the select list, but they don't insist on ORDER BY columns and expressions being in the same sequence as SELECT columns and expressions. If you changed the example so that it sorts first by *pub_id* and then by *price*, here's what you'd see:

SQL:

```
select price, title_id, pub_id
from titles
order by pub_id, price
```

Results:

```
price                   title_id pub_id
----------------------- -------- ------
                   2.99 BU2075   0736
                   7.00 PS2106   0736
                   7.99 PS7777   0736
                  10.95 PS2091   0736
                  19.99 PS3333   0736
                  21.59 PS1372   0736
                   NULL MC3026   0877
                   2.99 MC3021   0877
                  11.95 TC4203   0877
                  14.99 TC7777   0877
                  19.99 MC2222   0877
                  20.95 TC3218   0877
                   NULL PC9999   1389
                  11.95 BU1111   1389
                  19.99 BU1032   1389
                  19.99 BU7832   1389
                  20.00 PC8888   1389
                  22.95 PC1035   1389

(18 rows affected)
```

The columns are listed in the same order as in the previous results (*price* first, *title_id* second, and *pub_id* third), but the rows are arranged differently:

first you see all the rows with 0736, then all those with 0877, and finally those with 1389 as the publisher identification number.

Sort Up, Sort Down

You can specify a direction—low to high or high to low—for each individual sort by using the ascending (ASC) or descending (DESC) keyword immediately after the sort item. Ascending is the default, assumed to be in effect unless you type DESC, which means you don't really need to use ASC except to make the direction of the sort unavoidably explicit to others who read the query.

Here's how you'd get prices to display in descending order:

```
SQL:
select price, title_id, pub_id
from titles
order by price desc, pub_id

Results:
price                    title_id pub_id
------------------------ -------- ------
                   22.95 PC1035   1389
                   21.59 PS1372   0736
                   20.95 TC3218   0877
                   20.00 PC8888   1389
                   19.99 PS3333   0736
                   19.99 MC2222   0877
                   19.99 BU1032   1389
                   19.99 BU7832   1389
                   14.99 TC7777   0877
                   11.95 TC4203   0877
                   11.95 BU1111   1389
                   10.95 PS2091   0736
                    7.99 PS7777   0736
                    7.00 PS2106   0736
                    2.99 BU2075   0736
                    2.99 MC3021   0877
                    NULL MC3026   0877
                    NULL PC9999   1389

(18 rows affected)
```

Notice that *pub_id*s are still in ascending order within each price category. Depending on your system, NULL prices may be at the beginning or the end of the list. You could change the direction of the *pub_id* sort like this:

SQL:

```
select price, title_id, pub_id
from titles
order by price desc, pub_id desc
```

Results:

```
price                   title_id pub_id
----------------------- -------- ------
                  22.95 PC1035   1389
                  21.59 PS1372   0736
                  20.95 TC3218   0877
                  20.00 PC8888   1389
                  19.99 BU1032   1389
                  19.99 BU7832   1389
                  19.99 MC2222   0877
                  19.99 PS3333   0736
                  14.99 TC7777   0877
                  11.95 BU1111   1389
                  11.95 TC4203   0877
                  10.95 PS2091   0736
                   7.99 PS7777   0736
                   7.00 PS2106   0736
                   2.99 MC3021   0877
                   2.99 BU2075   0736
                   NULL PC9999   1389
                   NULL MC3026   0877
```

(18 rows affected)

What about Expressions?

What if you want to sort by an expression in the select list? SQL allows you to use the expression's position in the select list (represented with a number) or heading (also called alias or label) as the order element. Some systems also allow you to use the full expression.

Here's an example of the kind of query that could cause a problem for sorting, with `price * ytd_sales` an expression in the select list:

SQL:
```
select pub_id, price * ytd_sales, price, title_id
from titles
```

Results:

pub_id		price	title_id
1389	81,859.05	19.99	BU1032
1389	46,318.20	11.95	BU1111
0736	55,978.78	2.99	BU2075
1389	81,859.05	19.99	BU7832
0877	40,619.68	19.99	MC2222
0877	66,515.54	2.99	MC3021
0877	NULL	NULL	MC3026
1389	201,501.00	22.95	PC1035
1389	81,900.00	20.00	PC8888
1389	NULL	NULL	PC9999
0877	8,096.25	21.59	PS1372
0736	22,392.75	10.95	PS2091
0736	777.00	7.00	PS2106
0736	81,399.28	19.99	PS3333
0736	26,654.64	7.99	PS7777
0877	7,856.25	20.95	TC3218
0877	180,397.20	11.95	TC4203
0877	61,384.05	14.99	TC7777

```
(18 rows affected)
```

Sorting by Position. Let's say you want to see these results sorted by publisher and then by income (`price * ytd_sales`). Since income is an expression, you can't use a simple column name. Instead, use the number "2," because the expression is the second element in the select list. (When counting select list items, start with "1" and move from left to right. Signed numbers [–2, +4, etc.] are not allowed and don't make sense anyway.)

SQL:
```
select pub_id, price * ytd_sales, price, title_id
from titles
order by pub_id, 2
```

Results:

pub_id	price		title_id
0736	777.00	7.00	PS2106
0736	8,096.25	21.59	PS1372
0736	22,392.75	10.95	PS2091
0736	26,654.64	7.99	PS7777
0736	55,978.78	2.99	BU2075
0736	81,399.28	19.99	PS3333
0877	NULL	NULL	MC3026
0877	7,856.25	20.95	TC3218
0877	40,619.68	19.99	MC2222
0877	61,384.05	14.99	TC7777
0877	66,515.54	2.99	MC3021
0877	180,397.20	11.95	TC4203
1389	NULL	NULL	PC9999
1389	46,318.20	11.95	BU1111
1389	81,859.05	19.99	BU1032
1389	81,859.05	19.99	BU7832
1389	81,900.00	20.00	PC8888
1389	201,501.00	22.95	PC1035

```
(18 rows affected)
```

You can use numbers to represent columns as well as expressions, and freely mix the two styles (positional numbers and column headings) as the spirit moves. ASC and DESC work with numbers just as they do with column headings. Here's an example showing sorting on the *pub_id* column by name in ascending order and then the *price* column by number in descending order:

SQL:
```
select pub_id, price * ytd_sales, price, title_id
from titles
order by pub_id, 3 desc
```

Results:

pub_id	price		title_id
0736	8,096.25	21.59	PS1372
0736	81,399.28	19.99	PS3333
0736	22,392.75	10.95	PS2091
0736	26,654.64	7.99	PS7777
0736	777.00	7.00	PS2106
0736	55,978.78	2.99	BU2075
0877	7,856.25	20.95	TC3218
0877	40,619.68	19.99	MC2222
0877	61,384.05	14.99	TC7777
0877	180,397.20	11.95	TC4203
0877	66,515.54	2.99	MC3021
0877	NULL	NULL	MC3026
1389	201,501.00	22.95	PC1035
1389	81,900.00	20.00	PC8888
1389	81,859.05	19.99	BU1032
1389	81,859.05	19.99	BU7832
1389	46,318.20	11.95	BU1111
1389	NULL	NULL	PC9999

(18 rows affected)

One thing to watch out for with numbered ORDER BY items is modifications to the select list. The order of your results may well change dramatically when you add columns to or subtract columns from the select list.

Sorting by Expression Heading. If you assign headings (or labels) to expressions in the select list, you can sort by the headings. In fact, sorting by position will probably be phased out in favor of this method. In this example, which returns the same results as the previous one, price * ytd_sales is named *income*, and the ORDER BY clause makes use of the heading, rather than the select list number.

SQL:
```
select pub_id, price * ytd_sales as income, price, title_id
from titles
order by pub_id, income desc
```

Sorting by Expression.   Some systems allow you to sort by select list expressions—you don't need positions or headings. Check your system to see if this query is legal:

```
SQL:
select pub_id, price * ytd_sales, price, title_id
from titles
order by pub_id, price * ytd_sales desc
```

How Do You Sort Nulls?

Not all systems order nulls the same way. SQL-92 specifies that when nulls are sorted, they should be either greater than or less than all non-null values. Which you get depends on your implementation. In Sybase SQL Server, NULL is less than all non-null values, but in Sybase SQL Anywhere, nulls are grouped together at the beginning of the display, whether the sort is ascending or descending.

ELIMINATING DUPLICATE ROWS: DISTINCT AND ALL

The DISTINCT and ALL keywords in the select list let you specify what to do with duplicate rows in your results. ALL returns all qualified rows and is the default. DISTINCT returns only those that are unique.

For example, if you search for all the author identification codes in the *titleauthors* table using ALL, you'll find these rows:

```
SQL:
select all au_id
from titleauthors

Results:
au_id
-----------
172-32-1176
213-46-8915
213-46-8915
238-95-7766
267-41-2394
```

```
267-41-2394
274-80-9391
409-56-7008
427-17-2319
472-27-2349
486-29-1786
486-29-1786
648-92-1872
672-71-3249
712-45-1867
722-51-5454
724-80-9391
724-80-9391
756-30-7391
807-91-6654
846-92-7186
899-46-2035
899-46-2035
998-72-3567
998-72-3567

(25 rows affected)
```

Looking at the results, you'll see that there are some duplicate listings. You can eliminate them, and see only the unique *au_id*s, with DISTINCT.

```
SQL:
select distinct au_id
from titleauthors

Results:
au_id
-----------
172-32-1176
213-46-8915
238-95-7766
267-41-2394
274-80-9391
409-56-7008
427-17-2319
```

```
472-27-2349
486-29-1786
648-92-1872
672-71-3249
712-45-1867
722-51-5454
724-80-9391
756-30-7391
807-91-6654
846-92-7186
899-46-2035
998-72-3567

(19 rows affected)
```

Six rows from the first display are not in the second—they are duplicates.

DISTINCT Syntax

ALL is the default unless you explicitly specify DISTINCT. Here's what the basic syntax looks like:

```
SELECT [DISTINCT | ALL] select_list
```

Notice that you use DISTINCT or ALL only once in a select list and that it must be the first word in the select list. The following example will give you a syntax error:

```
SQL (illegal):
select state, distinct city
from authors
```

In other words, you can't select all the states but only the unique cities.

Make Distinctions

When there is more than one item in the select list, DISTINCT finds the rows where the combination of items is unique.

Here's an example that should make it clear. First, take a look at the listing of *pub_id*s and *type*s in the *titles* table.

```
SQL:
select pub_id, type
from titles
order by pub_id

Results:
pub_id type
------ ------------
0736   business
0736   psychology
0736   psychology
0736   psychology
0736   psychology
0736   psychology
0877   NULL
0877   mod_cook
0877   mod_cook
0877   trad_cook
0877   trad_cook
0877   trad_cook
1389   business
1389   business
1389   business
1389   popular_comp
1389   popular_comp
1389   popular_comp

(18 rows affected)
```

There are eighteen rows. Notice that there is some repetition. (The ORDER BY is there only to make the display easy to read.) If you query for distinct publisher numbers, you'll get just three rows:

```
SQL:
select distinct pub_id
from titles
order by pub_id
```

Results:
```
pub_id
------
0736
0877
1389

(3 rows affected)
```

If you query for distinct types, you'll get six rows:

SQL:
```
select distinct type
from titles
order by type
```

Results:
```
type
------------
NULL
business
mod_cook
popular_comp
psychology
trad_cook

(6 rows affected)
```

However, if you query for distinct combinations of publisher and type, you'll get seven rows:

SQL:
```
select distinct pub_id, type
from titles
order by pub_id
```

Results:
```
pub_id type
------ ------------
0736   business
```

```
0736    psychology
0877    NULL
0877    mod_cook
0877    trad_cook
1389    business
1389    popular_comp

(7 rows affected)
```

This display represents all the unique publisher-type combinations in the table. Publisher number 0736 has two types, publisher number 0877 has two types (and a NULL), and publisher number 1389 has two types, giving a total of seven rows. The DISTINCT applies to the select list as a whole, not to individual columns.

Are Nulls Distinct? Although null values are by definition unknown and never equal to each other, DISTINCT treats each null in a particular column as a duplicate of all other null values in that column. If publisher number 0877 had more than one book with a NULL type, and you ran a query with DISTINCT to retrieve the two columns, you'd still see the publisher/NULL combination listed only once.

DISTINCT *. If your system allows DISTINCT *, compare the results of two queries like these:

```
SQL:
select distinct *
from titles

SQL:
select *
from titles
```

Most likely, you'll get exactly the same results from each query, because each row in a table should be unique. If you don't, you should take another look at the database design. Why is there more than one row with a given set of values in a table? How can you retrieve a particular row if it is precisely the same as one or more other rows?

DISTINCT and Non-Select-List ORDER BY. In most SQL dialects, every element in the ORDER BY clause must appear in the select list. In systems that allow more flexibility (where non-select-list elements are allowed in the ORDER BY clause) you can run queries with DISTINCT in the select list and a non-select-list ORDER BY element.

With Sybase SQL Server, for example, sorting by a column not in the select list has the same effect as including that column in the DISTINCT select list: it increases the number of rows displayed. Take a look at this query (you'll get an error if you try to run it on SQL Anywhere):

```
SQL:
select distinct pub_id
from titles
order by type
```

Since there are only three publishers in the database, you'd probably expect three rows in the results. However, this is what you get:

```
Results:
pub_id
------
0877
0736
1389
0877
1389
0736
0877

(7 rows affected)
```

Why are there seven rows in the results? The clue is in the ORDER BY clause, where *type* stars: you get the same number of rows when you turn the query around, searching for distinct types but sorting by publishers.

```
SQL:
select distinct type
from titles
order by pub_id
```

```
Results:

type
- - - - - - - - - - - -
business
psychology
NULL
mod_cook
trad_cook
business
popular_comp

(7 rows affected)
```

Now it's clear where the seven rows come from. Transact-SQL handles the query as if it were a request for all possible unique combinations of the items in the DISTINCT select list and the non-select-list ORDER BY items. There are, in fact, seven unique combinations of *pub_id* and *type*.

If your system allows non-select-list elements in the ORDER BY clause, run a few experimental queries to see how it handles this kind of situation. Chapter 12 includes more examples of DISTINCT use.

AGGREGATE FUNCTIONS

Aggregates are functions you can use to get summary values. You apply aggregates to **sets** of rows: to all the rows in a table, to just those rows specified by a WHERE clause, or to groups of rows set up in the GROUP BY clause (discussed in the next chapter). No matter how you structure the sets, you get *a single value for each set of rows.*

Take a look at the difference in the results of these two queries: the first finds each individual yearly sale value in the *titles* table (one sale listing per row); the second calculates the total yearly sales for all books in the *titles* table (one total sale listing per set, and the table is the set).

```
SQL:
select ytd_sales
from titles
```

Results:
```
ytd_sales
- - - - - - - - - - -
        4095
        3876
       18722
        4095
        2032
       22246
        NULL
        8780
        4095
        NULL
         375
        2045
         111
        4072
        3336
         375
       15096
        4095

(18 rows affected)
```

SQL:
```
select sum(ytd_sales)
from titles
```

Results:
```
- - - - - - - - - - -
       97446

(1 row affected)
```

The first returns results for each qualified row in the table. The second summarizes all the qualified rows into one row. There is no column heading for the aggregate column unless your system generates one (as does SQL Anywhere). You can use a query like this to make the results easier to read:

```
SQL:
select sum(ytd_sales) as Total
from titles

Results:
Total
-----------
      97446

(1 row affected)
```

Most dialects of SQL (including SQL Anywhere) do not allow you to mix row-by-row results and set results. The select list must be pure, either all columns and expressions (row values) or all aggregates (set values). The only exception is for grouping columns—columns on which you base groups when you use a GROUP BY clause. (GROUP BY and aggregates are covered in Chapter 6.)

Here's a query that's usually not allowed, because it mixes a row value with a set value:

```
SQL (variant):
select price, sum(price)
from titles
```

The problem is that *price* returns a value for each row, while *sum(price)* returns a value for each set (here, the table as a whole). Unless your system was designed to handle this kind of query, it will find the two results incompatible and give you a syntax error.

If your system doesn't reject the query, it will probably give results like these (produced by Sybase SQL Server):

```
Results:
price
----------------------- -----------------------
                  19.99                   236.26
                  11.95                   236.26
                   2.99                   236.26
                  19.99                   236.26
                  19.99                   236.26
                   2.99                   236.26
```

```
     NULL                 236.26
    22.95                 236.26
    20.00                 236.26
     NULL                 236.26
    21.59                 236.26
    10.95                 236.26
     7.00                 236.26
    19.99                 236.26
     7.99                 236.26
    20.95                 236.26
    11.95                 236.26
    14.99                 236.26
```

```
(18 rows affected)
```

The unlabeled column on the right shows the grand total of all the prices in the table, while the column on the left shows the price for each row. Notice that the total price is the same in each row: this is because there is only one value for the sum, and it's based on the set (here the table as a whole), not the row.

To get summary and row results on most systems, you have to run two queries.

Aggregate Syntax

Since aggregates are functions, they always take an **argument**. The argument is an expression, and it is enclosed in parentheses.

The general syntax of the aggregate functions is this:

```
aggregate_function([DISTINCT] expression)
```

Figure 5-1 lists the aggregate functions.

You can use DISTINCT with any aggregate except COUNT(*). However, note that DISTINCT gives you no advantage with MIN and MAX, because the minimum distinct price is the same as the minimum price.

The expression in the general syntax statement is often a column name, but it can also be a constant, a function, or any combination of column names, constants, and functions connected by arithmetic (and in some systems by bit-wise) operators.

Aggregate Function	Result
SUM([DISTINCT] expression)	The total of (distinct) values in the numeric expression
AVG([DISTINCT] expression)	The average of (distinct) values in the numeric expression
COUNT([DISTINCT] expression)	The number of (distinct) non-null values in the expression
COUNT(*)	The number of selected rows
MAX(expression)	The highest value in the expression
MIN(expression)	The lowest value in the expression

Figure 5–1. Aggregate Functions

For example, with this statement, you can find what the average price of all books would be if the prices were doubled:

```
SQL:
select avg(price * 2)
from titles

Results:
- - - - - - - - - - - -
        29.53

(1 row affected)
```

COUNT and COUNT(*). The apparent similarity of COUNT and COUNT(*) can lead to confusion. However, the two are really not the same. COUNT takes an argument (a column or expression) and discovers all non-null occurrences of that argument, while COUNT(*) counts all rows, whether or not any particular column contains a null value. This example lets you compare the two:

```
SQL:
select count(price), count(*)
from titles

Results:
----------- -----------
        16          18

(1 row affected)
```

The results produced by the two functions are different because two rows in the *titles* table have NULL in the *price* column. If you used a column with no nulls instead, you'd get the same results from COUNT() and COUNT(*):

```
SQL:
select count(title_id), count(*)
from titles

Results:
----------- -----------
        18          18

(1 row affected)
```

The difference in function between the two counts can be useful for tracking null values in particular columns.

Aggregates and Datatypes.   You can use SUM and AVG with numeric columns only. MIN, MAX, COUNT, and COUNT(*) work with all types of data.

For example, you can use MIN (minimum) to find the lowest value—the one closest to the beginning of the alphabet—in a *char* column:

```
SQL:
select min(au_lname)
from authors
```

```
Results:
- - - - - - - - - - - - - - - - - - - - - - - - -
Bennet

(1 row affected)
```

Of course, there is no meaning in the sum or average of all author last names.

DISTINCT Aggregates.   You can use DISTINCT with SUM, AVG, COUNT, MIN, and MAX (it goes inside the parentheses and before the argument). As noted earlier, DISTINCT doesn't change the results with MIN and MAX.

DISTINCT eliminates duplicate values before calculating the sum, average, or count. Here's an example:

```
SQL:
select count(price)
from titles

Results:
- - - - - - - - - - -
          16

(1 row affected)

SQL:
select count(distinct price)
from titles

Results:
- - - - - - - - - - -
          11

(1 row affected)
```

The first query finds out how many non-null prices there are in the *titles* table. The second calculates the number of different non-null prices. Apparently there is some overlap: five books have the same price.

Some systems specify that when you use DISTINCT, the argument can't be an arithmetic expression; it must be a column name only. However, other systems are more lenient. Check your reference manual to find out what you can do. You might want to see if you can run both of these (rather silly) queries, or only the first:

```
SQL:
select count(price * 2)
from titles

Results:
-----------
         16

(1 row affected)

SQL (variant):
select count(distinct price * 2)
from titles

Results:
-----------
         11

(1 row affected)
```

The first query doubles all the prices and counts the total number of prices. The second does the same arithmetic, but counts only the unique prices. Systems that do not allow calculated columns with DISTINCT will rule the second query illegal.

DISTINCT does not work at all with COUNT(*). This is because COUNT(*) always returns one and only one row. DISTINCT has no meaning here.

Generally speaking, you can use DISTINCT no more than once in a select list. This is because, when no aggregates are involved, DISTINCT applies to the select list as a whole, and not to individual columns in the select list. But limiting DISTINCT to once per select list can cause some special problems when you use aggregates. For example, consider comparing the results of two aggregate operations. If you take the count and the sum of the *price* column, you'll get these results:

```
SQL:
select count(price), sum(price)
from titles

Results:
----------- ------------------------
         16                   236.26

(1 row affected)
```

It's easy to see that the average price is $236.26 divided by 16.

If you use DISTINCT with just one of the two columns, the results may not be so useful:

```
SQL:
select count(price), sum(distinct price)
from titles

Results:
----------- ------------------------
         16                   161.35

(1 row affected)
```

The difference between this and the previous sum value indicates that there are duplicate prices, and that they have not been included in this sum calculation. However, they still show up in the count column. Dividing the distinct sum by the count will not give an accurate value for average price. Putting DISTINCT on the count rather than the sum also gives incorrect data for calculating an average price.

```
SQL:
select count(distinct price), sum(price)
from titles

Results:
----------- ------------------------
         11                   236.26

(1 row affected)
```

It's clear that what you need here is either no DISTINCT or two DIS-
TINCTs. Because of this requirement, SQL-92 supports multiple
DISTINCTs when you have multiple aggregates. Here's an example:

SQL:

```
select count(distinct price), sum(distinct price)
from titles
```

Results:

```
----------- ------------------------
         11                    161.35
```

```
(1 row affected)
```

Note that DISTINCT in the select list and DISTINCT as part of an
aggregate do not give the same results:

SQL:

```
select count(au_id)
from titleauthors
```

Results:

```
-----------
         25
```

```
(1 row affected)
```

SQL:

```
select count(distinct au_id)
from titleauthors
```

```
-----------
         19
```

```
(1 row affected)
```

SQL:

```
select distinct count(au_id)
from titleauthors
```

```
Results:

-----------
          25


(1 row affected)
```

The first query finds all the author identification numbers in the table. The second counts the unique numbers only. Applying a DISTINCT to the select list as a whole, rather than in the aggregate, gives the same result as the first query. This is because the aggregate does its work first, returning one row, and then DISTINCT cheerfully eliminates any duplicates of this row. Since there is only one row of results, there are by definition no duplicates.

Aggregates and WHERE.   You can use aggregate functions in a select list, as in the previous examples, or in the HAVING clause of a SELECT statement (more about this in Chapter 6).

You can't use aggregate functions in a WHERE clause. If you do, you'll get a syntax error. However, you can use a WHERE clause to restrict the rows used in the aggregate calculation. Here's a statement that finds the average advance and total year-to-date sales for all the rows in the *titles* table.

```
SQL:
select avg(advance), sum(ytd_sales)
from titles

Results:

------------------------- -----------
              5,962.50          97446


(1 row affected)
```

To see the same figures for business books only, you could write this query:

```
SQL:
select avg(advance), sum(ytd_sales)
from titles
where type = 'business'
```

Results:

```
------------------------- -----------
                6,281.25       30788
```

(1 row affected)

Apparently, business writers do a little better than the average writer.

How do the aggregates and the WHERE clause interact? The WHERE clause does its job first, finding all business books. Then the functions perform their calculations on the retrieved rows.

Null Values and the Aggregate Functions. If there are any null values in the column on which the aggregate function is operating, they are ignored for the purposes of the function.

For example, if you ask for the COUNT of advances in the *titles* table, your answer is not the same as if you ask for the COUNT of title names, because of the null values in the *advance* column:

SQL:
```
select count(advance)
from titles
```

Results:
```
-------------
           16
```

(1 row affected)

SQL:
```
select count(title)
from titles
```

Results:
```
-------------
           18
```

(1 row affected)

The exception to this rule is COUNT(*), which counts each row, whether or not a column value is NULL. If no rows meet the query conditions, COUNT returns zero. The other functions all return NULL. Here are examples (there is no "poetry" type in the *titles* table):

```
SQL:
select count(distinct title)
from titles
where type = 'poetry'

Results:
- - - - - - - - - - - -
             0

(1 row affected)

SQL:
select avg(advance)
from titles
where type = 'poetry'

Results:
- - - - - - - - - - - -
           NULL

(1 row affected)
```

SCALAR AND VECTOR AGGREGATES

The next chapter explores the GROUP BY clause and the use of aggregate functions with groups to return an array of values (one per group).

The HAVING clause, closely bound to GROUP BY and vector aggregates, is also explored. Finally, NULL is taken apart and put back together one last time.

Chapter 6

Grouping Data and Reporting from It

GROUPING

The previous chapter discussed some SELECT features: the DISTINCT keyword and the ORDER BY clause. It also introduced the aggregate functions. There, aggregates were used only with the table as a whole—but that's just a small part of the aggregate story. In real life, aggregate functions are most frequently used in combination with the GROUP BY clause.

This chapter focuses on GROUP BY, which returns groups of rows, and on the HAVING clause, which puts conditions on GROUP BY results much as WHERE qualifies individual rows. The chapter concludes with a recapitulation of nulls in all their glory.

THE GROUP BY CLAUSE

The GROUP BY clause is intimately connected to aggregates. In fact, GROUP BY doesn't really have much use without aggregate functions. GROUP BY divides a table into sets, while aggregate functions produce summary values for each set. These values are called vector aggregates. (A scalar aggregate is a single value produced by an aggregate function as discussed in the previous chapter.) Figure 6-1 shows examples of scalar and vector aggregate queries.

GROUP BY Syntax

Here's what GROUP BY looks like in the context of a SELECT statement:

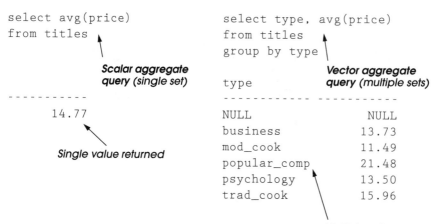

```
select avg(price)              select type, avg(price)
from titles                    from titles
                               group by type
```

Scalar aggregate   *Vector aggregate*
query (single set)   *query (multiple sets)*

```
                               type
-----------                    ------------ -----------
     14.77                     NULL              NULL
                               business         13.73
                               mod_cook         11.49
                               popular_comp     21.48
                               psychology       13.50
                               trad_cook        15.96
```

Single value returned

Multiple values returned

Figure 6-1. Scalar and Vector Aggregates

```
SELECT select_list
FROM table_list
[WHERE conditions]
[GROUP BY group_by_list]
[ORDER BY order_by_list]
```

In most SQL dialects, every item in the GROUP BY list must be equivalent to or a subset of select list items—you can make groups only out of things you select. Systems vary in what they allow in addition to column names: expressions, column headings, and select list position numbers are all possibilities. Check Appendix B for some varieties; see your reference manuals for precise details on your system. Here is an example with a single column in the GROUP BY clause:

SQL:
```
select pub_id, count(type)
from titles
group by pub_id
```

```
Results:
pub_id
------ -----------
0736              6
0877              5
1389              6

(3 rows affected)
```

You can include the grouping column (*pub_id*) as well as the aggregate in the select list. All the rows that make up the first group have 0736 in the *pub_id* column, all those in the second have 0877, and all those in the third have 1389. The COUNT generates a single value (the number of types) for each group. Both items in the select list (the publishers and the COUNT) are single-valued per set—there is only one publisher and one type total for each group.

Groups within Groups.   Just as you can sort by multiple items, so can you form groups within groups. Separate the grouping elements with commas and go from large groups to progressively smaller ones.

```
SQL:
select pub_id, type, count(type)
from titles
group by pub_id, type

Results:
pub_id type
------ ------------ -----------
0736   business               1
0736   psychology             5
0877   NULL                   0
0877   mod_cook               2
0877   trad_cook              3
1389   business               3
1389   popular_comp           3

(7 rows affected)
```

This example is much the same as the previous one, but it uses nested groups. Essentially, you are first dividing the rows in the table by publisher. Then you are separating the rows in each publisher group by type, ending up with seven groups, or sets. Once you have the sets established, you apply the aggregate to each, and come up with a number that reveals how many books belong to each type within each publisher.

Restrictions.   GROUP BY looks straightforward, but it's caused its share of headaches for SQL users.

Here, for example, is a query that seems reasonable but won't work on most systems:

```
SQL (variant):
select pub_id, type, count(type)
from titles
group by pub_id
```

Since the table is divided into sets by publisher (group by pub_id) and there are three publishers, the query must return no more than three rows, and each select list item must have a single value for the set. Unfortunately, there is more than one type per publisher, so most systems find the query impossible to answer. You could solve this problem by adding *type* to the GROUP BY clause, as shown in the example just before this one.

Another limitation in some SQL implementations concerns expressions. You're always safe with vanilla column names in the GROUP BY clause. Aggregate expressions, column headings, and select list position numbers may or may not be allowed.

How about multiple summary values for multiple levels of grouping? Let's say you're sorting by *pub_id* and *type*. You want to see the total number of books for each publisher, and the total number of books for each type of book the publisher carries. You might think something like this would do the trick:

```
SQL:
select pub_id, count(title_id), type, count(title_id)
from titles
group by pub_id, type
```

When you look at the results, however, it's clear you're on the wrong track:

```
Results:
pub_id              type
------ ----------- ------------ -----------
0736               1 business              1
0736               5 psychology            5
0877               1 NULL                  1
0877               2 mod_cook              2
0877               3 trad_cook             3
1389               3 business              3
1389               3 popular_comp          3

(7 rows affected)
```

The number of books is the same for publisher and for type, and the results don't make much sense in light of what you are trying to get. What you're seeing (in two columns) is the number of books for each publisher/type combination, since that is the bottom level of the group. To get the results you want, you need to run two queries: the first one grouped by publisher (to give the publisher totals) and the second grouped by publisher and then by type within each publisher (to give the publisher/type totals).

```
SQL:
select pub_id, count(title_id)
from titles
group by pub_id
```

The results of the first query make it clear that each publisher has six books.

```
Results:
pub_id
------ -----------
0736               6
0877               6
1389               6

(3 rows affected)
```

This set of results following the second query shows the total number of books for each publisher/type combination.

SQL:

```
select pub_id, type, count(title_id)
from titles
group by pub_id, type
```

Results:

```
pub_id type
------ ------------- -----------
0736   business                 1
0736   psychology               5
0877   NULL                     1
0877   mod_cook                 2
0877   trad_cook                3
1389   business                 3
1389   popular_comp             3
```

(7 rows affected)

If you group by type alone, you'll get different results for this data:

SQL:

```
select type, count(title_id)
from titles
group by type
```

Results:

```
type
------------- -----------
NULL                     1
business                 4
mod_cook                 2
popular_comp             3
psychology               5
trad_cook                3
```

(6 rows affected)

In this last set of results, there are four books in the business category. However, two publishers sell this type of book: one has a single business book and the other has three. The query results don't show how many are in each publisher/type combination.

Since the need to see multiple levels of summary values is so pervasive, many database vendors provide a report generator of some type. However, the report generator usually is an application program rather than a part of SQL, because report results with multiple levels of summary values are not able to be represented as relational tables.

Sybase SQL Server does provide an extension that represents a SQL-based approach to the problem. Here's an example:

```
SQL (extension):
select pub_id, type, title_id
from titles
order by pub_id, type
compute count(title_id) by pub_id, type
compute count(title_id) by pub_id
```

```
Results:
pub_id type          title_id
------ ------------  -----------
0736   business      BU2075
                     count
                     -----------
                               1
pub_id type          title_id
------ ------------  -----------
0736   psychology    PS1372
0736   psychology    PS2091
0736   psychology    PS2106
0736   psychology    PS3333
0736   psychology    PS7777
                     count
                     -----------
                               5
                     count
                     -----------
                               6
```

```
pub_id type          title_id
------ ------------- -----------
0877   NULL          MC3026
                     count
                     -----------
                               1

pub_id type          title_id
------ ------------- -----------
0877   mod_cook      MC2222
0877   mod_cook      MC3021
                     count
                     -----------
                               2

pub_id type          title_id
------ ------------- -----------
0877   trad_cook     TC3218
0877   trad_cook     TC4203
0877   trad_cook     TC7777
                     count
                     -----------
                               3
                     count
                     -----------
                               6

pub_id type          title_id
------ ------------- -----------
1389   business      BU1032
1389   business      BU1111
1389   business      BU7832
                     count
                     -----------
                               3

pub_id type          title_id
------ ------------- -----------
1389   popular_comp PC1035
1389   popular_comp PC8888
```

```
1389    popular_comp PC9999
                        count
                        - - - - - - - - - - -
                                       3
                        count
                        - - - - - - - - - - -
                                       6
(28 rows affected)
```

This report shows row values, subgroup totals, and group totals in one set of results. Note that these results, unlike the results of other SQL queries, are not a relation and cannot be further manipulated by other SQL statements.

Nulls and Groups.   Since nulls represent "the great unknown," there is no way to know whether one null is equal to any other null. Each unknown value may or may not be different from another.

However, if the grouping column contains more than one null, all of them are put into a single group.

The *type* column in the *titles* table contains a null. Here's an example that groups the rows by the *type* column and counts the number of rows in each group:

SQL:
```
select type, count(*)
from titles
group by type
```

Results:
```
type
- - - - - - - - - - - - -  - - - - - - - - - - -
NULL                       1
business                   4
mod_cook                   2
popular_comp               3
psychology                 5
trad_cook                  3

(6 rows affected)
```

Notice that there is one row that has a NULL type. If you used `count(type)` instead of `count(*)` in the query, you'd get 0 instead of 1 in the second column:

```
SQL:
select type, count(type)
from titles
group by type

Results:
type
- - - - - - - - - - - -  - - - - - - - - - - -
NULL                    0
business                4
mod_cook                2
popular_comp            3
psychology              5
trad_cook               3

(6 rows affected)
```

Why is there still a NULL group, even though it has a count of zero? While `count(*)` finds all rows in a group, independent of the value in any particular column, `count()` works with a specified column and tallies only the non-nulls for that column. GROUP BY registers the existence of a type called NULL and forms a group for it. `count(type)` duly calculates how many items are in the group. It finds only a NULL, which it doesn't include in the total, and hence records zero.

What happens if there's more than one null in a grouping column (like *advance*)? Here's a query that answers the question:

```
SQL:
select advance, count(*)
from titles
group by advance
```

```
Results:
advance
------------------------  -----------
                   NULL            2
                   0.00            1
               2,000.00            1
               2,275.00            1
               4,000.00            2
               5,000.00            3
               6,000.00            1
               7,000.00            3
               8,000.00            2
              10,125.00            1
              15,000.00            1
```

(11 rows affected)

Two books have null advances. Both of them are grouped under NULL advance. Note that, as expected, zero advance forms a separate group because zero is not the same as null.

GROUP BY without Aggregates.   Used without aggregates, GROUP BY is like DISTINCT. It divides a table into groups and returns one row for each group. Remember, whenever you use GROUP BY, each item in the select list has to produce a single value per set. Here are some examples to make the relationship to DISTINCT clearer. First, a listing of all the publishers in the *titles* table:

```
SQL:
select pub_id
from titles

Results:
pub_id
------
1389
1389
0736
1389
0877
```

```
0877
0877
1389
1389
1389
0877
0736
0736
0736
0736
0877
0877
0877
```

```
(18 rows affected)
```

Next, a listing of all the publishers grouped by publisher:

```
SQL:
select pub_id
from titles
group by pub_id
```

```
Results:
pub_id
------
0736
0877
1389
```

```
(3 rows affected)
```

The results are exactly the same as if you had selected all the unique publishers.

A listing of book types grouped by type and a listing of SELECT DISTINCT *type* produce the same results:

```
SQL:
select type
from titles
group by type
```

```
Results:

type
- - - - - - - - - - - -
NULL
business
mod_cook
popular_comp
psychology
trad_cook

(6 rows affected)
```

GROUP BY with Aggregates. The last chapter discussed basic aggregate syntax without GROUP BY; this chapter has covered GROUP BY syntax. Now we can put the two together. The fact is, GROUP BY and aggregates were made for each other. GROUP BY creates the sets, and aggregates calculate per-set values. The two together can give you some very useful information.

Let's examine some typical queries. This statement finds the average advance and sum of year-to-date sales for *each type of book*:

```
SQL:
select type, avg(advance), sum(ytd_sales)
from titles
group by type

Results:

type
- - - - - - - - - - - -   - - - - - - - - - -   - - - - - - - - - -
NULL          NULL          NULL
business      6,281.25      30788
mod_cook      7,500.00      24278
popular_comp  7,500.00      12875
psychology    4,255.00       9939
trad_cook     6,333.33      19566

(6 rows affected)
```

The summary values produced by SELECT statements with GROUP BY and aggregates appear as new columns in the results.

Here's a query looking for relationships between price categories and average advance:

SQL:

```
select price, avg(advance)
from titles
group by price
```

Results:

```
price
------------------------    ------------------------
            NULL                        NULL
            2.99                   12,562.50
            7.00                    6,000.00
            7.99                    4,000.00
           10.95                    2,275.00
           11.95                    4,500.00
           14.99                    8,000.00
           19.99                    3,000.00
           20.00                    8,000.00
           20.95                    7,000.00
           21.59                    7,000.00
           22.95                    7,000.00
```

(12 rows affected)

GROUP BY with WHERE.   You've seen that when there's no grouping and aggregates are working on the table as a whole, you can use the WHERE clause to specify which rows participate in the aggregate calculations. The same is true when you have groups.

The WHERE clause acts first to find the rows you want. Then the GROUP BY clause divides these favored few (or many) into groups. Rows that WHERE doesn't select don't make it into any groups. Here's an example:

SQL:

```
select type, avg(price)
from titles
```

```
where advance > 5000
group by type
```

Results:

```
type
------------  ------------------------
business                      2.99
mod_cook                      2.99
popular_comp                 21.48
psychology                   14.30
trad_cook                    17.97

(5 rows affected)
```

Now, the same query without the WHERE clause:

SQL:

```
select type, avg(price)
from titles
group by type
```

Results:

```
type
------------  ------------------------
NULL                          NULL
business                     13.73
mod_cook                     11.49
popular_comp                 21.48
psychology                   13.50
trad_cook                    15.96

(6 rows affected)
```

It returns an extra row (one with a NULL type and NULL average price) and different average price values for all but the popular computing type. The extra row is easy to explain—since the WHERE clause looked for rows with advances greater than $5,000, it didn't include any rows with NULL advances. The row with a NULL type has a NULL advance, so the first set of results, based on groups formed after the WHERE clause eliminated unqualified rows, does not include a group with a NULL type.

If you look at results from a query for *type*, *price*, and *advance*, and then apply the WHERE clause manually by marking with asterisks the rows in each group that have an advance greater than $5,000, you'll see how the results of the first query (the one with both WHERE and GROUP BY) were generated:

SQL:

```
select type, price, advance
from titles
```

Results:

type	price	advance
business	19.99	5,000.00
business	11.95	5,000.00
business	2.99	10,125.00***
business	19.99	5,000.00
mod_cook	19.99	0.00
mod_cook	2.99	15,000.00***
NULL	NULL	NULL
popular_comp	22.95	7,000.00***
popular_comp	20.00	8,000.00***
popular_comp	NULL	NULL
psychology	21.59	7,000.00***
psychology	10.95	2,275.00
psychology	7.00	6,000.00***
psychology	19.99	2,000.00
psychology	7.99	4,000.00
trad_cook	20.95	7,000.00***
trad_cook	11.95	4,000.00
trad_cook	14.99	8,000.00***

```
(18 rows affected)
```

Only the rows with advances greater than $5,000 are included in the groups that give rise to the query results. Since there's just one row in the *business* group, for example, with a qualifying advance, the average price is the same as the price in that row. In the *popular_comp* group, on the other hand, two rows meet the WHERE conditions, and the average is halfway between the two.

Notice that the column in the WHERE clause doesn't have to have anything to do with the select list or the grouping list.

Orderly Groups

GROUP BY divides rows into sets, but it doesn't necessarily put those sets in any order. If you want your results sorted in some particular way, use ORDER BY. Remember that the sequence of clauses in SELECT statements is fixed, and ORDER BY always goes after GROUP BY. For example, to find the average price for books of each type with advances over $5,000 and order the results by average price, the statement is this:

```
SQL:
select type, avg(price)
from titles
where advance > 5000
group by type
order by 2

Results:
type
------------ ------------------------
business                 2.99
mod_cook                 2.99
psychology              14.30
trad_cook               17.97
popular_comp            21.48

(5 rows affected)
```

THE HAVING CLAUSE

In its most common usage, the HAVING clause is a WHERE clause for groups. Just as WHERE limits rows, HAVING limits groups. Most of the time, you use HAVING with GROUP BY.

When there are aggregates in the select list of a query, WHERE clause conditions apply to the aggregates, while HAVING conditions apply to the query as a whole, after you've calculated the aggregates and set up the groups. One way to keep this difference in mind is to recall the order of the clauses in the SELECT statement. Remember that WHERE comes after FROM, and HAVING comes after GROUP BY. An example at the end of this section explores WHERE and HAVING interactions in some detail.

In terms of allowed elements, HAVING search conditions are identical to WHERE search conditions, with one exception: WHERE search conditions cannot include aggregates, while HAVING search conditions often do. In most systems, each element in the HAVING clause must also appear in the select list. WHERE, of course, does not have this limitation. You can put as many conditions as you want in a HAVING clause.

Garden-Variety HAVING

Here's the standard use of HAVING: GROUP BY divides the rows into sets (by type) and HAVING puts a condition on the sets, in this example eliminating those sets that include only one book:

```
SQL:
select type, count(*)
from titles
group by type
having count(*) > 1

Results:
type
------------ -----------
business          4
mod_cook          2
popular_comp      3
psychology        5
trad_cook         3

(5 rows affected)
```

Notice that you couldn't simply substitute WHERE for HAVING in this query, since WHERE does not allow aggregates. Here's an example of a HAVING clause without aggregates. It groups the *titles* table by type and eliminates those types that do not have "p" as the first letter:

```
SQL:
select type
from titles
group by type
having type like 'p%'

Results:
type
-----------
popular_comp
psychology

(2 rows affected)
```

When you want more than one condition included in the HAVING clause, you can combine conditions with AND, OR, or NOT. For example, to group the *titles* table by publisher, and to include only those groups of publishers with identification numbers greater than 0800, who have paid more than $15,000 in total advances, and whose books average less than $20 in price, the statement is this:

```
SQL:
select pub_id, sum(advance), avg(price)
from titles
group by pub_id
having sum(advance) > 15000
  and avg(price) < 20
  and pub_id > '0800'

Results:
pub_id
------  ----------------  ----------------
0877         34,000.00         14.17
1389         30,000.00         18.98
(2 rows affected)
```

The following statement illustrates the use of GROUP BY, HAVING, WHERE, and ORDER BY clauses in one SELECT statement. It produces the same groups and summary values as the previous example, but does so after eliminating the titles with prices under $5. It also orders the results by *pub_id*.

SQL:

```
select pub_id, sum(advance), avg(price)
from titles
where price >= 5
group by pub_id
having sum(advance) > 15000
   and avg(price) < 20
   and pub_id > '0800'
order by pub_id
```

Results:

pub_id		
0877	19,000.00	16.97
1389	30,000.00	18.98

```
(2 rows affected)
```

HAVING and WHERE

Although WHERE and HAVING look the same, it's important to remember the difference in their basic functions. For example, in the query just preceding, you'd get quite different results if you put the >= $5 qualification in the HAVING clause instead of the WHERE. (Many systems limit HAVING clause conditions to elements found in the select list. If yours is in this camp, the `price >= 5` qualifier will not be legal, because there is no unaggregated price in the select list.)

SQL(variant):

```
select pub_id, sum(advance), avg(price)
from titles
group by pub_id
```

```
having sum(advance) > 15000
  and avg(price) < 20
  and pub_id > '0800'
  and price >= 5
order by pub_id
```

The reason for this difference is that WHERE eliminates rows before grouping, but HAVING goes to work after grouping.

Here's a somewhat less complex query pair to puzzle over while figuring out the interaction of the two clauses. (The second query will not work on systems that require items in the HAVING clause to also appear in the select list.)

SQL:

```
select pub_id, type, count(advance)
from titles
where advance > 10000
group by pub_id, type
```

Results:

```
pub_id type
------ ------------ -----------
0736   business               1
0877   mod_cook               1

(2 rows affected)
```

SQL(variant):

```
select pub_id, type, count(advance)
from titles
group by pub_id, type
having advance > 10000
```

Results:

```
pub_id type
------ ------------ -----------
0736   business               1
0877   mod_cook               2

(2 rows affected)
```

The first query, using WHERE as the qualifier, finds two groups, each with one book. The second, using HAVING, also finds two groups, but one of the groups has two books. Why is this?

In essence, WHERE looks at all the rows and keeps only those with advances greater than $10,000 (the ones marked with stars in the following conceptual table).

```
pub_id type              advance
------ ------------      ------------------------
1389   business                    5,000.00
1389   business                    5,000.00
0736   business                   10,125.00  ***
1389   business                    5,000.00
0877   mod_cook                        0.00
0877   mod_cook                   15,000.00  ***
0877   NULL                            NULL
1389   popular_comp                7,000.00
1389   popular_comp                8,000.00
1389   popular_comp                    NULL
0736   psychology                  7,000.00
0736   psychology                  2,275.00
0736   psychology                  6,000.00
0736   psychology                  2,000.00
0736   psychology                  4,000.00
0877   trad_cook                   7,000.00
0877   trad_cook                   4,000.00
0877   trad_cook                   8,000.00

(18 rows affected)
```

Then, WHERE functions finished, it releases the two rows for grouping and aggregate calculation. Clearly there are two groups, each containing one book. Hence, the results.

HAVING, of course, pertains to the query as a whole, not to individual rows. That's why its results are a little different. The query using HAVING processes grouping and aggregate values first. The first step finds the groups.

```
pub_id type
------ ------------      -----------
0736   business              1
0736   psychology            5
```

```
0877    NULL                1
0877    mod_cook            2
0877    trad_cook           3
1389    business            3
1389    popular_comp        3
```

(7 rows affected)

Then, groups determined, the HAVING condition is applied: Which groups contain one or more rows with advances over $10,000? Two groups qualify: the first group (0736—business) publishes one business title; the second group (0877—mod_cook) publishes two modern cooking titles.

While WHERE eliminates rows first and then groups the data, HAVING groups first and then eliminates rows. If you paraphrased the two queries, the first would be something like "Show me, for all books with advances over $10,000, the number of advances paid per type within each publisher." The second might be closer to "Show me the number of advances paid per type within each publisher for each type that includes books receiving over $10,000 in advances."

Again, if your system restricts the HAVING clause to elements in the select list, you won't be able to run this kind of query at all (*advance* does not appear in the select list except as an aggregate).

MORE ON NULLS

Nulls and the quirks connected with them have come up several times in this chapter and in earlier chapters. In this section, we'll pull all those bits and pieces together and go into more detail about the conceptual problems of nulls, with the goal of helping you avoid some of the mistakes that often result from misunderstandings about nulls.

The first point to consider, though it is hardly reassuring, is that even the experts consider nulls a pesky problem. C. J. Date, for example, has been wrestling with nulls for years. In a 1986 paper ("Null Values in Database Management," *Relational Database: Selected Writings*, 313), he argues that nulls should be done away with altogether. The problem of nulls, he says, "is generally not well understood, and . . . any attempt to incorporate support for null values into an implemented system should be considered premature at this time."

Actually, there are a number of different kinds of incomplete information. Date offers several examples of data that may never be known: entries such as "date of birth unknown" in historical records, "to be announced" instead of a speaker's name in a meeting agenda, or "present whereabouts unknown" in a police blotter. Sometimes, a value that isn't known now will be determined later, as in the *price* and *advance* columns of the *titles* table in our sample database. Other data is missing in the sense that it is inapplicable. The attribute does not apply to the entity in question. Data for the "assessed value of house" will never make sense for a renter, for example. In today's database products, nulls are used to represent both missing and inapplicable values.

There are other wrinkles, too. Sometimes you don't know precisely what a value is, but you know something about what it's not. You might not know a person's exact birth date, for example, but you know it was between 1860 and 1880. Or negotiations with an author might have already gotten far enough along so that it's clear the advance is going to be larger than $10,000. These kinds of unknown pieces of information are called **distinguished nulls**—their values are not precisely known, but some things about them are clear.

Some types of computer programs—statistical packages, for example—support many kinds of distinguished nulls. In relational database management systems, however, distinguished nulls are very problematic in terms of both definition and implementation. To date, no system we know of supports them.

Some systems have refrained from implementing nulls altogether—because it's too much trouble to support them. Date suggests an alternative to the SQL concept of nulls that we'll consider briefly later in this section. But most of today's database management systems use nulls much as we've described them here. Let's summarize what we've said about nulls in earlier chapters.

Nulls and Database Design

In systems that support nulls, you can specify whether a column allows nulls when you create a table. Setting up columns that can accept nulls means that the database system can gracefully handle these two situations:

- A user is adding a new row to a table, but doesn't have the information to be entered in some of the fields. The database system automatically marks these positions as nulls.
- You're restructuring a table by adding a new column to it. What gets entered in that new column in all the existing rows? Again, the database system automatically marks nulls.

Comparisons Involving Nulls

We pointed out in Chapter 3 that since nulls represent the unknown, a null can't possibly be sure to match any other value, even another null. (Of course, you can't guarantee that a null doesn't match any other value, either.)

For example, the advance for the book called *Net Etiquette* is represented as NULL. Does this mean that it is larger than $5,000? Smaller than $5,000? Is it larger or smaller than the advance for *The Psychology of Computer Cooking*, also represented as NULL?

Based on the definition of NULL as unknown, of course, the answer to all these questions is unknown. You might also say that the answer is "maybe." That's what we mean when we say that null implies three-valued logic instead of the more intuitively understandable two-valued logic. With nulls, the possibilities are never just true and false; they're true, false, and maybe.

The counterintuitive nature of three-valued logic often leads to confusion. Consider the unsuspecting user who asks for a listing of all titles with advances greater than $5,000 and gets a list of eight titles. The user then asks for the titles with advances less than $5,000 and gets five. Finally, he or she determines that there are three titles with advances of exactly $5,000. The user then concludes that there are sixteen titles in all, forgetting that the titles with unknown advances are not reported by any of the queries. This is because, of course, the database system interpreted the first question as "Give me all titles *known* to have advances greater than $5,000."

Here are a few other likely sources of confusion. If you sort the books by advance, all those with null advances are shown at the beginning or the end of the report, depending on how your system sorts nulls. This implies pretty strongly both that these advances are less than (or more than) any of the others, and that all the nulls are equal to each other, since they are shown together.

Similarly (as far as confusion potential goes), when you select distinct values, all the nulls are eliminated except one. This suggests that the nulls in question are equal to each other!

One aspect of the problem of nulls is simply remembering that they may exist. For example, suppose you want to notify all the authors whose royalty payments for the year totaled less than $600 that they need not report this amount to the IRS. Those whose payments are unknown wouldn't show up in your report unless you specifically searched for them with an operator such as IS NULL.

Nulls and Computations

The really sticky problems associated with nulls become apparent when you try to figure out what to do with those unknown values when you operate on them.

It's easy enough to see that when you perform an arithmetic operation on an unknown value, the result can only be unknown. You can double all the advances, for example, and the advance for *Net Etiquette* is still NULL. You can subtract it from the advance for *The Psychology of Computer Cooking*, and you certainly can't say that the answer is zero: it is still NULL.

But what if you want to find the average of all advances? Here's what you'd do:

```
SQL:
select avg(advance)
from titles

Results:
-----------------------
            5,962.50

(1 row affected)
```

Let's check up on SQL, by querying it for the sum of all the advances, and then for the number of books:

```
SQL:
select sum(advance)
from titles

select count(*)
from titles

Results:
-----------------------
            95,400.00
```

```
(1 row affected)

- - - - - - - - - - -
           18

(1 row affected)
```

Don't reach for your calculator. What you'll find is that 95,400 divided by 18 does not give the answer that SQL did. The reason for the discrepancy is that SQL throws out the two null advances in the sum, and in the count that it does for the purposes of calculating the average. However, the nulls are included for the purposes of COUNT(*).

The situation is very confusing. You asked for the average of all the advances, and got a figure that looked very precise. But it cannot be precise, since the data on which it was based is itself incomplete and imprecise.

SQL does the best it can, as the rules for nulls and aggregates given earlier demonstrate. But it is extremely misleading in cases like the one just described.

Nulls and Groups

In many dialects of SQL, all nulls are put into a single group for the purposes of GROUP BY.

Defaults as an Alternative to Nulls

One alternative to a null is a default, a value entered by the database management system when the user provides no explicit value. SQL allows you to specify defaults in the CREATE TABLE command.

One of the advantages of defaults over nulls is that you can give a particular column an appropriate value, instead of having to rely on null everywhere. A good default for the *type* column might be "unknown," while one for the *date* column might be "TBD" or today's date.

Most observers agree that defaults will never provide a solution to the problems associated with nulls. But nulls, with all their complexities, will always be with us.

As a convenience, some database management systems allow you to assign particular display values to nulls. This can be done through an application program or as a SQL extension. For example, this query shows the types in the database, and the number of rows for each:

```
SQL:
select type, count(*)
from titles
group by type

Results:
type
- - - - - - - - - - - -  - - - - - - - - - - -
NULL                    1
business                4
mod_cook                2
popular_comp            3
psychology              5
trad_cook               3

(6 rows affected)
```

One of the types is unknown. Here's how you'd use a Transact-SQL function called ISNULL() to display a different value for the null:

```
SQL (variant):
select isnull(type, 'What?'), count(*)
from titles
group by type

Results:
- - - - - - - - - - - -  - - - - - - - - - - -
What?                   1
business                4
mod_cook                2
popular_comp            3
psychology              5
trad_cook               3

(6 rows affected)
```

The ISNULL() function has two arguments: the name of the column, and the value to display for any nulls found in that column. You can also use the function for doing "what if" math, substituting different display values for the original nulls. Of course, the actual value in the database is not affected.

Here's a query that shows *title_id*, *advance*, and *price* for titles that have an advance less than $6,000, or a null advance:

```
SQL:

select title_id, advance, price
from titles
where advance < 6000 or advance is null
order by price
```

```
Results:

title_id advance                          price
-------- -----------------------------    ------------------------
MC3026                            NULL                        NULL
PC9999                            NULL                        NULL
PS7777                        4,000.00                        7.99
PS2091                        2,275.00                       10.95
BU1111                        5,000.00                       11.95
TC4203                        4,000.00                       11.95
BU1032                        5,000.00                       19.99
BU7832                        5,000.00                       19.99
MC2222                            0.00                       19.99
PS3333                        2,000.00                       19.99

(10 rows affected)
```

Two rows show null advances and null prices. To see what the same data would look like with different values for the nulls, try something like this:

```
SQL (variant):
select title_id, isnull(advance, 4000), isnull(price, 35.00)
from titles
where advance < 6000 or advance is null
order by price
```

```
Results:
title_id
-------- ------------------------------- -----------------------------
  MC3026                  4,000.00                          35.00
  PC9999                  4,000.00                          35.00
  PS7777                  4,000.00                           7.99
  PS2091                  2,275.00                          10.95
  BU1111                  5,000.00                          11.95
  TC4203                  4,000.00                          11.95
  BU1032                  5,000.00                          19.99
  BU7832                  5,000.00                          19.99
  MC2222                      0.00                          19.99
  PS3333                  2,000.00                          19.99
(10 rows affected)
```

The values and the position of the two rows have changed. Check the manuals to see if a similar capability exists in your system.

WORKING WITH MULTIPLE TABLES

The next two chapters give more information about the SELECT statement. Chapter 7 focuses on joins, while Chapter 8 explores nested queries, or subqueries.

Chapter 7

Joining Tables for Comprehensive Data Analysis

WHAT IS A JOIN?

Joins complete the triad of operations that a relational query language must provide: selection, projection, and join. The join operation lets you retrieve and manipulate data from more than one table in a single SELECT statement. Joining two tables is a little like making a seam to join two pieces of material. Once you have made the seam, you can work with the whole cloth.

SQL-92 provides some keywords for joins (CROSS JOIN, NATURAL, INNER, OUTER), but they are not widely implemented. In most systems, you specify joins in the WHERE clause of a SELECT statement. Like projections, which are specified in the select list of the SELECT statement, joins are expressed implicitly rather than explicitly.

You specify each join (there can be more than one in a single SELECT statement) on two tables at a time, using a column from each table as a **connecting column** or **join column**. A connecting column should have values that match or compare easily, representing the same or similar data in each of the tables participating in the join. For example, the *title_id* column in the *titles* table matches the *title_id* column in the *salesdetails* table.

Connecting columns almost always have the same datatype. The values in connecting columns are **join-compatible**: their values come from the same general class of data.

Join Syntax

A skeleton version of join syntax is this:

```
SELECT select_list
FROM table_1, table_2 [, table_3]...
WHERE [table_1.]column  join_operator  [table2.]column
```

The FROM clause's table list must include at least two tables, and the columns specified in the WHERE clause must be join-compatible. When the join columns have identical names, you must qualify the columns with their table names in the select list and in the WHERE clause. For example, if you wanted to know the names of the editors of *Secrets of Silicon Valley*, you'd need a join on the *ed_id* column that appears in both tables:

SQL:

```
select ed_lname, ed_fname, ed_pos
from editors, titleditors
where editors.ed_id = titleditors.ed_id
   and titleditors.title_id = 'PC8888'
```

Results:

ed_lname	ed_fname	ed_pos
DeLongue	Martinella	project
Samuelson	Bernard	project
Kaspchek	Chistof	acquisition

(3 rows affected)

This join selects the names of editors who are connected to the *title_id* "PC8888" by joining on the *ed_id* column that appears in both the *editors* and the *titleditors* tables.

WHY JOINS ARE NECESSARY

In a database that has been designed according to the normalization rules, one table may not give you all the information you need about a particular entity. For comprehensive data analysis, you must assemble data from several tables. The relational model—having led you to partition your data into several single-subject tables following the rules of normalization and good, clean database design—relies on the join operation to enable you to perform ad hoc queries and produce comprehensible reports. Thus, the join operation is one of the key operations of the relational model.

Joins and the Relational Model

Joins are possible because of the relational model, and they are necessary because of the relational model.

Joins are possible in a relational database management system because the relational model's data independence permits you to bring data from separate tables into new and unanticipated relationships. Relationships among data values become explicit when the data is manipulated—when you *query* the database, not when you *create* it.

You need not know that data will join in advance. You can discover new relationships among data in different tables by joining them. For example, you could find out whether any names of an organization's board members match those of contributors to a political campaign with a query such as this:

```
SQL:
select board_members.name
from board_members, political_contributors
where board_members.name = political_contributors.name
```

Or, using the sample database, you could use a join query to find out whether any editor is also an author:

```
SQL:
select ed_lname
from editors, authors
where ed_id = au_id
```

This query is a little tricky. Since an editor and an author can have the same last name, you need to join on the ID column, which uniquely identifies each of the suspects. As a row's unique identifier, a primary key is often particularly useful in join queries.

Joins are necessary because during the process of analysis that distributes data over the relational database landscape, you cleanly separate information on separate entities. You can get a comprehensive view of your data only if you can reconnect the tables. That's the whole point of joins.

A corollary of the join capability is that it gives you unlimited flexibility in adding new kinds of data to your database. You can always create a new table that contains data about a different subject. If the new table has an eligible field, you can link it to existing tables by joining.

That's how relational databases grow: If tables need to split, you can always reconstruct the rows by joining. If new tables are needed, you can always link them into the rest of the database by joining.

For example, our *bookbiz* database might need an *invoices* table for billing stores. Such a table could link to the *sales* and *salesdetails* tables by *sonum* (sales order number) and (presumably) to a new *stores* table on the *stor_id* column.

Your database design should anticipate likely joins and build in eligible join columns, which are usually primary key or foreign key columns for their tables. Primary keys (*titles.title_id*) join to the corresponding foreign keys (*salesdetails.title_id*, *titleauthors.title_id*, and *titleeditors.title_id*). Without join columns available as links, it will be more difficult to run queries on multiple tables.

A PRELIMINARY JOIN EXAMPLE

In the SELECT syntax, the preconditions for a join are

- Naming more than one table in the FROM list
- Adding conditions in the WHERE clause to create the join on the connecting columns

You can use any of the relational operators to express the relationship between the join columns, but equality is the most common (in which a value in the join column from one table is equal to a value in the join column from another table). For example, if an author calls to ask which editors live close to a publisher's home office, a join query can provide the answer. This query finds the names of editors who live in the same city as Algodata Infosystems:

```
SQL:
select ed_lname, ed_id, editors.city, pub_name, publishers.city
from editors, publishers
where editors.city = publishers.city
and pub_name = 'Algodata Infosystems'
```

```
Results:
ed_lname  ed_id       city        pub_name             city
--------  ----------  ----------- -------------------- -------
DeLongue  321-55-8906 Berkeley    Algodata Infosystems Berkeley
Kaspchek  943-88-7920 Berkeley    Algodata Infosystems Berkeley

(2 rows affected)
```

The join query promptly reports that two editors, DeLongue and Kasp-chek, live in the same city (Berkeley) as Algodata Infosystems. This was information you didn't know before. In fact, all you had to know was the publisher's name, and the join supplied you with all that additional information. You told the system: "Join on the city, whatever that is, and tell me the editors' names, whoever they are."

Testing for Successful Joins

In relational theory, a join is the projection and restriction of the product. The product, or **Cartesian product**, is the set of all possible combinations of the rows from the two tables.

The system first examines all possible combinations of the rows from two tables, then eliminates all the rows that do not meet the conditions of the projection (selection of columns) and restriction (selection of rows). The actual procedure that a system follows is more sophisticated and varies from implementation to implementation. (For more information, see "How the System Processes Joins," at the end of this chapter.)

With join queries, more so than with other types of SQL queries, you should test your queries on a sample of your data to make sure that you're getting the results you really want. An insufficiently restricted join query can return results that need a good pruning before you can be sure that they are correct, and useful.

HOW TO GET A GOOD JOIN

What makes for a good join column? Ideally, a join column is a key column for its table, either a primary key or a foreign key. When a key is composite, you can join on all the columns of the key.

Since the primary key logically connects to related foreign key columns in other tables, key columns are usually ideal candidate columns on which to construct a join. Such a join is likely to be useful and logically appropriate, because the database designer planned ahead for it. Primary key–foreign key joins are based on the expectation that foreign keys will be kept consistent with their primary keys, in order to preserve the referential integrity of the database.

If a join is to have meaningful results, the columns being compared should have similar values—values drawn from the same general class of data. Such columns will have the same or similar datatypes, and the same or similar data values. In addition to considerations of type, of course, you must consider meaning. For example, you could join authors' ages (such as 25, 30, 50) to numbers in the *salesdetails* table's *qty_shipped* column, but the results would be meaningless. The columns have superficial similarities, but they are not logically related.

Columns being joined need not have the same name, though they often will. Join column datatypes must be **compatible**—types that the system easily converts from one type into the other. For example, the system may easily convert among any of the numeric type columns—such as *integer*, *decimal*, or *float*—and among any of the character type and date columns— such as *character*, *varchar*, or *datetime*. This implicit conversion enables easy joining of integer type columns to float type columns, or of character type columns to date type columns. Datatype-compatible join columns are, generally speaking, both character types, or both numeric types. You can specify explicit conversion with the type conversion function, described in Chapter 3.

Joins and Nulls

If there are nulls in the connecting columns of tables being joined, the nulls will never join because nulls represent unknown or inapplicable values (and there is no reason to believe one unknown value matches another).

IMPROVING THE READABILITY OF JOIN RESULTS

When you join tables, the system compares the data in the specified fields and displays the results of the comparison as a table of the qualifying rows.

The results show a row for each successful join. Data from any of the tables is duplicated as needed. In the earlier example, "Algodata Infosystems" appears twice in the results even though this publisher appears only once in the *publishers* table.

Join query results replicate data from qualifying rows as needed in order to regularize the table display. As with any query, the results of a join query display as a table without altering the database tables in any way. The join operation simply permits the system to manipulate data from multiple tables as if it were contained in a single table.

You don't have to name the join column twice in the select list, or even include it in the results at all, in order for the join to succeed. However, you may need to qualify the name of a join column with its table name in the select list or in the join specification of the WHERE clause.

The first example could be restated as this:

```
SQL:
select ed_lname
from editors, publishers
where editors.city = publishers.city
and pub_name = 'Algodata Infosystems'

Results:
ed_lname

- - - - - - - - - - - - - - - - - - - - - - - - - - - - - - - - - - - - - -

DeLongue
Kaspchek

(2 rows affected)
```

This would be the "just the facts, ma'am" version.

Choose Columns Carefully for Ad Hoc Join Queries

As with any SELECT statement, the columns you name after the SELECT keyword are the columns you want the query results to display, in their desired order.

If you use SELECT * the columns appear in their CREATE TABLE order. In a query to find the title or titles associated with sales order number 1, you might join the *salesdetails* table to *titles* on *title_id*:

```
SQL:
select *
from titles, salesdetails
```

```
where titles.title_id = salesdetails.title_id
  and sonum = 1
```

Results:

```
title_id
   title
   type            pub_id        price          advance
   ytd_sales  contract
   notes
   pubdate                       sonum          qty_ordered qty_shipped
   title_id   date_shipped
---------------------------------------------------------------------
PS2091
   Is Anger the Enemy?
   psychology     0736           10.95          2,275.00
   2045       1
   Carefully researched study of the effects of strong emotions
   on the body. Metabolic charts included.
   Jun 15 1985                   1              75            75
   PS2091     Sep 15 1985
(1 row affected)
```

The preceding display shows a table that has 1 row and 14 columns. Since this system wraps the results in the display, each row occupies multiple horizontal lines. A join that creates a very wide row can present you with results that are hard to read. If your system has a problem displaying such results in a readable form, you should choose columns carefully for ad hoc queries; indiscriminate use of the asterisk notation would not be advisable.

Both tables must be named in the table list in order for the system to perform the join. The FROM clause's table list sets the stage—it puts the system on alert to perform a join. The order of the tables (or views) in the list affects the results display only when you use SELECT * to specify the select list.

The table list should name all the tables that will participate in any of the query's joins. You can specify a join on more than two tables, as long as you join tables two at a time. Two-way joins are the most common, but we give some examples of three-way joins later in this chapter.

Aliases in the Table List Improve Readability

In order to make join queries easier to type and more readable, you may want to give the tables alias names (abbreviations to cut down on typing) in the table list. Assigning an alias to each table name is particularly helpful when you join on identically named columns, which have to be qualified with the table name each time they're used. Aliases can be letters or numbers in any combination. Most people make them short and easy to remember.

Here's how you could use aliases in a query to find authors who live in the same city as some publisher:

```
SQL:
select au_lname, au_fname
from authors a, publishers p
where a.city = p.city

Results:
au_lname                                      au_fname
-------------------------------------- -----------------

Carson                                        Cheryl
Bennet                                        Abraham

(2 rows affected)
```

If you wanted to display the city name, you'd also need to qualify it with one of the table name aliases (*a* or *p*) in the select list. The names in the table list can be those of tables or views.

SPECIFYING JOIN CONDITIONS

A join is often based on equality, or matching values in the joining columns. Joins based on equality are indicated with the "=" logical operator in the join part of the WHERE clause. Joins can also be constructed on other conditions: the join operator can be any one of the logical operators, or a special operator for specifying an **outer join** (which we'll discuss later).

In addition to the equality operator, the other logical operators that can be used to specify comparison conditions are

Symbol	Meaning
>	greater than
>=	greater than or equal to
<	less than
<=	less than or equal to
!= (or <>)	not equal to

Transact-SQL also provides the operators !> and !<, which are equivalent to <= and >=, respectively. In relational database jargon, joins that use any of the comparison operators are collectively called **theta** joins.

Joins Based on Equality

By definition, an **equijoin** joins on matching values and displays the join's seam—the connecting column from each table that participates in the join.

This query finds titles that are connected with a particular sales order number:

```
SQL:
select title, t.title_id, sonum, sd.title_id
from titles t, salesdetails sd
where sonum = 14
and t.title_id = sd.title_id

Results:
title
-----------------------------------------------------------------
title_id     sonum    title_id
--------     -------  --------

Computer Phobic and Non-Phobic Individuals: Behavior Variations
PS1372       14       PS1372

Life Without Fear
PS2106       14       PS2106

Prolonged Data Deprivation: Four Case Studies
PS3333       14       PS3333
```

```
Emotional Security: A New Algorithm
PS7777        14       PS7777
```

(4 rows affected)

Since there's really no need to display information redundantly, you can eliminate the display of one of the connecting columns by restating the query so that it displays the join column only once. Such a display is called a **natural join**. The natural join version of the previous query is this:

SQL:
```
select title, t.title_id, sonum
from titles t, salesdetails sd
where sonum = 14
and t.title_id = sd.title_id
```

Results:
```
title
- - - - - - - - - - - - - - - - - - - - - - - - - - - - - - - - - - - - - - - - - - - - - - - - - - - - - - - -
title_id      sonum
- - - - - - - -     - - - - - - -
Computer Phobic and Non-Phobic Individuals: Behavior Variations
 PS1372            14
 Life Without Fear
 PS2106            14
 Prolonged Data Deprivation: Four Case Studies
 PS3333            14
 Emotional Security: A New Algorithm
 PS7777            14
```

(4 rows affected)

Now we have a natural join, because the column *title_id* does not appear twice in the results. Some systems use the natural join display as the default display for a join, because it makes the results more readable. It doesn't matter which *title_id* column you include, but you have to qualify it in the select list with its table name.

The natural join is only one variant on the equijoin: in addition, we have all of the joins based on various kinds of inequality.

Joins Not Based on Equality

Joins not based on equality can be described by their comparison condition, as "less-than join," "greater-than join," and so forth. This example of a less-than join displays orders that were shipped on a date later than the sale:

SQL:
```
select distinct s.sonum, s.stor_id, s.sdate,
 sd.date_shipped
from sales s, salesdetails sd
where s.sdate < sd.date_shipped
 and s.sonum = sd.sonum
```

Results:

sonum	stor_id	date	date_shipped
1	7066	Sep 13 1985	Sep 15 1985
2	7067	Sep 14 1985	Sep 15 1985
3	7131	Sep 14 1985	Sep 18 1985
4	7131	Sep 14 1985	Sep 18 1985
6	8042	Sep 14 1985	Sep 22 1985
7	6380	Sep 13 1985	Sep 20 1985
9	8042	Mar 11 1988	Mar 28 1988
10	7896	Oct 28 1987	Oct 29 1987
11	7896	Dec 12 1987	Jan 12 1988
12	8042	May 22 1987	May 24 1987
14	7131	May 29 1987	Jun 13 1987
15	7067	Jun 15 1987	Jun 17 1987
19	7896	Feb 21 1988	Mar 15 1988

(13 rows affected)

The following example joins the *titles* table to the *roysched* table on the *title_id* column, then uses a greater-than join and a less-than join to find the appropriate *royalty* rate given the year-to-date sales recorded in the *ytd_sales* column from the *titles* table. The royalty figure shows what royalty rate is assigned to that unit sales range in the *roysched* table. (The author's royalty percentage can change as sales increase.) The results of this join could be extended to help calculate an author's royalty, based on the price (or net price) of each title. This example uses aliases for table names to make the query easier to read.

SQL:
```
select t.title_id, t.ytd_sales, r.royalty
from titles t, roysched r
where t.title_id = r.title_id
  and t.ytd_sales >= r.lorange and t.ytd_sales <= r.hirange
```

Results:
```
title_id ytd_sales    royalty
-------- -----------  --------------------
BU1032         4095           0.100000
BU1111         3876           0.100000
BU2075        18722           0.180000
BU7832         4095           0.100000
MC2222         2032           0.120000
MC3021        22246           0.200000
PC1035         8780           0.160000
PC8888         4095           0.100000
PS1372          375           0.100000
PS2091         2045           0.120000
PS2106          111           0.100000
PS3333         4072           0.100000
PS7777         3336           0.100000
TC3218          375           0.100000
TC4203        15096           0.140000
TC7777         4095           0.100000

(16 rows affected)
```

Joining a Table with Itself: The Self-Join

The **self-join** is another variant on the equijoin. A self-join compares values within a column of a single table.

For example, you can use a self-join to find out which authors in Oakland, California, have exactly the same zip code. Since this query involves a join of the *authors* table with itself, the *authors* table appears in two roles. You must distinguish these roles by giving the *authors* table two *different* aliases—*au1* and *au2*—in the FROM clause's table list. These aliases are also used to qualify the column names in the rest of the query. Here's how you could state this query:

SQL:
```
select au1.au_fname, au1.au_lname, au1.zip
from authors au1, authors au2
where au1.city = 'Oakland'
and au1.zip = au2.zip
```

Results:

au_fname	au_lname	zip
Marjorie	Green	94618
Dick	Straight	94609
Dick	Straight	94609
Dick	Straight	94609
Dirk	Stringer	94609
Dirk	Stringer	94609
Dirk	Stringer	94609
Stearns	MacFeather	94612
Livia	Karsen	94609
Livia	Karsen	94609
Livia	Karsen	94609

```
(11 rows affected)
```

These results are a bit hard to read and don't appear to be correct. In order to clarify the situation, let's first attempt to get rid of the duplicate rows. The results show duplicates for three of the authors: Straight, Stringer, and Karsen. To eliminate duplicate rows, use the keyword DISTINCT to modify the first column in the select list.

SQL:
```
select distinct au1.au_fname, au1.au_lname, au1.zip
from authors au1, authors au2
where au1.city = 'Oakland'
and au1.zip = au2.zip
```

Results:

au_fname	au_lname	zip
Livia	Karsen	94609
Dick	Straight	94609
Dirk	Stringer	94609
Marjorie	Green	94618
Stearns	MacFeather	94612

(5 rows affected)

Now the results are free from duplicates, but they show all five authors who live in Oakland, not just those who share a zip code! What's going on?

The self-join compares all the zip code values to themselves, so that each Oakland author's zip code automatically matches his or her own zip code. Therefore, all the Oaklanders appear in the results. In order to eliminate the authors that match only themselves, you need to add one more condition to the WHERE clause:

SQL:
```
select distinct au1.au_fname, au1.au_lname, au1.zip
from authors au1, authors au2
where au1.city = 'Oakland'
and au1.zip = au2.zip
and au1.au_id != au2.au_id
```

Results:

au_fname	au_lname	zip
Livia	Karsen	94609
Dick	Straight	94609
Dirk	Stringer	94609

(3 rows affected)

That looks better. In the first, unrestrained example, the duplicate rows for these three authors resulted from each author's match with himself or herself and with the other two qualifying authors. If you omitted the DISTINCT qualifier from the previous example, you would still get duplicates from each author's match with the other two qualifying authors.

```
SQL:
select au1.au_fname, au1.au_lname, au1.zip
from authors au1, authors au2
where au1.city = 'Oakland'
and au1.zip = au2.zip
and au1.au_id != au2.au_id
```

au_fname	au_lname	zip
Dick	Straight	94609
Dick	Straight	94609
Dirk	Stringer	94609
Dick	Straight	94609
Livia	Karsen	94609
Livia	Karsen	94609

```
(6 rows affected)
```

Eliminating duplicates could be important to an analysis of the validity of the results, in cases where you really want to know "How many?" as well as "Who?".

Not-Equal Comparison in Self-Joins

The clause that eliminates the self-joins of authors with themselves in the previous example uses a not-equal join—a join with the not-equal operator.

Not-equal joins are of particular value in restricting the rows returned by a self-join. A not-equal join can also be stated with the NOT keyword. The expression *NOT column_name = column_name* is equivalent to *column_name != column_name*. The previous query could be restated as the following:

```
SQL:
select distinct au1.au_fname, au1.au_lname, au1.zip
from authors au1, authors au2
where au1.city = 'Oakland'
and au1.zip = au2.zip
and not au1.au_id = au2.au_id
```

As another example of combining a not-equal join with a self-join, the following query reports *title_id*s and *author_id*s for books that have more than one author (that is, all the rows in the *titleauthors* table where there are two or more rows with the same *title_id*, but different *au_id* numbers).

SQL:
```
select distinct t1.title_id, t1.au_id
from titleauthors t1, titleauthors t2
where t1.title_id = t2.title_id
and t1.au_id != t2.au_id
order by t1.title_id
```

Results:
```
title_id au_id
-------- -----------
BU1032   213-46-8915
BU1032   409-56-7008
BU1111   267-41-2394
BU1111   724-80-9391
MC3021   722-51-5454
MC3021   899-46-2035
PC8888   427-17-2319
PC8888   846-92-7186
PS1372   724-80-9391
PS1372   756-30-7391
PS2091   899-46-2035
PS2091   998-72-3567
TC7777   267-41-2394
TC7777   472-27-2349
TC7777   672-71-3249

(15 rows affected)
```

The not-equal join is necessary here again in order for the results to make sense.

Joining More Than Two Tables

The *titleauthors* table of our sample database offers a good example of a situation that often requires more than two tables to participate in a join. The design of the *bookbiz* database dictates that you must join three tables in order to obtain complete information about books and their authors.

For example, to find the titles of all the books of a particular type (*trad_cook*) and the names of their authors, the query is this:

```
SQL:
select au_lname, au_fname, title
from authors a, titles t, titleauthors ta
where a.au_id = ta.au_id
and t.title_id = ta.title_id
and t.type = 'trad_cook'
```

```
Results:
au_lname              au_fname   title
----------------      --------   ------------------------------------
Panteley              Sylvia     Onions, Leeks, and Garlic: Cooking
                                 Secrets of the Mediterranean
Blotchet-Halls        Reginald   Fifty Years in Buckingham Palace
                                 Kitchens
O'Leary               Michael    Sushi, Anyone?
Gringlesby            Burt       Sushi, Anyone?
Yokomoto              Akiko      Sushi, Anyone?

(5 rows affected)
```

The database design uses *titleauthors* as an intermediate table that joins with both *authors* and *titles*. You need this three-way join in order to find out even so simple a fact as who wrote which book.

When there is more than one join condition in a statement, the join conditions are almost always connected with AND, as in the preceding examples. Connecting two join conditions with OR is rarely justified: the results are not likely to make sense because the conditions are not restrictive enough.

Outer Joins: Showing the Background

The joins we've discussed so far include only rows that satisfy the join condition in the results. Occasionally, you may want to display the rows of one table that do not satisfy the join condition. An outer join shows you the join rows against the background of rows that did not meet the join conditions. It is convenient for putting results in context, and makes visual scans easy.

An outer join typically shows you the join, plus all the rows that did not qualify from the first-named table in the join specification. Other outer join operators can display all the rows that did not qualify from the *second*-named table in the join specification, or even from both tables. SQL-92 provides language for retrieving either the LEFT (first-named) table for an outer join or the RIGHT (second-named) table. Vendors generally implemented this feature before the standard defined it, and implementations still vary: some systems mark the outer join in the FROM clause, and others in the WHERE clause. Check your reference manuals for information. Transact-SQL uses the WHERE clause and this notation:

Symbol	Meaning
*=	include all rows from the first-named table
=*	include all rows from the second-named table

SQL Anywhere supports this form and others.

Recall that the query for authors who live in the same city as a publisher returns two names, Abraham Bennet and Cheryl Carson.

To include all the names from the *authors* table, regardless of whether or not they qualify for the join, you would use an outer join, as follows:

```
SQL:
select au_fname, au_lname, pub_name
from authors, publishers
where authors.city *= publishers.city
```

```
Results:
au_fname          au_lname            pub_name
---------         ----------------    ----------------
Johnson           White               NULL
Marjorie          Green               NULL
Cheryl            Carson              Algodata Infosystems
Michael           O'Leary             NULL
Dick              Straight            NULL
```

```
Meander      Smith            NULL
Abraham      Bennet           Algodata Infosystems
Ann          Dull             NULL
Burt         Gringlesby       NULL
Chastity     Locksley         NULL
Morningstar  Greene           NULL
Reginald     Blotchet-Halls   NULL
Akiko        Yokomoto         NULL
Innes        del Castillo     NULL
Michel       DeFrance         NULL
Dirk         Stringer         NULL
Stearns      MacFeather       NULL
Livia        Karsen           NULL
Sylvia       Panteley         NULL
Sheryl       Hunter           NULL
Heather      McBadden         NULL
Anne         Ringer           NULL
Albert       Ringer           NULL
```

```
(23 rows affected)
```

The outer join operator "*=" tells the system to include all the rows from the first table in the join specification (here, *authors*) in the results, whether or not there is a match on the *city* column in the *publishers* table. (The symbol for this outer join operator is the one that Transact-SQL provides; other systems may use different notation.) The outer join results show "no match" for most of the authors listed, as the results indicate with null values in the *pub_name* column.

You can specify that an outer join show nonmatching rows either from the first table in the join specification (a "left" outer join) or from the second (a "right" outer join). The outer join operator "=*" includes all the rows in the second table in the join specification in the results, regardless of whether there is matching data in the first table.

Substituting the right outer join operator shows the publishers that do not coexist in the same city with any authors, as well as the publisher that did satisfy the join condition:

SQL:

```
select au_fname, au_lname, pub_name
from authors, publishers
where authors.city =* publishers.city
```

```
Results:
au_fname      au_lname   pub_name
---------     ---------  ----------------

NULL          NULL       New Age Books
NULL          NULL       Binnet & Hardley
Cheryl        Carson     Algodata Infosystems
Abraham       Bennet     Algodata Infosystems

(4 rows affected)
```

As in any join, the results of an outer join can be restricted by comparison to a constant. This means that you can zoom in on precisely the value or values you want to see, and use the outer join to show the rows that didn't make the cut. Let's look at the equijoin first, and then compare it to the outer join. For example, if you wanted to find out which title had sold more than fifty copies from any store, you'd use this query:

```
SQL:
select sonum, title
from salesdetails sd, titles t
where qty_ordered > 50
and sd.title_id = t.title_id
```

```
Results:
sonum         title
---------     ---------------------------

1             Is Anger the Enemy?

(1 row affected)
```

To show, in addition, the titles that didn't sell more than fifty copies in any store, you'd use an outer join query:

```
SQL:
select sonum, title
from salesdetails sd, titles t
where qty_ordered > 50
and sd.title_id =* t.title_id
```

Results:

```
sonum   title
-----   -------------------------------------------------------
NULL    The Busy Executive's Database Guide
NULL    Cooking with Computers: Surreptitious Balance Sheets
NULL    You Can Combat Computer Stress!
NULL    Straight Talk About Computers
NULL    Silicon Valley Gastronomic Treats
NULL    The Gourmet Microwave
NULL    The Psychology of Computer Cooking
NULL    But Is It User Friendly?
NULL    Secrets of Silicon Valley
NULL    Net Etiquette
NULL    Computer Phobic and Non-Phobic Individuals: Behavior
        Variations
1       Is Anger the Enemy?
NULL    Life Without Fear
NULL    Prolonged Data Deprivation: Four Case Studies
NULL    Emotional Security: A New Algorithm
NULL    Onions, Leeks, and Garlic: Cooking Secrets of the
        Mediterranean
NULL    Fifty Years in Buckingham Palace Kitchens
NULL    Sushi, Anyone?

(18 rows affected)
```

HOW THE SYSTEM PROCESSES JOINS

It's not all that uncommon to make a mistake in a join statement that results in an incomprehensible report. If your join results seem to contain too many rows, and include a great many duplicate rows, you probably need to restate your join query. The excess output—although it is not what you intended—does reveal something about the way a relational system processes joins.

Conceptually speaking, the first step in processing a join is to form the Cartesian product of the tables—all the possible combinations of the rows from each of the tables. Once the system obtains the Cartesian product, it uses the columns in the select list for the projection, and the conditions in the WHERE clause for the selection, to eliminate the rows that do not satisfy the join.

The Cartesian product is the matrix of all the possible combinations that could satisfy the join condition. If there is only one row in each table, there is only one possible combination. (This is very exciting.) To show the product of two tables having one row each, we use data values of *a, b* in one table and *c, d* in the other, with the column names *one, two* in the first table and *three, four* in the second table:

```
one two
--- ---
a   b


three four
----- ----
c     d
```

The Cartesian product is this:

```
one two three four
--- --- ----- ----
a   b   c     d
```

If you have two rows in each table, the Cartesian product is four rows (2 × 2):

```
First table:
one two
--- ---
a   b
c   d


Second table:
three four
----- ----
c     d
e     f
```

```
Cartesian product:
one two three four
--- --- ----- ----
a    b   c     d
a    b   e     f
c    d   c     d
c    d   e     f

(4 rows affected)
```

The number of rows in the Cartesian product increases geometrically in direct relation to the number of rows in the two tables. It equals the number of rows in the first table times the number of rows in the second table. As soon as you have any significant amount of data, a Cartesian product can produce an overwhelming amount of rows and columns.

All you have to do in order to create a Cartesian product right at your own terminal is to set up a join on two tables and omit the join condition. The query that produced the preceding Cartesian product was this:

```
select *
from test, test2
```

The Join Clause Constrains the Cartesian Product

A valid join in the WHERE clause is essential to producing comprehensible multitable query results. Without a valid join, precisely stated and refined, a query on two tables can produce an uncontrolled display of the whole multiplicity of possible connections between the two tables.

In the *bookbiz* database, the Cartesian product of the *publishers* table (3 rows) and the *authors* table (23 rows), shows a results display of 69 rows (3 rows × 23 rows). This result is not only excessive, but also downright misleading, since it seems to imply that every author in the database has a relationship with every publisher in the database—which is not true at all. Getting the Cartesian product represents a failure of communication between you and your system.

If you add the join to the earlier query, it properly constrains the results:

```
SQL:
select *
from test, test2
where one = three

Results:
one two three four
--- --- ----- ----
c   d   c     d

(1 row affected)
```

UNIONS

Although UNION isn't a join , it is a way of combining data from multiple queries into one display. UNION is useful when you want to see similar data from two or more tables in one display. The simplified syntax is this:

```
select_statement
UNION
select_statement
```

Here's a query that will give you a list of all the authors and editors who live in Oakland or Berkeley:

```
SQL:
select au_fname, au_lname, city
from authors
where city in ('Oakland', 'Berkeley')
union
select ed_fname, ed_lname, city
from editors
where city in ('Oakland', 'Berkeley')
```

Notice that the two select lists contain the same number of items, and the datatypes are compatible. Check your documentation for specifics on what datatype combinations you can use.

When you examine the query results, you'll see that there are seven rows from *authors* and three from *editors* (those for Bernard, Christof, and Martinella). The UNION display uses the column names from the first select list only:

```
Results:
au_fname       au_lname       city
- - - - - - - - - -    - - - - - - - - - -    - - - - - - - - -
Livia          Karsen         Oakland
Dick           Straight       Oakland
Dirk           Stringer       Oakland
Cheryl         Carson         Berkeley
Marjorie       Green          Oakland
Abraham        Bennet         Berkeley
Bernard        Samuelson      Oakland
Christof       Kaspchek       Berkeley
Stearns        MacFeather     Oakland
Martinella     DeLongue       Berkeley
```

Although each SELECT statement can have its own WHERE clause, the query as a whole takes only one ORDER BY clause. It comes in its normal position but must be in the last SELECT statement. It applies to all the output.

Here's a query that makes the display more readable by "generalizing" the column names in the first SELECT statement—there's no need to change those in the second, since the display is set up based on the names in the first select list only. The query also contains an ORDER BY clause to sort the results by city.

```
SQL:
select au_fname as First_name, au_lname as Last_name,
    city as City
from authors
where city in ('Oakland', 'Berkeley')
union
select ed_fname, ed_lname, city
from editors
where city in ('Oakland', 'Berkeley')
order by 3
```

```
Results:

First_name   Last_name    City
-----------  -----------  ---------
Abraham      Bennet       Berkeley
Cheryl       Carson       Berkeley
Christof     Kaspchek     Berkeley
Martinella   DeLongue     Berkeley
Bernard      Samuelson    Oakland
Dick         Straight     Oakland
Dirk         Stringer     Oakland
Livia        Karsen       Oakland
Marjorie     Green        Oakland
Stearns      MacFeather   Oakland
```

By default, UNION removes duplicate rows from the results display. This can be confusing when there is only one column in the query. For example, the *authors* table lists 23 cities and the *publishers* table lists 3. A UNION shows only 18 rows.

```
SQL:
select count(city)
from authors

Results:
-----
   23

SQL:
select count(city)
from publishers

Results:
-----
    3

SQL:
select city
from authors
union
```

```
select city
from publishers
```

Results:

```
city
-------------------
Gary
Boston
Covelo
Oakland
Berkeley
Lawrence
San Jose
Ann Arbor
Corvallis
Nashville
Palo Alto
Rockville
Vacaville
Menlo Park
Washington
Walnut Creek
San Francisco
Salt Lake City
```

Why only 18 rows? UNION removes all the duplicates from the display, no matter which table they were derived from. Since *authors* has 16 distinct entries for *city* and *publishers* has 3, with one duplicating an *authors* city, the union of the two comes to 18.

To display all rows, including duplicates, add the keyword ALL after UNION. Check your implementation's documentation for other rules applying to UNION.

If I Had a UNION

One final wrinkle: you can use UNION as a kind of IF statement to display different values for one field, depending on what's in another. Without UNION, you'd have to use several queries or some procedural elements to get the same effect.

For example, it's time to reduce inventory. You need to produce a list of books showing discount percent and new prices. Books under $7.00 are reduced by 20 percent, those between $7.00 and $15.00 are reduced by 10 percent, and those above $15.00 are reduced by 30 percent. Without UNION, you'd have to write three separate queries and put the results into a new table.

Here's a UNION query that will do it in one pass:

```
SQL:
select '20% off', title, price, price * .80
from titles
where price < 7.00
union
select '10% off', title, price, price * .90
from titles
where price between 7.00 and 15.00
union
select '30% off', title, price, price * .70
from titles
where price > 15.00
```

After you clean up the output by shortening the displays and adding column headings, you'll see something like this:

```
Results:
discount      title                   old      new
--------      ------------------      ------   ------
10% off       Sushi, Anyone?          14.99    13.49
10% off       Life Without Fear        7.00     6.30
10% off       Is Anger the Enemy?     10.95     9.86
20% off       The Gourmet Microwave    2.99     2.39
30% off       But Is It User Friendly? 22.95   16.07
10% off       Cooking With Computers: 11.95    10.76
10% off       Emotional Security: A Ne  7.99     7.19
10% off       Fifty Years in Buckingha 11.95   10.76
20% off       You Can Combat Computer   2.99     2.39
30% off       Computer Phobic and Non-P 21.59   15.11
30% off       Onions, Leeks, and Garlic 20.95  14.67
30% off       Prolonged Data Deprivatio 19.99  13.99
30% off       Secrets of Silicon Valley 20.00  14.00
```

```
30% off     Silicon Valley Gastronomi 19.99    13.99
30% off     Straight Talk About Compu 19.99    13.99
30% off     The Busy Executive's Data 19.99    13.99
```

Add an ORDER BY clause if you want to see the output sorted by price.

DIVING INTO SUBQUERIES

In the next chapter we turn our attention to subqueries. Subqueries are the other method that relational systems provide for querying multiple tables. Although joins and subqueries are often interchangeable, there are some cases in which only a subquery yields the desired results.

Chapter 8

Structuring Queries with Subqueries

WHAT IS A SUBQUERY?

A **subquery** is an additional method for handling multitable manipulations. It is a SELECT statement that nests

- Inside the WHERE, HAVING, or SELECT clause of another SELECT statement;
- Inside an INSERT, UPDATE, or DELETE statement; or
- Inside another subquery.

The ability to nest SQL statements is the reason that SQL was originally called the Structured Query Language. The term *subquery* is often used to refer to an entire set of statements that includes one or more subqueries, as well as to an individual nestling. Each enclosing statement, the next level up in a subquery, is the outer level for its inner subquery.

Subqueries are a complex topic, because there are two processing types—noncorrelated and correlated—and three subquery-to-outer-clause connection possibilities. After looking at general subquery syntax we'll examine how noncorrelated and correlated subqueries work, and compare them to joins. Then we'll dive into the connection issue, looking at noncorrelated and correlated examples of each.

Simplified Subquery Syntax

A simplified form of the subquery syntax (Figure 8-1) shows how a subquery nests in a SELECT statement. (Most of the examples in this chapter use this kind of WHERE clause subquery structure.)

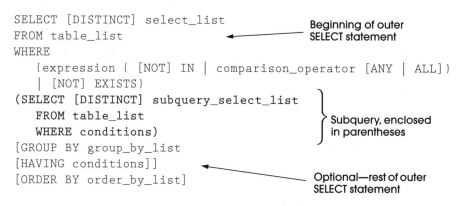

```
SELECT [DISTINCT] select_list                    ┌─── Beginning of outer
FROM table_list                          ◄────────     SELECT statement
WHERE
    {expression { [NOT] IN | comparison_operator [ANY | ALL]}
    | [NOT] EXISTS}
(SELECT [DISTINCT] subquery_select_list    ┐
    FROM table_list                        ├── Subquery, enclosed
    WHERE conditions)                      ┘   in parentheses
[GROUP BY group_by_list]
[HAVING conditions]]               ◄────────
[ORDER BY order_by_list]                   ┌─── Optional—rest of outer
                                                SELECT statement
```

Figure 8–1. A Subquery in an Outer SELECT

Other query search conditions (including joins) can also appear in the outer query WHERE clause, either before or after the inner query.

HOW DO SUBQUERIES WORK?

Subqueries return results from an inner query to an outer clause and come in two basic flavors: **noncorrelated** and **correlated**. The first is evaluated (conceptually) from the inside out. That is, the outer query takes an action based on the results of the inner query. You can think of the second (correlated) subquery as working the opposite way: The outer SQL statement provides the values for the inner subquery to use in its evaluation. Then the subquery results are passed back to the outer query. Both correlated and noncorrelated subqueries are divided into three types (more about this later), depending on elements in the outer query WHERE clause:

1. Subqueries that return zero or more items (introduced with IN or with a comparison operator modified by ANY or ALL)

2. Subqueries that return a single value (introduced with an unmodified comparison operator)

3. Subqueries that are an existence test (introduced with EXISTS)

Figure 8-2 compares a noncorrelated and a correlated subquery with identical results. Both are introduced with IN and find the names of the publishers who produce business books.

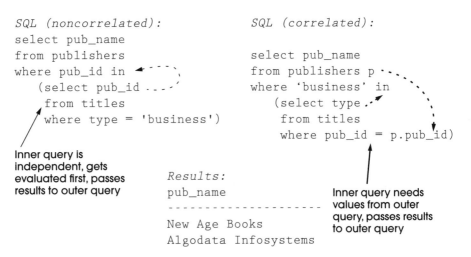

```
SQL (noncorrelated):              SQL (correlated):
select pub_name
from publishers                   select pub_name
where pub_id in                   from publishers p
   (select pub_id                 where 'business' in
    from titles                      (select type
    where type = 'business')         from titles
                                      where pub_id = p.pub_id)
```

Inner query is
independent, gets
evaluated first, passes   Results:
results to outer query   pub_name   Inner query needs
                                 --------------------   values from outer
                                                         query, passes results
                                 New Age Books   to outer query
                                 Algodata Infosystems

Figure 8–2. Noncorrelated and Correlated Subqueries

As with many subqueries, you could also formulate this query as a join query. To show publisher names only once, add DISTINCT to the select list.

```
SQL:

select distinct pub_name
from publishers p, titles t
where p.pub_id = t.pub_id
and type = 'business'
```

Noncorrelated Processing

Conceptually, the outer query and the noncorrelated subquery (or inner query) are evaluated in two steps. First, the inner query returns the identification numbers of those publishers that have published business books (1389 and 0736):

```
SQL:

select pub_id
from titles
where type = 'business'
```

Results:
```
pub_id
------
1389
1389
0736
1389

(4 rows affected)
```

Second, these values are substituted into the outer query, which finds the names that go with the identification numbers in the *publishers* table.

SQL:
```
select pub_name
from publishers
where pub_id in ('1389', '0736')
```

Results:
```
pub_name
---------------------------------------
New Age Books
Algodata Infosystems

(2 rows affected)
```

Qualifying Column Names. In subqueries, column names are implicitly qualified by the FROM clause table at the same level. This means the *pub_id* column in the outer query WHERE clause is implicitly qualified by the table name in the outer query FROM clause, *publishers*. The reference to *pub_id* in the subquery select list is qualified by the subquery's FROM clause—that is, by the *titles* table.

Here's what the queries look like with these implicit assumptions spelled out:

```
SQL:
select pub_name
from publishers
where publishers.pub_id in
    (select titles.pub_id
     from titles
     where type = 'business')
```

It is never wrong to state the table name explicitly, and you can always override implicit assumptions about table names with explicit qualifications.

Correlated Processing

Correlated queries are not as neat, but very valuable (they can handle problems you can't easily approach with joins or noncorrelated queries). For now, just understand the syntax and get an idea of how they work. As you experiment, you'll become comfortable with them.

In the correlated subquery, the inner query cannot be evaluated independently: it references the outer query and is executed once for each row in the outer query. In the example in Figure 8-2, the outer table (*publishers*) has three rows, so the inner query will run three times.

Conceptually, the processing follows these steps. The outer query finds the first name in the *publishers* table (say, New Age Books). The inner query joins the associated *publishers.pub_id* (0736) to *titles.pub_id* to find qualifying rows in the *titles* table (it finds six). Then the inner query passes this result back to the outer query IN clause, where *titles.type* is matched against the string "business". Only one of the six is a business book, but that's enough: New Age Books qualifies. The subquery then goes to work again, this time using the *pub_id* of the second row in *publishers* (0877). It retrieves an additional six rows, all with various cooking types; this publisher (Binnet & Hardley) does not meet the conditions. The subquery runs the third time with a *publishers.pub_id* of 1389 (Algodata Infosystems) and finds six more rows. Three of them have *type* "business". Algodata Infosystems will be in the final result set.

Qualifying Column Names.   Correlated queries require explicit naming for columns from the outer query (you can use aliases, as *p.pub_id* for *publishers.pub_id* in Figure 8-2). Columns belonging to the inner query table are implicitly qualified by it.

However, you can always specify both tables:

```
SQL (correlated):
select pub_name
from publishers
where 'business' in
    (select type
     from titles
     where titles.pub_id = publishers.pub_id)
```

JOINS OR SUBQUERIES?

As you develop your SQL style, you will use both joins and subqueries for your multitable queries. They can often be used interchangeably to solve a given problem; in these cases, whether you use a join or a subquery is simply a matter of individual preference. Some SQL users automatically reach for a subquery, while others prefer joins.

However, each has particular advantages and disadvantages.

Subqueries!

For example, consider the problem of listing all books with prices equal to the minimum book price. Using joins, you'd do the job in two steps.

1. Find the minimum price.

    ```
    SQL:
    select min (price)
    from titles

    Results:
    ------
    2.99
    ```

2. Get the names of all books selling for this price.

    ```
    SQL:
    select title, price
    from titles
    where price = 2.99
    ```

```
Results:

title                                          price
------------------------------------------     ------
You Can Combat Computer Stress!                2.99
The Gourmet Microwave                          2.99
```

With a subquery, you need only one statement.

```
SQL:
select title, price
from titles
where price =
    (select min(price)
     from titles)


Results:

title                                          price
------------------------------------------     ------
You Can Combat Computer Stress!                2.99
The Gourmet Microwave                          2.99
```

The ability to calculate an aggregate value on the fly and feed it back to the outer query for comparison is a subquery advantage; a join can't compete.

```
Join:                              Subquery:
select distinct pub_name           select pub_name
from publishers, authors           from publishers
where publishers.city =            where city in
    authors.city                       (select city
                                        from authors)



                    Results:

                    pub_name
                    --------------------

                    Algodata Infosystems
```

Figure 8-3. Comparing a Join and a Subquery

Joins!

But joins also have some special strengths. For example, the two queries in Figure 8-3 (both searching for the names of publishers located in the same city as some author) return identical results.

However, the join gives more options, because you can edit it to include results from both tables, which is not possible with the subquery.

SQL:
```
select pub_name, au_fname, au_lname
from publishers, authors
where publishers.city =
    authors.city
```

Results
```
pub_name                 au_fname            au_lname
---------------------    ----------------    ------------------
Algodata Infosystems     Cheryl              Carson
Algodata Infosystems     Abraham             Bennet
```

The subquery can display information from the outer table (*publishers*) only, so it reports the name of the publisher once and stops there. When you want results to include information about both tables, use a join.

Subqueries versus Self-Joins?

Many statements in which the subquery and the outer query refer to the same table can be alternatively stated as self-joins. For example, you can find authors who live in the same city as Livia Karsen by using a subquery:

SQL:
```
select au_lname, au_fname, city
from authors
where city in
    (select city
     from authors
     where au_fname = 'Livia'
     and au_lname = 'Karsen')
```

```
Results:
au_lname         au_fname        city
- - - - - - - - - - - - -   - - - - - - - - - - - - - -  - - - - - - - - - -
Green            Marjorie        Oakland
Straight         Dick            Oakland
Stringer         Dirk            Oakland
MacFeather       Stearns         Oakland
Karsen           Livia           Oakland

(5 rows affected)
```

Or you can use a self-join:

```
SQL:
select au1.au_lname, au1.au_fname, au1.city
from authors au1, authors au2
where au1.city = au2.city
    and au2.au_lname = 'Karsen'
    and au2.au_fname = 'Livia'
```

Which Is Best?

Deciding whether to use a subquery or a join when you are working with multiple tables is usually a matter of style. Most people find one—or the other—more intuitive. (Programmers, for example, often prefer subqueries because subqueries are like subroutines.) Nonetheless, there are times when you must choose:

- Subqueries shine when you need to compare aggregates to other values.
- Joins star when you're displaying results from multiple tables.

SUBQUERY RULES

Now that you've explored noncorrelated and correlated subqueries, and have compared them to joins, look at the rules governing subqueries more closely. They primarily concern the select list of the subquery, with some additional restrictions on functions you can specify in a subquery. Your SQL may have more or fewer restrictions, but here are some of the common ones:

- The select list of an inner subquery introduced with a comparison operator or IN can include only one expression or column name. The column you name in the WHERE clause of the outer statement must be join-compatible with the column you name in the subquery select list.

- The select list of a subquery introduced with EXISTS almost always consists of the asterisk (*). There is no need to specify column names, since you are only testing for the existence (or nonexistence) of any rows that meet the criteria. (You can qualify the rows in the subquery WHERE clause.) The select list rules for a subquery introduced with EXISTS are otherwise identical to those for a standard select list.

- Subqueries introduced by an unmodified comparison operator (a comparison operator not followed by the keyword ANY or ALL) cannot include GROUP BY and HAVING clauses unless you determine in advance that the grouping returns a single value.

- Subqueries cannot manipulate their results internally. That is, a subquery cannot include the ORDER BY clause or the INTO keyword. The optional DISTINCT keyword may effectively order the results of a subquery, since some systems eliminate duplicates by first ordering the results.

A survey of the three main types of subquery connections will clarify these restrictions and the reasons for them. As noted earlier, these connections involve

1. Subqueries that return zero or more items (introduced with IN or with a comparison operator modified by ANY or ALL)

2. Subqueries that return a single value (introduced with an unmodified comparison operator)

3. Subqueries that are an existence test (introduced with EXISTS)

The following sections address each connection type. (They can be noncorrelated or correlated.)

SUBQUERIES RETURNING ZERO OR MORE VALUES

This group includes subqueries introduced with IN, NOT IN, or a comparison operator and ANY or ALL.

Subqueries Introduced with IN

Subqueries introduced with the keyword IN take this general form:

```
Start of SELECT, INSERT, UPDATE, DELETE statement; or subquery
WHERE expression [NOT] IN (subquery)
[End of SELECT, INSERT, UPDATE, DELETE statement; or subquery]
```

The result of the inner subquery is a list of zero or more values. Once the subquery returns results, the outer query makes use of them.

Here's an example of a statement that you could formulate either with a subquery or with a join query. The English version of the query is "Find the names of all second authors who live in California and receive less than 30 percent of the royalties on the books they coauthor." Using a subquery, the statement is

```
SQL:

select au_lname, au_fname
from authors
where state = 'CA'
and au_id in
    (select au_id
     from titleauthors
     where royaltyshare < .30
     and au_ord = 2)


Results:

au_lname                      au_fname
------------------------      -----------
MacFeather                    Stearns

(1 row affected)
```

The inner query is evaluated, producing a list of the IDs of the two second authors who meet the qualification of earning less than 30 percent of the royalties. The system then evaluates the outer query.

Notice that it's legal to include more than one condition in the WHERE clause of both the inner and the outer query. A subquery can even include a join—joins and subqueries are by no means mutually exclusive.

Using a join, the query is expressed like this:

```
SQL:
select au_lname, au_fname
from authors, titleauthors
where state = 'CA'
and authors.au_id = titleauthors.au_id
and royaltyshare < .30
and au_ord = 2
```

```
Results:
au_lname                     au_fname
------------------------     ------------

MacFeather                   Stearns
```

```
(1 row affected)
```

"Which authors are both sole authors and coauthors?" is a question that may be easier to read and understand as a subquery, although you can get the same information with a complex join.

```
SQL:
select authors.au_id, au_lname, au_fname
from authors, titleauthors
where royaltyshare < 1.0
and authors.au_id = titleauthors.au_id
and authors.au_id in
    (select distinct authors.au_id
     from authors, titleauthors
     where titleauthors.royaltyshare = 1.0
     and authors.au_id = titleauthors.au_id)
```

```
Results:
au_id         au_lname             au_fname
-----------   -----------------    ---------------------
213-46-8915   Green                Marjorie
998-72-3567   Ringer               Albert
```

```
(2 rows affected)
```

First the inner query selects the identification numbers of authors whose royalty share is equal to 100 percent, and then the outer query compares these IDs to its selection of authors whose royalty share is less than 100 percent.

Here's a join that finds the same information. The select list is a little different, in order to list both royalty values (which is not possible with the subquery version—you'd only be able to display one):

SQL:

```
select a1.au_id, au_lname, ta1.royaltyshare, ta2.royaltyshare
from authors a1, titleauthors ta1, titleauthors ta2
where ta1.royaltyshare < 1.0
   and a1.au_id = ta1.au_id
   and a1.au_id = ta2.au_id
   and ta2.royaltyshare = 1.0
```

Results:

au_id	au_lname	royaltyshare	royaltyshare
212-46-8915	Green	0.400000	1.00000
998-72-3567	Ringer	0.500000	1.00000

Subqueries Introduced with NOT IN

Subqueries introduced with NOT IN also return a list of zero or more values. This query finds the names of the publishers who have *not* published business books (the inverse of an earlier example):

SQL:

```
select distinct pub_name
from publishers
where pub_id not in
   (select pub_id
    from titles
    where type = 'business')
```

```
Results:
pub_name
----------------------------------------
Binnet & Hardley

(1 row affected)
```

The query is exactly the same as the earlier one except that NOT IN is substituted for IN. However, you cannot convert this NOT IN statement to a "not equal" join. The analogous "not equal" join has a different meaning: it finds the names of publishers who have published *some* book that is not a business book.

```
SQL:
select distinct pub_name
from publishers, titles
where publishers.pub_id = titles.pub_id
and type != 'business'

Results:
pub_name
----------------------------------------
New Age Books
Binnet & Hardley
Algodata Infosystems

(3 rows affected)
```

To refresh your memory about joins based on inequality, refer to Chapter 7.

Correlated Subqueries with IN

You can find the names of all authors who earn 100 percent royalty on a book with this statement:

```
SQL:
select distinct au_lname, au_fname
from authors
```

```
where 1.00 in
    (select royaltyshare
     from titleauthors
     where au_id = authors.au_id)
```

Results:

au_lname	au_fname
Carson	Cheryl
Ringer	Albert
Straight	Dick
White	Johnson
Green	Marjorie
Panteley	Sylvia
Locksley	Chastity
del Castillo	Innes
Blotchet-Halls	Reginald

(9 rows affected)

Unlike most of the previous subquery examples, you cannot evaluate this statement's subquery independently. The value that the subquery needs for *authors.au_id* is a *variable*: it changes as the system examines different rows of the *authors* table.

Conceptually, that's exactly how the system processes this query: The system tests each row of the *authors* table against the condition. Say that the system first examines the row for Cheryl Carson. The variable *authors.au_id* takes the value "238-95-7766," which the system substitutes into the inner query:

SQL:
```
select royaltyshare
from titleauthors
where au_id = '238-95-7766'
```

The result is 1.00, so the outer query evaluates to

SQL:
```
select au_lname, au_fname
from authors
where 1.00 in (1.00)
```

Since this is true, the row for Cheryl Carson is included in the results. If you go through the same procedure with the row for Abraham Bennet, you will see that this row is not eligible for the results.

Correlated IN Subqueries on a Single Table.   You can use a correlated subquery introduced with IN on a single table, for example to find which types of books are common to more than one publisher:

```
SQL:
select distinct t1.type
from titles t1
where t1.type in
    (select t2.type
     from titles t2
     where t1.pub_id != t2.pub_id)

Results:
type
-------------------
business

(1 row affected)
```

Aliases are required here to distinguish the two different roles in which the *titles* table appears. This nested query is equivalent to the self-join statement:

```
SQL:
select distinct t1.type
from titles t1, titles t2
where t1.type = t2.type
and t1.pub_id != t2.pub_id
```

Correlated IN Subqueries in a HAVING Clause.   You can also use a correlated subquery in a HAVING clause. This kind of formulation will, for example, find types of books in which the maximum advance is at least twice the average advance for that type.

```
SQL:
select t1.type
from titles t1
group by t1.type
having max(t1.advance) in
  (select 2 * avg(t2.advance)
   from titles t2
   where t1.type = t2.type)

Results:
type
----------
mod_cook

(1 row affected)
```

In this case, the subquery is evaluated once for each group defined in the outer query—once for each type of book.

Subqueries Introduced with Comparison Operators and ANY or ALL

Another kind of subquery, which returns zero or more rows, uses a comparison operator modified with keywords ALL or ANY. Subqueries introduced with a modified comparison operator take this general form:

```
Start of SELECT, INSERT, UPDATE, DELETE statement; or subquery
WHERE expression comparison_operator [ANY | ALL] (subquery)
[End of SELECT, INSERT, UPDATE, DELETE statement; or subquery]
```

Understanding ALL and ANY. Using the ">" comparison operator as an example, "> ALL" means greater than every value—in other words, greater than the largest value. In this way, "> ALL (1, 2, 3)" means greater than 3. "> ANY" means greater than at least one value—in other words, greater than the minimum. So "> ANY (1, 2, 3)" means greater than 1. Figure 8-4 compares ANY and ALL.

ALL and ANY can be tricky because computers won't tolerate the ambiguity that these words sometimes have in English.

ALL	Results	ANY	Results
> ALL (1, 2, 3)	>3	> ANY (1, 2, 3)	>1
< ALL (1, 2, 3)	<1	< ANY (1, 2, 3)	<3
= ALL (1, 2, 3)	=1 and =2 and =3 (all at the same time)	= ANY (1, 2, 3)	=1 or =2 or =3

Figure 8–4. Comparing ANY and ALL

Subqueries with ALL. For example, you might ask the question, "Which books commanded an advance greater than any book published by New Age Books?" This question can be paraphrased to make the SQL "translation" of it more clear: "Which books commanded an advance greater than the largest advance paid by New Age Books?" The ALL keyword (*not* the ANY keyword) is what's required here:

```
SQL:
select title
from titles
where advance > all
   (select advance
    from publishers, titles
    where titles.pub_id = publishers.pub_id
    and pub_name = 'New Age Books')

Results:
title
-----------------------------------------
The Gourmet Microwave

(1 row affected)
```

For each title, the inner query finds a list of advance amounts paid by New Age. The outer query looks at the largest value in the list and determines whether the title currently being considered has commanded an even bigger advance.

If an inner subquery introduced with ALL and a comparison operator returns NULL as one of its values, the entire query fails. For example, the advances for Algodata Infosystems books look like this:

SQL:
```
select advance
from publishers, titles
where titles.pub_id = publishers.pub_id
    and pub_name = 'Algodata Infosystems'
```

Results:
```
advance
-----------------------
5000.00
5000.00
5000.00
7000.00
8000.00
NULL

(6 rows affected)
```

If you query for advances greater than all of those provided by Algodata Infosystems, you get no results, because it's impossible to tell what's greater than NULL.

SQL:
```
select title
from titles
where advance > all
    (select advance
     from publishers, titles
     where titles.pub_id = publishers.pub_id
     and pub_name = 'Algodata Infosystems')
```

Results:
```
title
-------------------------------------------------------

(0 rows affected)
```

Check your system to see what happens when the inner query returns no results, as in the following example, with a false condition (there is no publisher called "Demo Books").

SQL:
```
select title
from titles
where advance > all
   (select advance
    from publishers, titles
    where titles.pub_id = publishers.pub_id
    and pub_name = 'Demo Books')
```

Subqueries with ANY. A query with ANY finds values greater than "some" value of a subquery. The following query finds the titles that got an advance larger than the minimum advance amount ($5,000) paid by Algodata Infosystems.

SQL:
```
select title, advance
from titles
where advance > any
   (select advance
    from titles, publishers
    where titles.pub_id = publishers.pub_id
    and pub_name = 'Algodata Infosystems')
```

Results:

title	advance
Sushi, Anyone?	8,000.00
Life Without Fear	6,000.00
The Gourmet Microwave	15,000.00
But Is It User Friendly?	7,000.00
Secrets of Silicon Valley	8,000.00
You Can Combat Computer Stress!	10,125.00
Computer Phobic and Non-Phobic Individuals: Behavior Variations	7,000.00

```
Onions, Leeks, and Garlic: Cooking
    Secrets of the Mediterranean        7,000.00
```

```
(8 rows affected)
```

For each title, the inner query finds a list of advance amounts paid by Algodata. The outer query looks at all the values in the list and determines whether the title currently being considered has commanded an advance larger than any of those amounts.

If the subquery does not return any values, the entire query fails.

Comparing IN, ANY, and ALL.   The "= ANY" operator is exactly equivalent to IN. For example, to find authors that live in the same city as some publisher, you can use either IN or = ANY:

```
SQL:
select au_lname, au_fname, city
from authors
where city in
   (select city
    from publishers)
order by city
```

```
or
```

```
SQL:
select au_lname, au_fname, city
from authors
where city = any
   (select city
    from publishers)
order by city
```

```
Results:
au_lname        au_fname                city
------------    --------------------    -----------------
Carson          Cheryl                  Berkeley
Bennet          Abraham                 Berkeley

(2 rows affected)
```

However, the "<> ANY" operator (or "!= ANY" operator, depending on the syntax your system likes) is different from NOT IN. "<> ANY" means "not = a *or* not = b *or* not = c." NOT IN means "not = a *and* not = b *and* not = c." Say you want to find the authors who live in a city where no publisher is located. You might try this query:

SQL:

```
select au_lname, au_fname
from authors
where city <> any
    (select city
     from publishers)
```

Results:

au_lname	au_fname	city
del Castillo	Innes	Ann Arbor
Carson	Cheryl	Berkeley
Bennet	Abraham	Berkeley
Blotchet-Halls	Reginald	Corvallis
Gringlesby	Burt	Covelo
DeFrance	Michel	Gary
Smith	Meander	Lawrence
White	Johnson	Menlo Park
Greene	Morningstar	Nashville
Karsen	Livia	Oakland
Straight	Dean	Oakland
Stringer	Dirk	Oakland
Green	Marjorie	Oakland
MacFeather	Stearns	Oakland
Dull	Ann	Palo Alto
Hunter	Sheryl	Palo Alto
Panteley	Sylvia	Rockville
Ringer	Anne	Salt Lake City
Ringer	Albert	Salt Lake City
Locksley	Chastity	San Francisco
O'Leary	Michael	San Jose
McBadden	Heather	Vacaville
Yokomoto	Akiko	Walnut Creek

(23 rows affected)

The results include all 23 authors. This is because every author lives in *some* city where no publisher is located, since each author lives in one and only one city. The inner query finds all the cities in which publishers are located, and then, for *each* city, the outer query finds the authors who don't live there. Here's what happens when you substitute NOT IN in this query:

SQL:

```
select au_lname, au_fname, city
from authors
where city not in
    (select city
     from publishers)
order by city
```

Results:

au_lname	au_fname	city
del Castillo	Innes	Ann Arbor
Blotchet-Halls	Reginald	Corvallis
Gringlesby	Burt	Covelo
DeFrance	Michel	Gary
Smith	Meander	Lawrence
White	Johnson	Menlo Park
Greene	Morningstar	Nashville
Karsen	Livia	Oakland
Straight	Dean	Oakland
Stringer	Dirk	Oakland
Green	Marjorie	Oakland
MacFeather	Stearns	Oakland
Dull	Ann	Palo Alto
Hunter	Sheryl	Palo Alto
Panteley	Sylvia	Rockville
Ringer	Anne	Salt Lake City
Ringer	Albert	Salt Lake City
Locksley	Chastity	San Francisco
O'Leary	Michael	San Jose
McBadden	Heather	Vacaville
Yokomoto	Akiko	Walnut Creek

(21 rows affected)

These are the results you want. They include all the authors except Cheryl Carson and Abraham Bennet, who live in Berkeley, where Algodata Infosystems is located.

SUBQUERIES RETURNING A SINGLE VALUE

A subquery introduced with an **unmodified comparison operator** (a comparison operator not followed by ANY or ALL) must resolve to a single value. (If it doesn't, you'll get an error message, and the query won't be processed.) These subqueries take this general form:

```
Start of SELECT, INSERT, UPDATE, DELETE statement; or subquery
WHERE expression comparison_operator (subquery)
[End of SELECT, INSERT, UPDATE, DELETE statement; or subquery]
```

Ideally, in order to use this kind of subquery, you must be familiar enough with your data and with the nature of the problem to know that the subquery will return exactly one value. When you expect more than one value, use IN or a modified comparison operator.

For example, if you suppose each publisher to be located in only one city, and you wish to find the names of authors who live in the city where Algodata Infosystems is located, you can write a SQL statement with a subquery introduced with the simple comparison operator "=":

```
SQL:
select au_lname, au_fname
from authors
where city =
   (select city
    from publishers
    where pub_name = 'Algodata Infosystems')
```

```
Results:
au_lname         au_fname
--------------   --------------
Carson           Cheryl
Bennet           Abraham

(2 rows affected)
```

Aggregate Functions Guarantee a Single Value

Comparison operator subqueries often include aggregate functions because these functions are guaranteed to return a single value. For example, to find the names of all books with prices that are higher than the current minimum price:

```
SQL:
select title
from titles
where price >
    (select min(price)
     from titles)
```

```
Results:
title
-----------------------------------------------------------------
The Busy Executive's Database Guide
Cooking with Computers: Surreptitious Balance Sheets
Straight Talk About Computers
Silicon Valley Gastronomic Treats
But Is It User Friendly?
Secrets of Silicon Valley
Computer Phobic and Non-Phobic Individuals: Behavior Variations
Is Anger the Enemy?
Life Without Fear
Prolonged Data Deprivation: Four Case Studies
Emotional Security: A New Algorithm
Onions, Leeks, and Garlic: Cooking Secrets of the Mediterranean
Fifty Years in Buckingham Palace Kitchens
Sushi, Anyone?

(14 rows affected)
```

First the inner query finds the minimum price in the *titles* table, then the outer query uses this value to select qualifying titles.

GROUP BY and HAVING Must Return a Single Value

Comparison operator subqueries cannot include GROUP BY and HAVING clauses unless you know that they return a single value. For example, this query finds the books priced higher than the lowest-priced book in the *trad_cook* category:

```
SQL:
select title, type
from titles
where price >
    (select min(price)
     from titles
     group by type
     having type = 'trad_cook')
```

```
Results:
title                                            type
-----------------------------------------------  ------------
The Busy Executive's Database Guide              business
Straight Talk About Computers                    business
Silicon Valley Gastronomic Treats                mod_cook
But Is It User Friendly?                          popular_comp
Secrets of Silicon Valley                         popular_comp
Computer Phobic and Non-Phobic Individuals:
   Behavior Variations                            psychology
Prolonged Data Deprivation: Four Case Studies    psychology
Onions, Leeks, and Garlic: Cooking Secrets of the
   Mediterranean                                  trad_cook
Sushi, Anyone?                                    trad_cook

(9 rows affected)
```

Correlated Subqueries with Comparison Operators

To find sales where the quantity ordered is less than the average order for sales of that title, the query is this:

```
SQL:
select s1.sonum, s1.title_id, s1.qty_ordered
from salesdetails s1
where qty_ordered <
  (select avg(qty_ordered)
   from salesdetails s2
   where s1.title_id = s2.title_id)
order by title_id
```

Results:

sonum	title_id	qty_ordered
8	BU1032	5
5	MC3021	15
2	PS2091	10
3	PS2091	20
7	PS2091	3

(5 rows affected)

The outer query selects the rows of the *salesdetails* table (that is, of *s1*) one by one. The subquery calculates the average quantity for each order being considered for selection in the outer query. For each possible value of *s1*, the system evaluates the subquery and includes the row in the results if the quantity is less than the calculated average for that table.

In this query and in the next one, a correlated subquery mimics a GROUP BY statement. It is not necessary to group by type explicitly, because the self-join in the WHERE clause of the subquery effectively evaluates average prices by type. To find titles whose price is greater than the average for books of its type, the query is this:

```
SQL:
select t1.type, t1.title
from titles t1
where t1.price >
  (select avg(t2.price)
   from titles t2
   where t1.type = t2.type)
```

Results:

```
type                   title
-----------------      -------------------------------------
business               The Busy Executive's Database Guide
business               Straight Talk About Computers
mod_cook               Silicon Valley Gastronomic Treats
popular_comp           But Is It User Friendly?
psychology             Computer Phobic and Non-Phobic Individuals:
                         Behavior Variations
psychology             Prolonged Data Deprivation: Four Case
                         Studies
trad_cook              Onions, Leeks, and Garlic: Cooking Secrets
                         of the Mediterranean

(7 rows affected)
```

For each possible value of *t1*, the system evaluates the subquery and includes the row in the results if the price value in that row is greater than the calculated average.

SUBQUERIES TESTING EXISTENCE

When a subquery is introduced with the keyword EXISTS, the subquery functions as an "existence test." The EXISTS keyword in a WHERE clause tests for the existence or nonexistence of data that meets the criteria of the subquery.

A subquery introduced with EXISTS takes this general form:

```
Start of SELECT, INSERT, UPDATE, DELETE statement; or subquery
WHERE [NOT] EXISTS (subquery)
[End of SELECT, INSERT, UPDATE, DELETE statement; or subquery]
```

To find the names of all the publishers who publish business books, the query is this:

SQL:
```
select distinct pub_name
from publishers
```

```
where exists
   (select *
    from titles
    where pub_id = publishers.pub_id
    and type = 'business')
```

Results:

```
pub_name
----------------------------------------

New Age Books
Algodata Infosystems


(2 rows affected)
```

EXISTS tests for the presence or absence of "the empty set" of rows. If the subquery returns at least one row, the subquery evaluates to "true." This means that an EXISTS phrase will succeed and a NOT EXISTS phrase will fail. If the subquery returns the empty set (no rows), the subquery evaluates to "false." This means that a NOT EXISTS phrase will succeed and an EXISTS phrase will fail.

In this case, the first publisher's name is Algodata Infosystems, with an identification number of 1389. Does Algodata Infosystems pass the existence test? That is, are there any rows in the *titles* table in which *pub_id* is 1389 and *type* is business? If so, "Algodata Infosystems" should be one of the values selected. The same process is repeated for each of the other publishers' names.

Notice that the syntax of subqueries introduced with EXISTS differs a bit from the syntax of other subqueries, in these ways:

- The keyword EXISTS is not preceded by a column name, constant, or other expression.
- The select list of a subquery introduced by EXISTS almost always consists of an asterisk (*). There is no real point in listing column names, since you are simply testing for the existence of rows that meet the subquery's conditions, and these are spelled out in the subquery WHERE clause, not in the subquery SELECT clause.

The EXISTS keyword is very important, because there is often no alternative, nonsubquery formulation. In practice, an EXISTS subquery is almost always a correlated subquery. Instead of having the outer query operate on

```
SQL:                              SQL:
select title                      select title
from titles                       from titles
where pub_id in                   where exists
   (select pub_id                    (select *
    from publishers                   from publishers
    where city like 'B%')             where pub_id = titles.pub_id
                                      and city like 'B%')
```

Figure 8–5. Comparing Subqueries with IN and EXISTS

values that the inner query supplies, the outer query presents values, one by one, that the inner query tests.

You can use EXISTS to express all "list" subqueries that would use IN, ANY, or ALL. Some examples of statements using EXISTS and their equivalent alternatives follow.

Figure 8-5 shows two queries that find titles of books published by any publisher located in a city that begins with the letter *B*:

Both queries produce the same results. The results show that twelve of the books in the *titles* table are published by a publisher located in either Boston or Berkeley.

```
Results:

title
----------------------------------------------------
You Can Combat Computer Stress!
Computer Phobic and Non-Phobic Individuals: Behavior Variations
Is Anger the Enemy?
Life Without Fear
Prolonged Data Deprivation: Four Case Studies
Emotional Security: A New Algorithm
The Busy Executive's Database Guide
Cooking with Computers: Surreptitious Balance Sheets
Straight Talk About Computers
But Is It User Friendly?
Secrets of Silicon Valley
Net Etiquette

(12 rows affected)
```

NOT EXISTS Seeks the Empty Set

NOT EXISTS is the inverse of EXISTS. NOT EXISTS queries succeed when the subquery returns no rows.

For example, to find the names of publishers who do not publish business books, the query is this:

```
SQL:
select pub_name
from publishers
where not exists
    (select *
     from titles
     where pub_id = publishers.pub_id
     and type = 'business')
```

```
Results:
pub_name
---------------------------------------
Binnet & Hardley

(1 row affected)
```

This query finds the titles for which there have been no sales:

```
SQL:
select title
from titles
where not exists
    (select title_id
     from salesdetails
     where title_id = titles.title_id)
```

```
Results:
title
-----------------------------------------------------------
The Psychology of Computer Cooking
Net Etiquette

(2 rows affected)
```

Using EXISTS to Find Intersection and Difference

Subqueries introduced with EXISTS and NOT EXISTS can be used for two set theory operations: **intersection** and **difference**. The intersection of two sets contains all elements that belong to both of the two original sets. The difference contains the elements that belong only to the first of the two sets.

The intersection of *authors* and *publishers* over the *city* column is the set of cities in which both an author and a publisher are located:

```
SQL:
select distinct city
from authors
where exists
  (select *
   from publishers
   where authors.city = publishers.city)

Results:
city
-------------------
Berkeley

(1 row affected)
```

The difference between *authors* and *publishers* over the *city* column is the set of cities where an author lives but no publisher is located (that is, all the cities except Berkeley):

```
SQL:
select distinct city
from authors
where not exists
  (select *
   from publishers
   where authors.city = publishers.city)
```

Results:

```
city
-------------------
Gary
Covelo
Oakland
Lawrence
San Jose
Ann Arbor
Corvallis
Nashville
Palo Alto
Rockville
Vacaville
Menlo Park
Walnut Creek
San Francisco
Salt Lake City

(15 rows affected)
```

SUBQUERIES IN MULTIPLE LEVELS OF NESTING

A subquery may itself include one or more subqueries. You can nest any number of subqueries.

An example of a problem that can be solved using a statement with multiple levels of nested queries is "Find the names of authors who have participated in writing at least one popular computing book."

SQL:

```
select au_lname, au_fname
from authors
where au_id in
  (select au_id
   from titleauthors
   where title_id in
      (select title_id
       from titles
       where type = 'popular_comp') )
```

```
Results:
au_lname                au_fname
---------------------   ------------
Carson                  Cheryl
Dull                    Ann
Hunter                  Sheryl
Locksley                Chastity

(4 rows affected)
```

The innermost query returns the title ID numbers PC1035, PC8888, and PC9999. The query at the next level up is evaluated with these title IDs and returns the author ID numbers. Finally, the outer query uses the author IDs to find the names of the authors.

You can also express this query as a join:

```
SQL:
select au_lname, au_fname
from authors, titles, titleauthors
where authors.au_id = titleauthors.au_id
  and titles.title_id = titleauthors.title_id
  and type = 'popular_comp'
```

SUBQUERIES IN UPDATE, DELETE, AND INSERT STATEMENTS

Subqueries can nest in UPDATE, DELETE, and INSERT statements as well as in SELECT statements.

The following query doubles the price of all books published by New Age Books. The statement updates the *titles* table; its subquery references the *publishers* table.

```
SQL:
update titles
set price = price * 2
where pub_id in
  (select pub_id
   from publishers
   where pub_name = 'New Age Books')
```

An equivalent UPDATE statement using a join (for systems that allow a FROM clause in UPDATE) is this:

```
SQL:

update titles
set price = price * 2
from titles, publishers
where titles.pub_id = publishers.pub_id
  and pub_name = 'New Age Books'
```

You can remove all records of sales orders for business books with this nested SELECT statement:

```
SQL:

delete salesdetails
where title_id in
  (select title_id
   from titles
   where type = 'business')
```

An equivalent DELETE statement using a join (for systems that allow a FROM clause listing multiple tables in DELETE) is this:

```
SQL:

delete salesdetails
from salesdetails, titles
where salesdetails.title_id = titles.title_id
  and type = 'business'
```

ON TO VIEWS

Now that you can write plain and fancy queries using functions, joins, and subqueries, you have most of the power of the SQL language at your command. The remaining issues are how to customize your view of your data and how to preserve database integrity and security.

Views, covered in the next chapter, are a means of naming a specific selection of data from one or more tables so that it can be treated as a virtual table. Views can also be used as a security mechanism (discussed in Chapter 10).

Chapter 9

Creating and Using Views

WITH A VIEW TOWARD FLEXIBILITY

Like the join operation, the view is a hallmark of the relational model. A view creates a virtual table from a SELECT statement, and opens up a world of flexibility for data analysis and manipulation. You can think of a view as a movable frame or window, through which you can see data. This metaphor explains why people speak of looking at data or of changing data "through" a view.

Previous chapters have demonstrated how to use a SELECT statement to choose rows, combine tables, rename columns, and make calculations until you've derived specific information in a specific form. Creating a view based on a SELECT statement gives you an easy way to examine and handle just the data you (or others) need—no more, no less. In effect, a view "freezes" a SELECT statement.

Views are not separate copies of the data in the table(s) or view(s) from which they're derived. In fact, views are called virtual tables because they do not exist as independent entities in the database, as do "real" tables. (The ANSI term for a view is a **viewed table**; a native database table is a **base table**.) You can query views much as you query tables. Modifying data through views is limited, however.

The data dictionary stores the *definition* of the view—the view's SELECT statement. When a view is called by a user, the database system associates the appropriate data with it. A view presents the end result of this process, hiding all its technical underpinnings. Its beauty lies in its transparency: naive users aren't frightened by joins, crafty users aren't tempted to look at (or try to alter) data that is none of their business, and impatient users aren't slowed down by the need to type long SQL statements.

CREATING VIEWS

Here's the simplified syntax of a view definition statement:

```
CREATE VIEW view_name [(column_name [, column_name]...)]
AS
SELECT_statement
```

This example creates a view that displays the names of authors who live in Oakland, California, and their books:

```
SQL:
create view oaklanders
as
select au_fname, au_lname, title
from authors, titles, titleauthors
where authors.au_id = titleauthors.au_id
  and titles.title_id = titleauthors.title_id
  and city = 'Oakland'
```

```
SQL:
select *
from oaklanders
```

```
Results:
au_fname      au_lname      title
-----------   -----------   ------------------------------------

Marjorie      Green         The Busy Executive's Database Guide
Marjorie      Green         You Can Combat Computer Stress!
Dick          Straight      Straight Talk About Computers
Stearns       MacFeather    Cooking with Computers: Surreptitious
                               Balance Sheets
Stearns       MacFeather    Computer Phobic and Non-Phobic
                               Individuals: Behavior Variations
Livia         Karsen        Computer Phobic and Non-Phobic
                               Individuals: Behavior Variations

(6 rows affected)
```

When you name a view, be sure to follow your system's rules for identifiers. The first line of the CREATE VIEW statement names the view; the SELECT statement that follows defines it. As you've already seen, the SELECT statement need not be a simple selection of the rows and columns of one particular table. You can create a view using more than one table, other views, or both, with a SELECT statement of almost any complexity, using projection and selection to define the columns and rows you want to include.

Dropping Views

Most versions of SQL have a command for removing views with syntax something like this:

```
DROP VIEW view_name
```

If a view depends on a table (or on another view) that has been dropped, you won't be able to use the view. However, if you create a new table (or view) with the same name to replace the dropped one, you may be able to use the view again so long as the columns referenced in the view definition still exist. Check your system's reference manuals for details.

ADVANTAGES OF VIEWS

To clarify the advantages of using views, consider several different types of users of the *bookbiz* database. Let's say that the promotion manager needs to know which authors are connected to which books, and who has first, second, and third billing on the cover. Prices, sales, advances, royalties, and personal addresses are not of interest, but the promotion manager does need some information from each of the three tables: *titles*, *authors*, and *title-authors*. Without a view, a query something like this might be used:

```
SQL:
select titles.title_id, au_ord, au_lname, au_fname
from authors, titles, titleauthors
where authors.au_id = titleauthors.au_id and
      titles.title_id = titleauthors.title_id
```

This query involves a lot of typing, and there are any number of places where an error might slip in. Quite a bit of knowledge of the database is required, too. Creating a view called *books* that is based on this SELECT statement would facilitate the use of this particular set of data. Here's the statement that creates the view:

```
SQL:
create view books
as
select titles.title_id, au_ord, au_lname, au_fname
from authors, titles, titleauthors
where authors.au_id = titleauthors.au_id and
      titles.title_id = titleauthors.title_id
```

Now the promotion manager can use the view to get the same results, without thinking about joins or select lists or search conditions:

```
SQL:
select *
from books

Results:
title_id  au_ord au_lname     au_fname
--------- ------ ------------ --------------------
BU1032        1  Bennet       Abraham
BU1032        2  Green        Marjorie
BU1111        1  MacFeather   Stearns
BU1111        2  O'Leary      Michael
  .
  .
  .
TC7777        1  Yokomoto     Akiko
TC7777        2  O'Leary      Michael
TC7777        3  Gringlesby   Burt

(25 rows affected)
```

A view can be used in a SELECT statement just as if it were a table. For example, the promotion manager might want to order the results of the view alphabetically by author's last name, like this:

```
SQL:

select *
from books
order by au_lname
```

An accountant might want to create a different view. He or she doesn't care who the first or second author is. Let's assume that all the accountant needs to know is the bottom line: to whom should checks be written, and for how much. The query involves computing how many books were sold at what price, with what percentage rate for each author:

```
SQL:

select au_lname, au_fname,
  sum(price*ytd_sales*royalty*royaltyshare) as Total_Income
from authors, titles, titleauthors, roysched
where authors.au_id = titleauthors.au_id
  and titles.title_id = titleauthors.title_id
  and titles.title_id = roysched.title_id
  and ytd_sales between lorange and hirange
group by au_lname, au_fname
```

If the accountant uses this SELECT statement to create a view named *royaltychecks*, the equivalent query is this:

```
SQL:

select *
from royaltychecks
```

The results (who gets a check and for how much) are as follows:

```
Results:
```

au_lname	au_fname	Total_Income
Bennet	Abraham	4,911.54
Blotchet-Halls	Reginald	25,255.61

Carson	Cheryl	32,240.16
DeFrance	Michel	9,977.33
Dull	Ann	4,095.00
Green	Marjorie	13,350.54
Gringlesby	Burt	1,841.52
Hunter	Sheryl	4,095.00
Karsen	Livia	607.22
Locksley	Chastity	2,665.46
MacFeather	Stearns	2,981.50
O'Leary	Michael	3,694.25
Panteley	Sylvia	785.63
Ringer	Albert	1,421.27
Ringer	Anne	4,669.34
Straight	Dick	8,185.91
White	Johnson	8,139.93
Yokomoto	Akiko	2,455.36
del Castillo	Innes	4,874.36

```
(19 rows affected)
```

Finally, consider an executive at the parent publishing company who needs to find out how the different categories of books are doing at each subsidiary. A query something like this can be used:

```
SQL:
select pub_id, type, sum(price*ytd_sales),
   avg(price), avg(ytd_sales)
from titles
group by pub_id, type
```

However, the executive may not want to bother with anything so complex. A much simpler statement could be used:

```
SQL:
select *
from currentinfo
```

```
Results:
PUB# TYPE          INCOME      AVG_PRICE AVG_SALES
---- ------------  ----------  --------- ---------
0736 business       55,978.78      2.99      18722
0736 psychology    139,319.92     13.50       1987
0877 NULL                NULL      NULL       NULL
0877 mod_cook      107,135.22     11.49      12139
0877 trad_cook     249,637.50     15.96       6522
1389 business      210,036.30     17.31       4022
1389 popular_comp  283,401.00     21.48       6437

(7 rows affected)
```

Using this view, the busy executive can quickly see which publishing lines are making money, and compare the relationship among income, average price, and average sales.

Why View?

As the previous examples demonstrate, you can use views to focus, simplify, and customize each user's perception of the database. In addition, views provide a security mechanism. Finally, they can protect users from the effects of changes in the database structure.

Focus, Simplification, and Customization. Views allow the promotion manager, the accountant, and the executive in the previous examples to focus in on the particular data and tasks. No extraneous or distracting information gets in the way.

Working with the data is simpler, too. When favorite joins, projections, and/or selections are already defined as views, it's relatively simple to add other clauses. Constructing the entire underlying query, on the other hand, could be a daunting prospect.

Views are a good way of customizing a database, or tailoring it to suit a variety of users with dissimilar interests and skill levels. Our three users see the data in different ways, even when they're looking at the same three tables at the same time.

Security. Views provide security by hiding sensitive or irrelevant parts of the database. If permissions are set up properly, the accountant can find out

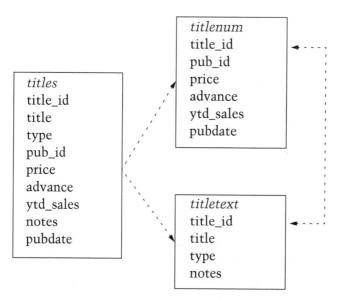

Figure 9–1. Splitting a Table into Two Tables

how big an author's check should be, but can't look at the underlying figures or compare his or her own paycheck to a coworker's. You can restrict the accountant's access in the database to just those views that are relevant to accounting. Using views as a security mechanism is discussed in more detail in Chapter 10.

Independence. Finally, there's the issue of independence. From time to time, you may have to modify the structure of the database. But there's no reason that users should suffer from these changes. For example, say you split the *titles* table into two new tables and drop *titles*. The new tables are shown in Figure 9-1.

Notice that the old *titles* table can be regenerated by joining the *title_id* columns of the two new tables. To shield the changed structure of the database from users, you can create a view that is the join of the two new tables (Figure 9-2). You can even name it *titles* (though here it's called *titlesview*)— and in most systems, doing so means you won't have to change any views that were based wholly or in part on the old *titles*.

Restrictions on updating data through views (explained later in this chapter) limit the independence of this kind of view. Certain data modification statements on the new *titles* may not be allowed.

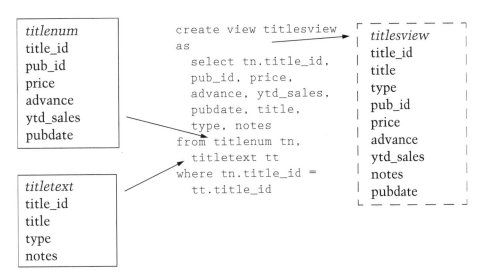

Figure 9-2. Uniting Two Base Tables in a Single View

HOW VIEWS WORK

What actually happens in the database when you create a view, and what happens when you use it?

Creating a view means defining it in terms of its base tables. The definition of the view is stored in the data dictionary, without any data stored in association with it. When you access data through the view, you are accessing the data that is stored in association with the underlying tables. In other words, creating a view does not generate a copy of the data, neither at the time the view is defined nor at the time the view is accessed.

When you query a view, it looks exactly like any other database table. You can display it much as you can any other table, with few restrictions.

Changing data through a view has some limitations (explained later in this chapter). For now, consider the simplest case: a view based on a single table. When you modify the data you see through a view, you are actually changing the data in the underlying base table. Conversely, when you change the data in the base tables, these changes are automatically reflected in the views derived from them.

Suppose you are interested only in books priced higher than $15 and for which an advance of more than $5,000 was paid. This straightforward SELECT statement would find the rows that qualify:

```
SQL:
select *
from titles
where price > $15
  and advance > $5000
```

Now suppose you have a slew of retrieval and update operations to do on this collection of data. You could, of course, combine the conditions shown in the previous query with any command that you issue. However, for convenience, you can create a view in which just the records of interest are visible:

```
SQL:
create view hiprice
as
select *
from titles
where price > $15
  and advance > $5000
```

When SQL receives this command, it does not actually execute the SELECT statement that follows the keyword AS. Instead, it stores the SELECT statement (which is in fact the definition of the view *hiprice*) in the data dictionary.

Now, when you display or operate on *hiprice*, SQL combines your statement with the stored definition of *hiprice*. For example, you can change all the prices in *hiprice* just as you can change any other table:

```
SQL:
update hiprice
set price = price*2
```

SQL actually finds the view definition in the data dictionary and converts this update command into this statement:

```
SQL:
update titles
set price = price*2
where price > $15
  and advance > $5000
```

In other words, SQL knows from the view definition that the data to be updated is in *titles*. It also knows that it should increase the prices only in those rows that meet the conditions on the *price* and *advance* columns given in the view definition.

Having issued the first update statement—the update to *hiprice*—you can see its effect either through the view or in the *titles* table. Conversely, if you had created the view and then issued the second update statement, which operates directly on the base table, the changed prices would also be visible through the view.

If you update a view's underlying table in such a way that more rows qualify for the view, they become visible through the view. For example, say you increase the price of the book *You Can Combat Computer Stress* to $25.95. Since this book now meets the qualifying conditions in the view definition statement, it becomes part of the view.

Rules for Naming View Columns

Assigning alias names to a view's columns is optional. If you don't give names in the CREATE VIEW clause, the view's columns inherit their names from the columns in the underlying table(s). If you do want to choose new names, put them inside parentheses following the view name, separated by commas. (In some systems, you can also rename columns in the select list as usual.)

There are a couple of circumstances in which new names for the view's columns are required. (If you rename any column you must list all of them.)

- One or more of the view's columns is derived from an arithmetic expression, a built-in function, or a constant
- The view would wind up with more than one column of the same name (usually because the view definition's SELECT statement includes a join, and the columns from the joined tables have the same name)

The first circumstance can be illustrated with the CREATE VIEW statement for the view called *currentinfo* used by the executive we discussed earlier in this chapter:

```
SQL:
create view currentinfo (PUB#, TYPE, INCOME,
  AVG_PRICE, AVG_SALES)
as
select pub_id, type, sum(price*ytd_sales),
  avg(price), avg(ytd_sales)
from titles
group by pub_id, type
```

The computed columns in the select list don't really have names, so you must give them new names in the CREATE VIEW clause. Otherwise, you'd have no way to refer to them. When you work with the view *currentinfo*, always use the new names, like this:

```
SQL:
select PUB#, AVG_SALES
from currentinfo
```

Using the old names, such as *pub_id* or *avg(ytd_sales)*, won't work.

The second circumstance in which assigning new column names is required usually arises when there's a join in the SELECT statement and the joining columns have the same name. Even though they are qualified with different table names in the SELECT statement, you have to rename them in order to resolve the ambiguity:

```
SQL:
create view cities (Author, Authorcity, Pub, Pubcity)
as
select au_lname, authors.city, pub_name, publishers.city
from authors, publishers
where authors.city = publishers.city
```

Of course, you are free to rename columns in a view definition statement whenever it's helpful to do so. Just remember that when you rename any column in a view, you have to list all of them: the number of column names inside the parentheses has to match the number of items in the select list.

Whether or not you rename a view column, its datatype and null status depend on how it was defined in its base table(s).

Creating Views with Joins and Subqueries

The examples shown so far include views defined with computed columns, aggregates, and joins. Views defined with joins and views defined with subqueries are also possible. Check your reference manuals for restrictions. Here's an example of a view definition that includes three joins and a subquery. It finds the author ID, title ID, publisher, and price of each book with a price that's higher than the average of all the books' prices. (Including the author ID means that you'll see more than one row for books with multiple authors.)

```
SQL:
create view highaverage
as
select authors.au_id, titles.title_id, pub_name, price
from authors, titleauthors, titles, publishers
where authors.au_id = titleauthors.au_id and
      titles.title_id = titleauthors.title_id and
      titles.pub_id = publishers.pub_id and
      price >
          (select avg(price)
           from titles)
```

Now that the view has been created, you can use it to display the results:

```
SQL:
select *
from highaverage
```

```
Results :
au_id       title_id pub_name                 price
----------- -------- ------------------------ ------------
213-46-8915 BU1032   Algodata Infosystems     19.99
409-56-7008 BU1032   Algodata Infosystems     19.99
274-80-9391 BU7832   Algodata Infosystems     19.99
712-45-1867 MC2222   Binnet & Hardley         19.99
238-95-7766 PC1035   Algodata Infosystems     22.95
427-17-2319 PC8888   Algodata Infosystems     20.00
846-92-7186 PC8888   Algodata Infosystems     20.00
724-80-9391 PS1372   New Age Books            21.59
```

```
756-30-7391 PS1372   New Age Books           21.59
172-32-1176 PS3333   New Age Books           19.99
807-91-6654 TC3218   Binnet & Hardley        20.95
267-41-2394 TC7777   Binnet & Hardley        14.99
472-27-2349 TC7777   Binnet & Hardley        14.99
672-71-3249 TC7777   Binnet & Hardley        14.99

(14 rows affected)
```

Let's use *highaverage* to illustrate one more variety of view: a view derived from another view. Here's how to create a view that displays all the higher-than-average-priced books published by Binnet & Hardley:

```
SQL:
create view highBandH
as select *
from highaverage
where pub_name = 'Binnet & Hardley'

select *
from highBandH

Results:
au_id         title_id  pub_name                  price
----------    --------  ----------------------    ------------
712-45-1867 MC2222   Binnet & Hardley        19.99
807-91-6654 TC3218   Binnet & Hardley        20.95
267-41-2394 TC7777   Binnet & Hardley        14.99
472-27-2349 TC7777   Binnet & Hardley        14.99
672-71-3249 TC7777   Binnet & Hardley        14.99

(5 rows affected)
```

Restrictions on Creating Views

In spite of the many kinds of views that can be created, there are always limits, varying from SQL to SQL. Basically, restrictions have two sources:

- Elements not allowed in CREATE VIEW statements (ORDER BY and sometimes clauses with UNION, SELECT INTO, or COMPUTE). Check your system manuals for specifics.
- Elements permitted in CREATE VIEW statements (computed columns, aggregates), which can limit the data modification permitted through the view because of the problem of interpreting data modification statements. The view-updating problem is explained and illustrated later in this chapter. If you want users to be able to perform most functions through a view, you may decide to modify a perfectly legal CREATE VIEW statement to avoid these limitations.

The Check Option

One of the problems with updating a view is that it is possible to change its values in such a way as to make them ineligible for the view. For example, consider a view that displays all books with prices less than $5.00. What happens if you update one of those book prices through the view, changing its price to $5.99? The optional WITH CHECK OPTION clause, which appears after the SELECT statement in the CREATE VIEW syntax, is designed to prevent such a problem:

```
CREATE VIEW view_name [(column_name [, column_name]...)]
AS
SELECT_statement
[WITH CHECK OPTION]
```

The WITH CHECK OPTION clause tells SQL to reject any attempt to modify a view in a way that makes one or more of its rows ineligible for the view. In other words, if a data modification statement (UPDATE, INSERT, or DELETE) causes some rows to disappear from the view, the statement is considered illegal.

As an example, recall the view *hiprice*, which includes all titles whose price is greater than $15 and whose advance is greater than $5,000:

```
SQL:
create view hiprice
as
select title, price, advance
from titles
```

```
where price > $15
and advance > $5000

select *
from hiprice
```

Results:

title	price	advance
But Is It User Friendly?	22.95	7,000.00
Secrets of Silicon Valley	20.00	8,000.00
Computer Phobic and Non-Phobic Individuals: Behavior Variations	21.59	7,000.00
Onions, Leeks, and Garlic: Cooking Secrets of the Mediterranean	20.95	7,000.00

```
(4 rows affected)
```

This statement updates one of the books visible through *hiprice,* changing its price to $14.99.

SQL:
```
update hiprice
set price = $14.99
where title = 'Secrets of Silicon Valley'
```

If WITH CHECK OPTION had been part of the definition of *hiprice,* the UPDATE statement would be rejected because the new price of *Secrets of Silicon Valley* would make it ineligible for the view. Since the definition of *hiprice* does not include the WITH CHECK OPTION clause, the UPDATE statement is accepted. But the next time you look at the data through *hiprice,* you'll no longer see *Secrets of Silicon Valley.*

The check option can be included only if the view being defined is otherwise updatable. In effect, WITH CHECK OPTION allows you to specify rules for modifying data through views. If the conditions specified in the view definition are violated by a data modification statement, the statement is considered illegal. Check your system manuals for specific details.

View Resolution

The process of combining a query on a view with its stored definition and translating it into a query on the view's underlying tables is called view resolution. Several problems can arise during this process.

If any of the tables, views, or columns that underlie a view has been dropped or renamed, or if any datatype incompatibilities have been introduced by restructuring, the system won't be able to resolve the view and you won't be able to use it. Instead, SQL generates an error message.

If you add columns to a view's underlying table, the new columns may not appear in a view defined with a SELECT * clause unless you delete and redefine the view. This is because many dialects of SQL interpret and expand the asterisk shorthand at the time they create the view. In Transact-SQL, for example, the expansion of the asterisk shorthand is the only kind of interpretation that is done when a view is created, rather than when it's queried or modified. Check your system's reference manuals for details on how your implementation works.

Redefining Views

Since views can be defined in terms of other views, it's possible to wind up with a chain of views, each dependent on another. Just as an actual chain can break at any link, so can a chain of views. Any one of the views in the chain might be redefined in such a way that its dependent views no longer make sense.

As an example, three generations of views derived on the *authors* table are shown here.

```
SQL:
create view number1
as select au_lname, phone
from authors
where zip like '94%'

SQL:
select * from number1
```

Results:

au_lname	phone
White	408 496-7223
Green	415 986-7020
Carson	415 548-7723
Straight	415 834-2919
Bennet	415 658-9932
Dull	415 836-7128
Locksley	415 585-4620
Yokomoto	415 935-4228
Stringer	415 843-2991
MacFeather	415 354-7128
Karsen	415 534-9219
Hunter	415 836-7128

(12 rows affected)

SQL:

```
create view number2
as select au_lname, phone
from number1
where au_lname like '[M-Z]%'
```

SQL:

```
select * from number2
```

Results:

au_lname	phone
White	408 496-7223
Straight	415 834-2919
Yokomoto	415 935-4228
Stringer	415 843-2991
MacFeather	415 354-7128

(5 rows affected)

```
SQL:
create view number3
as select au_lname, phone
from number2
where au_lname = 'MacFeather'

SQL:
select * from number3

Results:
au_lname                                           phone
----------------------------------------------     ------------
MacFeather                                         415 354-7128

(1 row affected)
```

What would happen if you redefined view *number2* with different selection criteria, such as a zip code matching "947*nn*"? Would view *number3*, which depends on view *number2*, still be accessible? The answer is that it depends on the implementation. In some systems, view *number3* would be fine, though the data seen through it would be different. When you used a query that referenced either *number2* or *number3*, view resolution would take place as usual.

Of course, it would be possible to redefine view *number2* in such a way that view *number3* becomes impossible to use. For example, if the new version of *number2* included only the *au_lname* column (eliminating *phone*), view *number3* could no longer be used in a query, since it cannot derive the *phone* column from the object on which it depends. However, view *number3* would still exist, and in some systems would become usable again by dropping and re-creating view *number2*, adding the *phone* column back to it.

In short, some systems allow you to change the definition of an intermediate view without affecting dependent views as long as the *target list* of the dependent views remains valid. If you violate this rule, a query that references the invalid view produces an error message.

DATA MODIFICATION THROUGH VIEWS

Changing data through views is a thorny issue. The general problem, as we'll demonstrate here, is that commands to change data in a view sometimes can't be understood by SQL in an unambiguous way. Such updates are disallowed by every version of SQL. In other words, some views are inherently and logically not updatable.

There are other views that are logically updatable but that many versions of SQL rule non-updatable. Disallowing a wide range of data modification statements makes for more severe restrictions but simpler rules about what you can and cannot do. Other SQL implementations go to great lengths to let you make as many kinds of changes as possible, in spite of the complications inevitably introduced into rules about data modification.

The kinds of data modification statements that are allowed vary a great deal from SQL to SQL. So treat the rules we give here as guidelines, and check your system's reference manuals for details.

The Rules according to ANSI

The ANSI standard declares that views are read-only (not modifiable) if the CREATE VIEW statement contains any of the following:

- DISTINCT in the select list
- Expressions (computed columns, aggregates, functions, and so on) in the select list
- References to more than one table, either in the FROM clause or in a subquery or in a UNION clause
- References to a view that is itself not updatable, either in the FROM clause or in a subquery
- A GROUP BY or HAVING clause

Some dialects of SQL are less restrictive than the ANSI standard; others may be more restrictive. You can consult your reference manual, or you can experiment. When you try to modify data through a view, SQL checks to make sure that no restrictions are violated. If it detects a violation, it rejects the data modification statement and informs you of an error.

The best way to understand the rationale for these restrictions is to look at some examples of non-updatable views. Let's start with the restriction that prohibits updating views with columns derived from computed columns.

The *gross_sales* column in the view *accounts* is computed from the *price* and *ytd_sales* columns of the *titles* table:

```
SQL:

create view accounts (title, advance, gross_sales)
as
select title_id, advance, price*ytd_sales
from titles
where price > $15
  and advance > $5000
```

The rows visible through *accounts* are these:

```
SQL:

select *
from accounts

Results:

title   advance                    gross_sales
------  -------------------------  -------------------------
PC1035               7,000.00                    201,501.00
PC8888               8,000.00                     81,900.00
PS1372               7,000.00                      8,096.25
TC3218               7,000.00                      7,856.25

(4 rows affected)
```

Think about what it would mean to update the *gross_sales* column. How could the system deduce the underlying values for price or year-to-date sales from any value you might enter? There's no way for the system to know, and no way for you to tell it. Thus, updates on this view are declared illegal.

Now let's turn to a view with a column derived from an aggregate—that is, a view whose definition includes a GROUP BY clause. Such views (and any view derived from them) are called **grouped views**. A variety of restrictions may apply to grouped views, depending on the particular version of SQL you're using. Here's the view definition statement:

```
SQL:
create view categories (Category, Average_Price)
as select type, avg(price)
from titles
group by type
```

Here's what the view looks like:

```
SQL:
select *
from categories
```

```
Results:
Category          Average_Price
- - - - - - - - - - - - - - -   - - - - - - - - - - - - - -
UNDECIDED         NULL
business          13.73
mod_cook          11.49
popular_comp      21.48
psychology        13.50
trad_cook         15.96
```

```
(6 rows affected)
```

It would make no sense to insert rows into the view *categories*. To what group of underlying rows would an inserted row belong? Updates on the *Average_Price* column cannot be allowed either, because there is no way to know from any value you might enter there how the underlying prices should be changed. Theoretically, updates to the *Category* column and deletions could be allowed, but they are not supported by many versions of SQL.

Some SQL dialects place restrictions not only on updating grouped views, but also on querying through them. For example, the following query would be illegal in such SQLs:

```
SQL (possibly illegal):
select *
from categories
where Average_Price > $12.00
```

Such a query presents problems when it is translated or expanded: the SELECT statement that results is illegal because aggregates are not allowed in the WHERE clause. Here's what the (illegal) statement would look like:

```
SQL (illegal):
select type, avg(price)
from titles
where avg(price) > $12.00
group by type
```

Another restriction on view modifications disallows updates and insertions through a view if the statement would modify columns that are derived from more than one object. This is because updates and insertions on more than one object in a single statement are never allowed.

Some systems allow you to modify the view if you change columns from only one of the underlying tables. For example, if a view contains three columns from *titles* and two columns from *publishers*, these systems would allow an update operation on the view if it changed only the columns from *titles*. You couldn't write an UPDATE statement that changed one column from *titles* and one column from *publishers*.

CREATING COPIES OF DATA

We've stressed in this chapter that views are not copies of data, but rather are virtual tables with no physical data associated with them. If an independent copy of data is what you want, check to see what your system provides. Transact-SQL offers this facility through the INTO clause in a SELECT statement. It allows you to define a table and put data into it (based on existing definitions and data) without going through the usual data definition process. The new table (named in the INTO clause) is based on the columns you specify in the select list, the table(s) you name in the FROM clause, and the rows you choose in the WHERE clause. However, this use of the INTO clause is not widespread; the following examples work for Transact-SQL only.

As an example, imagine that you need a new table called *newbooks* that is made up of two of the columns in *titles* and a subset of its rows. Here's how you'd create it:

```
SQL:
select title_id, type
into newbooks
from titles
where price > $20
```

Here's what *newbooks* looks like:

```
SQL:
select *
from newbooks
```

```
Results:
title_id type
-------- ------------
PC1035   popular_comp
PS1372   psychology
TC3218   trad_cook

(3 rows affected)
```

The new table, with a real (physical) copy of the data from the parent table, becomes part of the database. The data in the parent table is not affected in any way.

The SELECT INTO statement is useful for creating test tables, new tables that resemble existing tables, and tables that have some or all of the columns in several other tables.

You can also use a SELECT INTO statement to create a skeleton table with no data by putting a false condition in the WHERE clause. For example:

```
SQL:
select *
into newpubs
from publishers
where 1 = 2
```

```
SQL:
select *
from newpubs
```

Results:

```
pub_id                  pub_name         address    city       state
----------------------- ---------------- ---------- ---------- -----
```

DATABASE ADMINISTRATION ISSUES

The next chapter is a roundup of some remaining database management issues: security, transactions, performance, and integrity.

Chapter 10

Security, Transactions, Performance, and Integrity

DATABASE MANAGEMENT IN THE REAL WORLD

This chapter is devoted to four issues that are of particular importance in production-oriented, on-line database applications.

The first of these issues, security, is handled in nearly every relational database management system by two mechanisms: the assignment of **permissions** (also called **privileges**) with the SQL GRANT and REVOKE commands, and the creation of views (through which users can be granted selective access to the database). Some systems also use procedures (sets of extended, often procedural, SQL statements that may accept parameters) as a method to control user actions. Different database management systems deal with the other three issues—transactions, performance, and integrity—in a wide variety of ways. For that reason, this chapter emphasizes concepts rather than syntax details in its discussion of them.

Security and one aspect of transaction management are primarily of concern in multiuser situations: granting permissions to other users is an issue only when there are other users. Transaction management allows the database system to run interference among simultaneous requests for the same data from different users (a capability known as **concurrency control**). Database management systems also rely on transaction management for **recovery** purposes—in case of software or media failure. Recovery is important for both single-user and multiuser systems.

The integrity of data is important whether you're in a single-user system or a shared one. Performance is particularly critical in large multiuser database environments, but it also can become a problem in single-user systems.

In the past, performance was considered a weak point of the relational model. Now some relational products perform as well as or better than systems based on other data models. These high-performance relational systems tend to provide tools, some of them SQL-based, for monitoring and improving the speed and efficiency of data retrieval and modification.

Relational systems have also been criticized for failing to provide adequate assurances of data integrity. Unlike most of the critics of performance, however, the commentators most vocally addressing the integrity issue are strong relational supporters. In fact (as you may recall from Chapter 1), Dr. E. F. Codd, the originator of the relational model, has included stringent integrity requirements in his twelve rules for relational database systems. But the ANSI SQL-92 standard includes language for defining some integrity constraints, and most vendors have enhanced their SQLs to meet other integrity needs.

DATA SECURITY

Security is an important issue in database management because information is a valuable commodity. Much of the data worth entrusting to a database management system needs to be protected from unauthorized use—that is, from being seen, changed, or removed by anyone not certified to do so.

If you're the sole user of a database, the security issue boils down to figuring out how to protect the database as a whole—a project not in the province of SQL. With a personal computer, for example, your main line of defense may be as low-tech as a lock and key.

On the other hand, even if you're the only authorized user of a database, the database management system may be running in a shared environment (on either a multiuser computer or one that's linked into a network). Most such computers provide security facilities at the operating system level. Typically, they require passwords for logging on to the computer in the first place; often they flag each file according to which users have permission to read, write, and execute it.

When you're sharing a database with other users, you turn to SQL and the database management system to meet your security needs with two mechanisms. The first is the control of privileges (also called permissions): the use of the SQL GRANT and REVOKE commands to specify which users are to be allowed to perform which commands on which tables, views, and columns. A second security mechanism is the use of views in conjunction with GRANT and REVOKE to provide selective access to subsets of the data.

Both mechanisms assume the database system has a way to know who you are—to recognize its users and verify their identities.

User Identification and Special Users

Database management systems vary widely in their approaches to identifying users, both in basic concept and in detail. Not much can be said that applies across the board; a broad outline of the major variations is about the best that can be done.

Some systems rely on the user's identity at the operating system level: in other words, they recognize as an authorized user anyone who can log on to the computer. That's not to say, however, that anyone who can access the database system will be able to do much of anything in it.

More sophisticated database management systems have their own identification and authorization mechanisms, which require each user to have an established name (sometimes called an account or login) and password on the system itself and/or in each database on the system (assuming the system supports the concept of multiple interacting databases). Application programs can supply additional layers of protection.

What happens once the database management system recognizes your on-line identity and verifies it by requesting and receiving your password? At that point, what you can do depends on the kind of user you are and the permissions you've explicitly been granted by other users.

Most multiuser database management systems recognize at least two kinds of specially privileged users: a super user, often known as the database administrator (DBA) or system administrator, and the owners of database objects. Some database systems recognize additional special users and establish a hierarchy in which privileges to execute various commands are assigned to users depending on their position in the hierarchy.

The existence of the database administrator is established at the time the system is installed. The identity of the DBA is not exactly the same as that of ordinary mortals; DBA is actually a special position that can be (temporarily) filled by any user who knows the correct account name and password. In many database installations, the role of DBA is shared by several people. Each of these users might log in as DBA in order to accomplish administrative tasks but use his or her own name for other functions in the database. Alternatively, the system may support a number of roles. This way, users can have individual database identities such as "Stacy" and "Tom" and also be assigned functional roles (DBA, operator, and the like). Under such a plan, users have the power they need to do specialized work, and role activities can be traced to specific individuals.

The DBA typically is blessed with many special privileges and burdened with many responsibilities for the maintenance and smooth operation of the database application. For the purposes of this discussion on security, the DBA (in most systems) automatically holds all permissions that the system recognizes, on all database objects and for all commands. Which of these permissions the DBA can pass along to other users varies from system to system.

The other special category of users that's important for security purposes is the owner of a table or view. In many systems, the user who creates a table or view is its owner. (Some systems support the additional concept of a database owner.) A table owner or view owner may automatically be entitled to do anything to the table or view, (usually) including the granting of permissions on it to other users.

Users other than the owners of a table or view (and the DBA) need explicit permission to perform any operation on it. These permissions are controlled with the SQL GRANT and REVOKE commands, which are supported by virtually every multiuser implementation of SQL.

Information about user identification and permissions may be stored in the data dictionary.

The GRANT and REVOKE Commands

The phrases "granting privileges" or "assigning permissions" are often associated with discussions of GRANT and REVOKE. In most implementations of SQL, you can't do anything for which you don't have explicit authorization—either by virtue of being an object owner or a database administrator, or by virtue of having been granted authorization with the GRANT command.

The GRANT and REVOKE commands specify which users can perform which operations on which tables, views, or columns. In some versions of SQL, permission must also be explicitly granted (usually by the database administrator) in order to execute commands such as CREATE TABLE and DROP INDEX.

The operations associated with GRANT and REVOKE include SELECT, UPDATE, INSERT, DELETE, and REFERENCES. The database objects to which permissions for these operations apply are tables and views. Authorization to grant these permissions originates with the object owner and is optionally transferable along with the permission itself. Here are two variants on the GRANT syntax, differing in the location of the column list.

```
GRANT {ALL | privilege_list}
ON {table_name [(column_list)] | view_name [(column_list)]}
TO {PUBLIC | user_list}
[WITH GRANT OPTION]

GRANT {ALL | privilege_list [(column_list)]}
ON {table_name | view_name}
TO {PUBLIC | user_list}
[WITH GRANT OPTION]
```

The REVOKE command is similar:

```
REVOKE {ALL | privilege_list}
ON {table_name [(column_list)] | view_name [(column_list)]}
FROM {PUBLIC | user_list}

REVOKE {ALL | privilege_list [(column_list)]}
ON {table_name | view_name}
FROM {PUBLIC | user_list}
```

As is often the case in SQL, the syntax looks much more complicated than the majority of statements you'll need to write. Before we explain it in detail, here's a simple example that grants permission to Mary to insert into and update the *titles* table:

```
SQL:
grant insert, update
on titles
to mary
```

Figure 10-1 shows the slight variation in statements from two SQL dialects that revoke Mary's permission to update the *advance* and *price* columns of the *titles* table. For more syntax variants, see Appendix B.

```
SQL:                                       SQL:
revoke update (advance, price)             revoke update
on titles                                  on titles (advance, price)
from mary                                  from mary
```

Figure 10-1. Comparing Two REVOKE Statements

Now let's take a closer look at the GRANT and REVOKE syntax. The first line includes the keyword GRANT or REVOKE and either the keyword ALL or a list of (one or more) privileges being granted or revoked. If you include more than one privilege in the privilege list, separate them with commas. If the keyword ALL is used, every one of the privileges applicable to the object (that is, every privilege held by the grantor or revoker) is granted or revoked.

The ON clause specifies the table or view for which the privilege is being granted or revoked—one table or one view per statement.

Different versions of SQL allow the inclusion of somewhat different sets of privileges. SELECT, UPDATE, DELETE, and INSERT are always in that set, and SQL-92 has added REFERENCES (the right to reference a table in the CREATE TABLE statement of another table for foreign keys). Less frequently included privileges are ALTER, INDEX, and EXECUTE. SQLs differ in whether permissions for some, all, or none of these operations can be controlled on the level of columns as well as tables and views. When permissions are being granted on columns, the column name or names are listed in parentheses.

Privileges can be granted for more than one column at a time, but all the columns must be in the same table, or in the same view. If you don't include a list of column names, the privilege is being granted or revoked for the entire table or view. (In some systems, the column list belongs in the first line.)

The next line in the syntax begins with the keyword TO (for the GRANT command) or FROM (for the REVOKE command). The keyword PUBLIC refers to all the users of the system.

The alternative to PUBLIC is a list of the names of the users to whom you want to grant the privileges, or from whom you want to revoke them. As always, each name in the list is separated from the next by a comma. Some SQL dialects support the concept of user groups, roles, or both; in these SQLs the name of a group or role may be included in the user list.

The optional WITH GRANT OPTION clause governs whether the grantee can in turn pass that privilege (with or without the grant option) on to other users. For example, here's a statement that grants Mary permission to SELECT from the *authors* table, and allows her to pass that privilege to other users:

```
SQL:
grant select
on authors
to mary
with grant option
```

Whenever you set up permissions on a table or view that you own, it's good practice to issue the GRANT and REVOKE commands according to a plan to which you've given some thought, rather than to GRANT and REVOKE haphazardly, on the spur of the moment.

Here are some examples that show how to use GRANT and REVOKE statements to set up permissions on a table. Suppose you are the owner of the *titles* table and that you've decided that most of the system's users should be allowed access to the table—except those columns dealing with money and sales. You want to restrict permission to modify those columns to three specific users (Sara, John, and Leslie).

To handle this situation, you can choose between two approaches. The most straightforward is to assign specific permissions to specific users—which in this case would mean writing several GRANT statements, including one with a very long user list. You'd need one statement to grant all the permissions to Sara, John, and Leslie:

```
SQL:

grant select, insert, delete, update
on titles
to sara, john, leslie
```

Now you'd need a statement to grant SELECT permissions to all those other users:

```
SQL:

grant select
on titles
to linda, pat, steve, chris, cathy, peter, lee, carl, karen
```

The list of users could be very long—and you still need another statement to grant all of them permission to modify all the columns in *titles* except *advance, price,* and *ytd_sales.* Depending on the syntax rules your system follows, you'd use one of the two following statements:

```
SQL:

grant update
on titles (title_id, title, type, pub_id,
  contract, notes, pubdate)
to linda, pat, steve, chris, cathy, peter, lee, carl, karen
```

```
grant update (title_id, title, type, pub_id,
 contract, notes, pubdate)
on titles
to linda, pat, steve, chris, cathy, peter, lee, carl, karen
```

Since most users are going to be granted most privileges, it's easier to assign all permissions to all users and then revoke specific permissions from specific users. Here's how: Begin with a statement that grants all users permission to select from, insert into, delete from, and update *titles*:

SQL:

```
grant all
on titles
to public
```

You've been very generous: now any user can modify *titles* at will. To protect the more sensitive columns, issue a statement to change the situation created by the previous statement. These statements revoke permission for all users to update the *price* and *ytd_sales* and *advance* columns of the *titles* table. The other privileges granted in the previous statement are unaffected.

SQL:

```
revoke update
on titles (price, advance, ytd_sales)
from public
```

Now, to give Sara, John, and Leslie permission to update those columns, you might issue this command:

SQL:

```
grant update
on titles (price, advance, ytd_sales)
to sara, john, leslie
```

You will want to include your own name in the user list as well, since the revocation from PUBLIC also applies to you.

Conflicting GRANT and REVOKE Statements.   As the previous examples imply, GRANT and REVOKE statements are order-sensitive (in most implementations of SQL). In case of a conflict, the most recently issued statement supersedes all others. So, for example, if PUBLIC has been granted SELECT permission on the *titles* table and then Joe's permission to select the *advance* column has been revoked, Joe can select all the columns except *advance*, while all the other users can still select all the columns. Similarly, a GRANT or REVOKE statement issued to PUBLIC will change all previously issued permissions that conflict with the new regime.

The consequence of this rule is that the same GRANT and REVOKE statements issued in different orders can create entirely different situations. For example, this set of statements leaves Joe (who is, of course, part of PUBLIC) without any SELECT permission on *titles*:

```
SQL:

grant select
on titles
to joe

revoke select
on titles
from public
```

In contrast, consider the same statements issued in the opposite order:

```
SQL:

revoke select
on titles
from public

grant select
on titles
to joe
```

Now only Joe has SELECT permission.

Remember that when you use the keyword PUBLIC, you are including yourself. You could even deny yourself permission to modify your own table, while giving yourself permission to access a view built on it or a stored procedure that references it. (You can always change your mind and reinstitute the permission with a GRANT statement.) You will probably use PUBLIC more frequently as a quick way of revoking permissions and then defining some exceptions, as in the previous example.

Views as Security Mechanisms

The second major security mechanism in most relational database management systems involves using views in conjunction with GRANT and REVOKE. Permission to access the subset of data in a view must be explicitly granted or revoked, regardless of the set of permissions in force on the view's underlying table or tables.

Through a view, users can query and modify only the data they can see. The rest of the database is neither visible nor accessible. For example, you might not want some users to be able to access the columns in the *titles* table that have to do with money and sales. You could create a view of the *titles* table that omits those columns (call it *bookview*) and then give all users permission on the view, but give only some members of the sales group permission on the table. Here's how:

```
SQL:
revoke all
on titles
from public

grant all
on bookview
to public

grant all
on titles
to mccann, himmelwright, brady, mandelbaum
```

By defining different views and selectively granting permissions on them, a user (or any combination of users) can be restricted to different subsets of data:

- Access can be restricted to a subset of the rows of a base table (a value-dependent subset). For example, you might define a view that contains only the rows for business and psychology books, in order to keep information about other types of books hidden from some users.

- Access can be restricted to a subset of the columns of a base table (a value-independent subset). For example, you might define a view that contains all the rows of the *titles* table but omits the *ytd_sales* and *advance* columns, since this information is sensitive.
- Access can be restricted to a row-and-column subset of a base table. For example, you might define a view that contains information only about business and psychology books, and only nonfinancial information about them.
- Access can be restricted to the rows that qualify for a join of more than one base table. For example, you might define a view that joins the *titles*, *authors*, and *titleauthors* tables in order to display the names of the authors and the books they have written. This view would hide personal data about authors and financial information about the books.
- Access can be restricted to a statistical summary of data in a base table. For example, you might define a view that shows the average price of each type of book.
- Access can be restricted to a subset of another view, or of some combination of views and base tables. For example, you might define a view on the view described in the previous example, containing the average price of cooking and computer books.

Creating views and setting up authorizations on them and on base tables is often done as part of the data definition process. However, you can change the authorization scheme at any time, defining new views and writing new GRANT and REVOKE statements. For more details on views, you may want to review Chapter 9.

TRANSACTIONS

A **transaction** is a logical unit of work. **Transaction management** means ensuring that a set of SQL statements is treated as a unit—as an indivisible entity. In other words, transaction management guarantees either that all the operations within a set (a transaction) are completed or that none of them is completed: a transaction is an all-or-nothing proposition.

Transactions are necessary for the purposes of concurrency control (keeping users who are simultaneously accessing the database from colliding with each other) and recovery (allowing the database system to bring the database back to a consistent state after a software failure).

SQL automatically manages all commands, including single-step change requests, as transactions. You can also group a set of SQL statements into a **user-defined transaction** with transaction commands (syntax varies from system to system, but they usually contain keywords such as BEGIN, COMMIT, and ROLLBACK).

Transactions and Concurrency

In multiuser systems, more than one user and/or transaction can access the same data at the same time. Preventing simultaneous transactions from interfering with each other—controlling concurrency—means making sure that data is never seen nor operated on by another user until a change is completed.

The purchase of airline tickets provides a classic example of one of the situations in which concurrency can be a problem. (It's so classic that it has a name: the **lost-update problem**.)

Say you call your favorite airline and ask for a ticket to Tahiti. The ticketing clerk submits a query to the database that selects all the available seats, and tells you that there's one left on tonight's flight. As you ponder, another desperate tourist has called his travel agent to find out whether he can get to Tahiti tonight. The travel agent has submitted the query to the database— the same one submitted by your ticketing clerk—and gets the same results. The travel agent informs the customer of the availability of a single seat. By now you've made up your mind, and the airline's ticketing clerk updates the database to reflect the fact that the last seat has been sold. You start packing—unaware that the travel agent, who has no way to know about the update made by the ticketing clerk, has just sold the same ticket. In fact, the update made by the travel agent overwrites the update submitted by your ticketing clerk. When you get to the airport, no one has heard of you.

This example demonstrates one of the dangers posed by concurrency demands in large, shared database systems. To handle concurrency problems, most relational database management systems rely on a mechanism called **locking**. The details of locking are outside the scope of this book, especially since most database systems handle it automatically, leaving users little say (if any) about it. Therefore, we'll give only an overview of this mechanism.

Locking. Basically, the way locks work is that when a user selects some data from the database, the database management system automatically puts a lock on it so that no other user can update that data until the lock is released.

There are many kinds of locks, but the most important distinction to understand is the difference between an **exclusive** lock and a **shared** lock. Database systems apply exclusive locks during data modification (also called write) operations: UPDATE, INSERT, DELETE. When an exclusive lock is applied to a set of data, no other transaction can acquire any kind of lock on that data until the original lock is released at the end of the data modification transaction.

Shared locks are applied during nonupdate, or read, operations, usually SELECT. A shared lock on a set of data prevents a write operation from acquiring an exclusive lock on that data, but allows other read operations to acquire their own shared locks even though the first transaction hasn't completed.

For the most part, the database system handles the application and release of locks automatically—the whole mechanism is invisible to users. Some systems, however, let users control certain aspects of locking. They may provide SQL commands for choosing the level at which locking is automatically applied (for example, the table level or the row level), or the length of time that certain kinds of locks are held.

Transactions and Recovery

A transaction is not only a unit of work, but also a unit of recovery. Recovery refers to the database system's ability to get the database back on its feet after a system failure—that is, into the most current state of affairs that can be guaranteed to be consistent.

System failures are those that affect all transactions in progress but that don't damage the database physically. Physical damage to a database is caused by media failure; protection against this kind of failure is provided by regularly backing up your database and its **transaction log**. The SQL commands used for these purposes are discussed later in this chapter.

In the case of system failure, the problem facing the database system's recovery mechanism is to figure out two things:

- Which transactions were incomplete at the time of the failure and should therefore be undone
- Which transactions were complete at the time of the failure but had not yet been written from the system's internal buffers to the physical database itself, and should therefore be redone

The recovery mechanism is largely invisible to users, though some systems give users a command such as CHECKPOINT, which forces the system to write to disk all the completed transactions in its buffers.

User-Defined Transactions

User-defined transactions allow users to instruct the database management system to process any number of SQL statements as a single unit. Check your system for specific SQL commands. The beginning of a transaction may be marked with a statement (such as BEGIN TRANSACTION or BEGIN WORK) or may be implicit. The end of a transaction may include commands with the keywords COMMIT (for a successful command) or ROLLBACK (for a command you wish to reverse).

A classic illustration of the need for user-defined transactions is the situation faced by a bank when a customer transfers money from a savings account to a checking account. In database terms, this banking transaction consists of two operations: first updating the savings balance to reflect a debit, then updating the checking balance with the credit. Unless these two updates are treated as a single transaction to the database, the danger exists that some other user might submit a query during the interval between them. If a bank officer happened to submit a query requesting the customer's balance after the money was deducted from the savings account but before it was added to the checking account, the results would be incorrect. Putting the two operations into a user-defined transaction ensures that the transfer of money is either accomplished completely or not at all.

In addition to giving the user control over transaction management, user-defined transactions also improve performance, since system overhead is incurred only once for a set of transactions, rather than once for each individual command.

Certain SQL commands cannot be included inside user-defined transactions. Check your system's reference manuals for details.

Handling Transactions. The SQL commands for beginning and ending transactions can enclose any number of SQL statements. Depending on the syntax your system supports, it'll look something like this:

```
[begin transaction statement]
   SQL statement
   SQL statement
   SQL statement
commit transaction statement
```

ROLLBACK Transaction. If a transaction must be canceled before it is committed—either because of some failure or because of a change of heart by the user—all of its statements that have been completed must be undone. A transaction can be canceled or rolled back with the ROLLBACK transaction command at any time before the COMMIT transaction command has been given. You can cancel either an entire transaction or part of it (if you have a savepoint mechanism). However, you can't cancel a transaction after it has been committed.

In most systems, the syntax of the ROLLBACK transaction command looks something like this:

```
[begin transaction statement]
   SQL statement
   SQL statement
   SQL statement
rollback transaction statement
```

Backup and Recovery

Backup and recovery are very system dependent. Here's a quick summary of how one system (Sybase) handles them. Your system may approach these problems differently.

Every change to the database, whether it is the result of a single SQL UPDATE statement (a system-defined transaction) or a grouped set of SQL statements (a user-defined transaction), is automatically recorded in the transaction log, which is, in the Sybase system, a table in the data dictionary.

The transaction log records data modification requests (UPDATE, INSERT, or DELETE statements) on a moment-to-moment basis. When a transaction begins, a BEGIN transaction event is recorded in the log. As each data modification statement is received, it is recorded in the log.

In the Sybase system, the change is recorded in the log before any change is made in the database itself. This type of log, called a write-ahead log, ensures that the database can be recovered completely in case of a failure.

When a failure occurs, the log can be played back against a copy of the database restored from a backup. Starting from the backup, all the transactions in the log can be redone. The SQL commands for backing up and restoring databases and their transaction logs are usually called something like DUMP DATABASE, DUMP TRANsaction, LOAD DATABASE, and LOAD TRANsaction. Once the appropriate LOAD commands are issued, the database system handles all aspects of the recovery process.

PERFORMANCE

Performance is a critical issue in relational database management systems. Multiuser, production-oriented applications are especially sensitive to performance problems: databases running on these systems tend to be larger, their operations tend to be more complex, the number of users and transactions puts heavy demands on the system, and the tasks for which the applications are responsible are often time-critical. However, performance sometimes becomes a matter of concern even for single-user database systems. No one wants to wait an unreasonable length of time for the results of a query or the execution of a data modification statement.

Unfortunately, many aspects of performance are outside the control of users. Instead, people depend on the features and capabilities built into the system by the vendor. If you're currently shopping for a relational database management system, you'll be particularly interested in the next section, which briefly discusses the use of **benchmarking** to compare the performance of different database systems. Benchmarking can also be used to evaluate how different database designs and indexes affect performance.

Following the discussion of benchmarking, the rest of this section mentions some of the ways that users can influence performance:

- A good logical database design can make a big difference in how well your system performs.
- The way you structure your queries can affect performance.
- Some database systems provide tools for monitoring and fine-tuning performance, including some control of physical design (where and how data is physically stored).

Performance is a huge subject. This book can only touch on it lightly, mainly in order to alert you to topics that you may need to research if performance becomes an issue for you.

Benchmarking

If you're in the market for a high-volume, production-oriented relational database management system, you've probably heard vendors making claims about the number of transactions per second their systems deliver. The numbers they bandy about are based on the results of benchmarks, or tests that measure the performance of a system in a controlled environment using a standard methodology.

Interpreting and analyzing claims about performance benchmarks are notoriously difficult. Benchmarking is technically complex, and the results announced by vendors inevitably reflect the tendency of any interested party to show his or her product at its best. The technical details of benchmark evaluation are beyond the scope of this book, but you'll find some suggested readings in the bibliography.

Here are a few nontechnical questions you can ask about performance claims based on benchmarking:

- Is one of the accepted standard tests used? Or has the vendor selected the test on the basis of how well its product does on it?
- Are the benchmark process and results validated by an independent and reputable organization?
- Is the hardware configuration that was used for the benchmark similar to what you'll be running on? Consider not only the type of computer, but also how its memory is configured, whether it was in a network, and so on.
- Is the software that was used for the benchmark the commercially available version of the product, or was the benchmark test run on a preproduction or special release?
- Are the results of the benchmark consistent and repeatable?

Benchmarks are typically associated with database systems that will be used for mission-critical applications involving dozens to hundreds of users and very large databases—hundreds or thousands of megabytes. They are used not only for making performance comparisons among products, but also for planning the kind of hardware you'll need for a given level of performance, and for making decisions about database design and indexing. Two versions of a database design, for example, can be created and tested against a benchmark to determine which is best for your purposes.

Design and Indexing

You can greatly enhance performance by paying close attention to logical database design. The importance of design for performance (as well as in other areas) belies the often-repeated notion that with a relational database system, you need specify only what you want, not how to get it. Relational expert Robert Epstein goes so far as to call this a "myth" and to state that "the relational database is no smarter than the design you came up with."

Chapters 2 and 3 explain how to analyze your data and follow the normalization guidelines in order to wind up with a good, clean database design. You may remember from the discussion in these chapters that indexes speed retrieval considerably while slowing down data modification to some extent, and that splitting tables for the purposes of normalization can slow the retrieval of data when a query that could have been answered by looking at one table now requires the system to look at more than one. Multi-table queries can adversely affect performance for several reasons. Since the data is dispersed among several tables, additional disk reads may be required to find it. Then, once the data is located, the system must join it. Finally, accessing more tables incurs the overhead of setting more locks.

Thus, with respect to performance, the basic principle is to consider how the database will primarily be used. If the number of queries to be run far surpasses the number of data modification statements, build a lot of indexes and minimize the number of joins that are required by designing fewer and larger tables. More specifically, find out which queries will be run often and put all the columns used by a given query in the same table. For the fastest response to data modification statements, use as few indexes as possible and normalize thoroughly.

Queries

When you submit a SQL statement to the database management system, a lot of work gets done that you don't see. In fact, SQL is considered a **nonprocedural language** precisely because it does not require the user to specify the steps the system must take to execute the command. Instead, the user simply states what is being sought.

The strength of the nonprocedural approach is the same as its drawback. To state it positively, the system does the work for you. The bad news is that once you're committed to a particular database design, you usually have no choice but to trust the system's intelligence rather than your own.

The part of the database management system responsible for analyzing a SQL statement is called the **query optimizer**. The query optimizer decomposes each query into its constituent parts and rearranges it to run as efficiently as possible. It evaluates several search strategies or access paths, deciding on the most useful indexes to use and on the path that requires the smallest number of logical page accesses. In other words, the query optimizer generates a plan, determining the most efficient path between the user's SQL statement and the data needed to carry out the assigned task.

The query optimizers of various relational database management systems have at their disposal a library of standard query-processing strategies (for example, to use the column's clustered index) that are applied in various query situations. If none of the strategies known to the system applies to the SQL statement being examined, the system resorts to the default strategy of reading every row of the table or tables referenced by the query. Whole-table scans always produce the desired results, but on a table of any size at all, they are horribly slow.

Early implementations provided no protection against inefficient structuring of queries by users. Most now have diagnostic tools that can help you see how commands are processed so that you can make adjustments in indexes, table structure, or data distribution. The query optimizer is often smart enough to "rephrase" SQL statements into forms that run most efficiently.

Some commercial systems support special "procedures": named collections of SQL statements including extensions for procedural code and input parameters. (In Transact-SQL, these objects are called stored procedures or system procedures and are precompiled, offering real performance advantages as well as functional flexibility.)

Other Tools for Monitoring and Boosting Performance

Relational database management systems that have been developed for production-oriented, multiuser, on-line applications often provide a variety of tools for monitoring and fine-tuning performance. Many of these features are outside the province of SQL per se; some systems expect you to accomplish these tasks using operating system facilities rather than those provided by the database system. A sampling of performance tools is offered briefly here, to give you a taste of the facilities that may be available.

Caches. The configuration of your computer's internal memory, especially the amount of memory allocated to the **data cache** or **buffer cache**, can markedly affect performance. In some systems, the cache is the area of memory where the most recently used data pages and index pages are stored. These database systems always look in the cache first for a page that they need; if they find what they are looking for there, they save a disk access. In other words, holding commonly used pages in a cache can boost performance by minimizing disk accesses.

Data caches are usually managed in what is called an **LRU-MRU** (least recently used, most recently used) fashion: the most recently used pages are put into the cache, displacing the least recently used ones. It makes sense to experiment with the data cache: increasing its size may speed up your application. Some systems also allow you to adjust the size of a page to your application. The smaller the pages, the more of them the cache can hold.

Logging. Most relational database management systems allow you to turn off the logging of database transactions, which speeds updates by saving the time it takes to enter the changes in the log. Of course, in case of a media failure, you can't rely on the database system to recover any of the changes that have been made if there is no log.

It makes sense to suspend logging temporarily before you load a large amount of data into the database—if the operation can be easily repeated in case of a media failure. But remember to make a backup copy before you begin, so that you can easily start over.

Monitoring Execution Plans. Check to see if your system provides a facility that allows you to monitor a query's execution plan. You can use this tool to check on SQL's work, and to see how its plan varies depending on where you put indexes and how you have written the statement.

Other monitoring tools may display information about how a given SQL statement was processed: how many table scans, logical accesses (cache reads) and physical accesses (disk reads) the system did for each table or view that is referenced in a query; how many pages it wrote for each data modification command; how much CPU time it took to parse and compile each command or to execute each step of the command.

Index Statistics.   Many systems provide a tool or utility that lets you look closely at index performance. This may include examining an index to determine its minimum value, maximum value, and the number of distinct values. In Transact-SQL, UPDATE STATISTICS calculates the distribution of index key values in the specified index.

Whether SQL calculates simple statistics or distribution statistics for an index, it stores this information in order to estimate how long a search using that index will take. By ranking the indexes for which it compiles statistics, the system can intelligently select the best one to use.

Statistics based on the distribution of key values give a much better estimate of retrieval time than simple statistics, which assume that the index's key values are uniformly distributed. If you're using a version of SQL that uses distribution statistics, it's important to remember to reissue the UPDATE STATISTICS command whenever you've added, deleted, or modified a bunch of new data, since those actions are likely to change the distribution of the index keys. If the system's information about key distribution is not kept up-to-date, it uses the old information and may make a bad choice about how to process a query.

You may also have additional commands that give you control of how the indexes are set up. For example, indexing options provided by Transact-SQL (FILLFACTOR, MAX_ROWS_PER_PAGE) allow you to control how full to make each page of a new index. This number affects performance because of the time it takes for the system to split index pages when they become 100 percent full.

Another reason to use a feature like FILLFACTOR is to physically spread the data in small but frequently accessed tables and thus cut down on lock contention. Let's say an important table takes up only a couple of data pages, and locking is on the page level. Specifying a clustered index with a few rows per page distributes the data over many more pages and decreases competition for locks.

The disadvantage of small fillfactor values is that each index takes more storage space and hence is slower.

DATA INTEGRITY

Broadly speaking, data integrity refers to the accuracy and consistency of the data in the database. Ideally, database software would provide a variety of mechanisms for checking on data integrity; unfortunately, several important kinds of integrity are unsupported by most relational systems.

In practice, many requirements for integrity are often met through special-purpose application code. The disadvantages of assigning the task of integrity control to application programs include the amount of extra work involved in writing and maintaining integrity-checking code, the potential for both duplicating work and introducing inconsistencies when more than one application uses the same database, and the ease with which constraints coded into applications can be bypassed by users with access to the underlying database.

There are several kinds of data integrity. At the most basic level, all database systems (not just relational ones) should be able to guarantee that a value being entered is the correct datatype and that it's within the range of values supported by the system. Different relational systems provide different assortments of datatypes, but all of them check values being entered and reject the data modification statement if the value is wrong for the specified datatype. The null status of the column is also checked on data entry. Finally, certain datatypes—usually character types—can (or must) be associated with user-specified lengths. Some systems reject data entries that exceed the maximum length for the datatype; others truncate the entered value to fit.

Three other kinds of integrity are discussed in this section:

- Domain constraints
- Entity integrity
- Referential integrity

Domain Constraints

A **domain** is the set of logically related values from which the value in a particular column can be drawn. Here are some examples of domains in the *bookbiz* database:

- The domain of the *authors.au_id* column is all the Social Security numbers issued by the U.S. government.
- The domain of the *authors.city* and *publishers.city* columns is all the cities in the United States; for *authors.state* and *publishers.state*, it's all the states in the United States. (Note the assumption that all authors live in the United States.)
- The domain of *titles.type* is the following set of values: *business, popular_comp, psychology, mod_cook,* and *trad_cook.*

- The domain of *titles.title_id* is the set of values with the following format: the first two characters are capitalized letters of the alphabet from the set *BU, PC, PS, MC, TC*; the next four characters are integers between 0 and 9, inclusive.
- The domain of *titleauthors.royaltyshare* is all numbers between 0 and 1, inclusive.

Notice the different kinds of logical relationships among the values in these domains. Some of the domains represent application-determined constraints—that is, business rules and regulations. For example, the constraints on the format of the title ID numbers were determined by someone in the publishing company. The publisher might also decide that the prices of books must be no less than $1.99 and no greater than $99.99; dollars-and-cents amounts between those two values would then be the domain for *titles.price*.

Other domains are based not on business rules but on physical or mathematical constraints. The values in *titleauthors.royaltyshare*, for example, represent percentages, so they must be numbers between 0 and 1. As another example, suppose the publisher wanted to record the sex of each author in the database. The domain for that column would be limited by (widely accepted interpretations of) human biology to the values *female, male,* and *unknown*.

The descriptions of the domains in the preceding list were deduced from an examination of the values in the *bookbiz* database. You can use the CHECK constraint in the CREATE TABLE statement to express many of them. Transact-SQL supports an additional mechanism for specifying domains, the CREATE RULE command. A rule is a named database object that can be associated with any number of columns or with all columns of a specified datatype. Like a CHECK constraint, a rule definition can include any expression that is valid in a WHERE clause—arithmetic operators, comparison operators, LIKE, IN, BETWEEN, and so on. This flexibility in defining rules allows you to base domains on lists of values (like the domain for *titles.type*), ranges (like the domain for *titleauthors.royaltyshare*), or format (like the domain for *titles.title_id*).

The Transact-SQL rule mechanism is limited, however, in that the rule definition cannot reference another column in the database. However, defining rules outside of the CREATE TABLE statement is convenient for rules that change frequently.

One last note: Recall from Chapter 7 that if the values in two columns have the same domains, joins between these columns are usually logical.

For example, *publishers.city* and *authors.city* have the same domain (all cities in the United States); therefore it would be meaningful to join on them.

Entity Integrity

Entity integrity requires that no component of a primary key be allowed to have a null value. That is, a single-column primary key can't accept nulls, nor can any of the columns in a composite primary key.

The entity-integrity constraint derives from the relational model, not from the requirements of any particular application. Nor is entity integrity a concern in other models of database management, the way domain constraints are. The requirement that no primary key contain a null value is based on the fact that real-world entities are distinguished from each other by primary keys that serve as unique identifiers. In fact, entity integrity is as much a design issue as it is an integrity issue.

You should guarantee entity integrity by designating a primary key that will not accept null values when you design your database. You can implement it by specifying NOT NULL in the CREATE TABLE statement and using the PRIMARY KEY constraint or by creating a unique index for the column. (See Chapters 2 and 3 for a review of these concepts.)

Referential Integrity

Informally speaking, referential integrity concerns the relationship between the values in logically related tables. In the relational model, it means guaranteeing the logical consistency of the database by making sure that the values of a primary key and the foreign keys that point to it always match.

Here's E. F. Codd's definition: "For each distinct non-null foreign key value in a relational database, there must exist a matching primary key value from the same domain."

Chapter 2 explains that foreign key–primary key relationships are planned during the design of a database; they represent the logical relationships among data (although their presence in no way limits the possible access paths among the data). In considering referential integrity, the question is what the database system can do to guarantee the maintenance of matching values between foreign keys and the primary key to which they point (that is, that referential constraints are not violated). Chapter 3 introduces the REFERENCES and FOREIGN KEY constraints in the CREATE TABLE statement. These clauses ensure some referential integrity—they allow you to set up checks that prevent a foreign key from being added if it does not correspond to a primary key. But this is only one issue in referential integrity.

For example, changing an author ID can present a problem, since the alteration would destroy the connection between the *authors*, *titles*, and *titleauthors* tables. The REFERENCES clause prevents this kind of change in the foreign key (*titleauthors.au_id*), but not in the primary key (*authors.au_id*). How do you deal with the primary key—changing the ID in the *authors* table, or deleting or updating a publisher ID in the *publishers* table when books in the *titles* table still reference the old ID? One approach is to decide that primary keys should never be changed, and prevent these updates.

Another answer is to automatically "cascade" the update or delete operation to the matching foreign keys. For example, if a publisher's ID number changes, the system would change the matching IDs in *titles.pub_id* in exactly the same way, without intervention by the user.

A third possibility is to accept data modification operations to primary key values even if they upset referential integrity, but first to change the matching foreign key values to NULL. (Of course, if the foreign key has been defined so as not to accept null values, this course of action is out.) Using a variation on the previous example: in response to a DELETE command that removes the row for Algodata Infosystems from the *publishers* table, the *titles.pub_id* values for all books published by Algodata would be set to NULL.

To summarize briefly, there are in general three possible responses to an attempt to delete or update a primary key to which a foreign key points:

- **Restrict**—the delete or update operation on the primary key is rejected unless there are no matching foreign key values.
- **Cascade**—the delete or update operation is automatically applied to the foreign keys whose values matched the "old" value of the deleted or updated primary key.
- **Nullify**—before the delete or update operation on the primary key is committed, the value(s) of matching foreign key(s) are set to NULL.

Unfortunately, many SQL dialects do not provide mechanisms for controlling primary key referential integrity. In these cases, the closest you can come to guaranteeing referential integrity is to revoke all permissions for deleting and updating a primary key column.

However, as the importance of referential integrity becomes more and more widely recognized, vendors are beginning to address it with special procedures or triggers. Transact-SQL was one of the first to do so. While the details of the Transact-SQL trigger mechanism are not important for our purposes, the description in the next section gives an idea of how triggers can be used to enforce referential integrity.

Triggers. A Transact-SQL trigger is a named collection of SQL statements that describes an action to be carried out when a specified data modification operation is attempted on a given column or table.

Triggers are automatic. They work no matter what causes the data modification—a clerk's entry, an application action, a report calculation. Each trigger is specific to one or more of the data modification operations: UPDATE, INSERT, or DELETE.

Creating a trigger involves specifying the data modification command that "fires" the trigger, the table that is its "target," and the action or actions the trigger is to take. Here's the CREATE TRIGGER syntax:

```
CREATE TRIGGER trigger_name
  ON table_name
  FOR {INSERT | UPDATE | DELETE}
    [, {INSERT | UPDATE | DELETE}]...
  AS SQL_statements
    [IF UPDATE (column_name)
    [{AND | OR} UPDATE (column_name)]...]
```

The ON clause gives the name of the table that activates the trigger—the trigger table. The FOR clause specifies which data modification command(s) on the trigger table activate the trigger.

The SQL statements in the AS clause specify **trigger actions** and **trigger conditions**. The trigger actions can consist of any number and any kind of SELECT statements, including the control-of-flow language that is part of Transact-SQL.

Trigger conditions can specify additional criteria that determine whether the attempted INSERT, DELETE, or UPDATE will cause the trigger action(s) to be carried out. Trigger conditions often include a subquery preceded by the keyword IF. The IF UPDATE (column_name) clause tests whether the specified column has been modified, allowing trigger actions to be associated with changes to particular columns.

The names of two logical (or conceptual) tables—*deleted* and *inserted*—are used in CREATE TRIGGER statements. When a DELETE command is issued on a trigger table (for example, an attempt is made to remove primary key values), the deleted rows are removed from the trigger table and transferred to the *deleted* table. Then the trigger can examine the rows in *deleted* to determine whether or how the trigger action(s) should be carried out.

When an INSERT or UPDATE command is attempted, rows representing the new values are added to the trigger table and to *inserted* at the same time. The rows in *inserted* can then be examined by the trigger mechanism.

Here's an example of a trigger that performs a cascading delete when a primary key value in *titles* is deleted. When a DELETE statement on *titles* is executed, the trigger removes the row from *titles* and adds it to *deleted*. Then it checks the tables—*titleauthors*, *salesdetails*, and *roysched* to see if they have any rows with a foreign key *title_id* that matches the *title_id* removed from *titles* (now stored in the *deleted* table). If the trigger finds any such rows, it removes them.

```
SQL (extension):
create trigger delcascadetrig
on titles
for delete
as
delete titleauthors
from titleauthors, deleted
where titleauthors.title_id = deleted.title_id
        /* Remove titleauthors rows
        ** that match deleted (titles) rows.*/

delete salesdetails
from salesdetails, deleted
where salesdetails.title_id = deleted.title_id
        /* Remove sales order rows
        ** that match deleted (titles) rows.*/

delete roysched
from roysched, deleted
where roysched.title_id = deleted.title_id
        /* Remove roysched rows
        ** that match deleted (titles) rows.*/
```

Here's another example of a referential control trigger. This one is not absolute, however: it prevents updates to the primary key column of the *titles* table on certain days of the week. (Such a trigger might be desirable for any type of column, not just for a primary key.)

The IF UPDATE clause focuses this trigger on a particular column, *titles.title_id*. Modifications to that column cause the trigger to go into action, canceling the update and printing a message.

```
SQL (extension):
create trigger stopupdatetrig
on titles
for update
as
if update (title_id)
   and datename(dw, getdate())
   in ("Saturday", "Sunday")
begin
   rollback transaction
   print "We don't allow monkeying with primary keys on
   the weekend!"
end
        /* If titles.title_id changes on
        ** Saturday or Sunday, cancel the update. */
```

As just illustrated, Transact-SQL triggers are often used to control referential integrity threatened by updates or deletions to a primary key. However, triggers actually represent a more generalized method for dealing with integrity issues:

- Triggers can enforce restrictions much more complex than those defined with rules, CHECK constraints, or REFERENCES constraints. For example, a trigger can reject updates that attempt to increase a book's price by more than 1 percent of its advance, or prevent all price increases greater than 100 percent.
- Triggers can be used to recalculate ongoing tallies. For example, you might write a trigger that updates the *ytd_sales* column in the *titles* table whenever a row is added to the *salesdetails* table.

FROM GENERIC SQL TO THE REAL WORLD

This chapter has brought the discussion of generic SQL closer to the real world by touching on topics such as performance, transaction control, and tools for maintaining referential integrity. We will not explore these issues further, since relational database management systems differ widely from each other in their implementations of backup and recovery tools, transaction control, and access strategies.

The next two chapters pull together many of the SQL statements you have learned so far, presenting more complex pieces of code.

Chapter 11

Solving Business Problems

USING SQL ON THE JOB

When you get right down to it, whatever you know about SQL is useful only to the degree that it helps you get your work done. SQL is a business tool.

Earlier chapters focused on teaching you SQL's capabilities; now it's time to look at how people really use SQL on the job. Most of the material in this chapter was collected from discussions (sometimes heated!) on the Internet: Puzzled SQL users submitted SQL questions to the world of network subscribers, often including code samples and background descriptions with their appeals for help. Readers volunteered solutions, added to or vigorously disagreed with previous answers, and occasionally "flamed" the inquirer for poorly analyzed materials.

Out of all this give-and-take, some common themes emerged. Certain questions came up over and over, such as how to format results. It became clear that a "cookbook" with code "recipes" for dealing with common issues could prove quite valuable.

This book deals with generic or industry SQL, rather than any particular vendor's implementation. However, code recipes require attention to the specific if they are going to have any real value, and they need testing. Sybase's Transact-SQL is the SQL dialect with which we are most familiar, so we've used it in our examples, running them on both Sybase SQL Server and SQL Anywhere. You may need to modify some of the items in the cookbook if you are using a different database system. However, we have avoided questions that are strictly Sybase-specific (stored procedure or trigger code).

You won't find indexing or performance discussions here either: They are too tightly coupled to SQL dialects and environment issues to make much sense as isolated pieces of code. "Religious" arguments, those concerning the correct and incorrect implementations of various features, have also been eliminated, because they don't fit the practical orientation of the book.

In short, this chapter is a collection of brief pieces of as-generic-as-possible SQL code. Each one is based on a real question posted to the Internet. The problems and solutions are modified to work with the sample database, *bookbiz*. They are not terribly difficult, but they represent the kind of things typical users get stuck on. The assumption is that if someone had the problem, you may too.

Use this chapter as a SQL cookbook, but be a creative chef: find interesting recipes and modify the ingredients to suit your palate.

The general categories are

- Formatting and displaying data
- Retrieving data (mostly by matching patterns)
- Using complex joins and subqueries
- Working with the GROUP BY clause
- Creating sequential numbers

FORMATTING AND DISPLAYING DATA

The way you store data isn't always the best way to display it. If you have application programs such as report generators connected to your database, they may provide all the formatting that you need. Sometimes, however, it makes sense to use the string, number, and date functions that most database vendors support. Many of them became part of the ANSI SQL standard in 1992.

But remember: SQL is *not* a display tool! It was designed to retrieve data, not to make it look good. If some of the recipes in this section look convoluted, it's because they are.

This section includes code for

- Displaying one field as two
- Right-justifying a character string
- Specifying the number of digits after the decimal point

Displaying One Field as Two

Sometimes data stored in the database as one field makes more sense to users when it appears as two or more separate fields. This is particularly true when the field consists of data that seems to be of mixed types, as in some composite identification fields (a health insurance number, for example, may consist of the familiar nine-digit Social Security number, plus an alphabetic company or geographic code).

In the *titles* table, the *title_id* field comes close to this situation. It contains six characters: two letters followed by four digits. Here's some sample data (the WHERE clause limits the data returned):

```
SQL:
select title_id
from titles
where price > 19.99

Results:
title_id
--------
PC1035
PC8888
PS1372
TC3218
```

To display the letter part of the field separately from the numeric part, you can use string functions in your SELECT. Once you have the data looking the way you want it, create a view. That way, users always see the divided fields instead of the original ones.

The first step is to define the two field subsets with a string function called SUBSTRING, which returns part of a character or binary string. The syntax is this:

```
SUBSTRING (expression, start, length)
```

You can see how SUBSTRING works by running a SELECT on *title_id*, giving each fragment of the field a new name:

```
SQL:
select substring(title_id,1,2) as alpha,
  substring(title_id,3,4) as num
from titles
where price > 19.99
```

```
Results:
alpha    num
-----    -------
PC       1035
PC       8888
PS       1372
TC       3218
```

Now hide this work from users by creating a view. When they run queries, they'll be unaware that *alpha* and *num* are actually parts of *title_id*. The CREATE VIEW looks like this (once again, the WHERE clause is included only to limit the number of rows returned for this example):

```
SQL:
create view split
as
select substring(title_id,1,2) as alpha,
    substring(title_id,3,4) as num
from titles
where price > 19.99
```

After you revoke permission to use the table and grant rights to use the view, users can see the two fields with this query:

```
SQL:
select   *
from split
```

```
Results:
alpha    num
-----    -----
PC       1035
PC       8888
PS       1372
TC       3218
```

Of course, *num* is still a character field, so you won't be able to perform mathematical operations on it. A query like the next one returns an error (unless your system can average character numerics):

```
SQL:
select avg(num)
from split
```

One way to get around this is to create a view in which you treat *num* as an integer datatype. Use the *split* view SQL plus one important addition: the CONVERT function. CONVERT changes one datatype to another. The syntax is this:

```
CONVERT(datatype[length], expression)
```

When you apply that formula to *num*, changing it to an integer datatype, you get this:

```
convert (int, num)
```

But remember, *num* is actually a SUBSTRING of *title_id*. To complete the work, substitute the SUBSTRING expression for *num* in the CONVERT phrase.

```
convert (int, substring(title_id,3,4))
```

The full query now reads:

```
SQL:
select substring(title_id,1,2) as alpha,
    convert(int, substring(title_id,3,4)) as num
from titles
where price > 19.99
```

If you create another view with this query variant, you'll be able to use numeric functions such as AVG on the *num* field:

```
SQL:
select avg(num)
from split2

Results:
- - - - - - - - - - -
        3628
```

Depending on how your system handles averaging and integers, you may get a different value.

Right-Justifying a Character String

Now for a more complex problem: How do you right-justify character strings? The easiest (and most sensible) way is to use a reporting tool or a display application. If neither is available or appropriate, or if you're just interested in pushing your SQL envelope, try this recipe.

Here's the default display (left-justified) of first and last names from the *authors* table. The WHERE clause limits results to people whose first name starts with the letter *A*.

```
SQL:
select au_fname, au_lname
from authors
where au_fname like 'A%'

Results:
au_fname            au_lname
-------             --------
Abraham             Bennet
Ann                 Dull
Akiko               Yokomoto
Anne                Ringer
Albert              Ringer
```

To right-justify the data, you need to go through these steps for each name field:

1. Find the defined size of the column (as in the CREATE TABLE statement) and the actual size of the data stored in the column.

2. For each column, calculate the difference between the defined column size and the actual data size.

3. Pad the left side of the display with spaces equal to that difference.

4. Add the data to the right of the spaces—the sum of the spaces on the left and the actual data on the right will be equal to the defined column size.

Most vendors provide a way to get information about a column's defined length and actual data length. In Transact-SQL, you can use two system functions, COL_LENGTH and DATALENGTH. The syntax is this:

```
COL_LENGTH ('object_name', 'column_name')

DATALENGTH (expression)
```

Check your manuals for details about your system.
Here's an example of how the two functions work:

```
SQL:
select au_fname,
   col_length ('authors', 'au_fname') as col,
   datalength(au_fname) as data,
   col_length ('authors', 'au_fname') -
       datalength(au_fname) as diff
from authors
where au_fname like 'A%'

Results:
au_fname     col     data    diff
--------     ---     ----    ----
Abraham      20      7       13
Ann          20      3       17
Akiko        20      5       15
Anne         20      4       16
Albert       20      6       14
```

The results show the *au_fname* data, the column length, the actual data size, and the difference between the column length and data length. The first function returns the column size, while the second finds the number of characters in each column. The difference between the two numbers equals the number of spaces you need to have in the left side of the field in order to push the names to the end of the field so that they will line up on the right.

Now that you know the data size and the difference between it and the column size, your next move is to pad the field with the correct number of leading spaces. REPLICATE is the Transact-SQL function for repeating characters. The syntax is this:

```
REPLICATE (char_expr, integer_expr)
```

In this example, *char_expr* is a space (" ") and *integer_expr* is the number of times to repeat *char_expr*. Use the difference between *col_length* and *datalength* as *integer_expr*. This is how the elements fit together so far:

```
SQL:
select replicate(' ', col_length('authors','au_fname')
         - datalength(au_fname)) as Personal_name,
       replicate(' ', col_length('authors','au_lname')
         - datalength(au_lname)) as Surname
from authors
where au_fname like 'A%'


Results:
Personal_name            Surname
--------------------     --------------------------------
```

This query runs fine, but all you get are the column titles and a blank screen! What you've done is set up the padding with blanks on the left; to see anything, you need to add the data.

Tack it on with a concatenating function. In Transact-SQL, you use the plus sign (+). The syntax is simply this:

```
expression + expression
```

Now you have code like this:

```
SQL:
select replicate(' ', col_length('authors','au_fname')
          - datalength(au_fname)) + au_fname as Personal_name,
replicate(' ',
      col_length('authors','au_lname')
          - datalength(au_lname)) + au_lname as Surname
from authors
where au_fname like 'A%'
```

This version gives you column headings and right-justified data. However, the fields are very large. To get what you really want, add CONVERT to control the display size:

```
SQL:
select convert(varchar(20),
        replicate(' ',
            col_length('authors', 'au_fname')
            - datalength(au_fname))
        + au_fname) as Personal_name,
        convert(varchar(40),
        replicate(' ',
            col_length('authors', 'au_lname')
            - datalength(au_lname))
        + au_lname) as Surname
from authors
where au_fname like 'A%'

Personal_name            Surname
-------------            --------
      Abraham            Bennet
          Ann            Dull
        Akiko            Yokomoto
         Anne            Ringer
       Albert            Ringer
```

(Because of font and alignment issues, some front-end tools do not show the columns as neatly aligned as this display. If this is true of your situation, send the results to an ASCII-format file and check them there.)

Specifying the Number of Digits after the Decimal Point

The default floating point display may not always be what you want. The precision (total number of digits) and scale (number of digits after the decimal point) may force a very wide display. In addition, the approximate nature of floating point numbers may cause hard-to-understand numbers. When your goal is to show the numbers in a consistent format, even if that means sacrificing some accuracy, you can use functions to control the display.

Here's how data was entered into a table containing a float datatype column:

```
one
-------------------
   22.1
    1.1
4444.20
   22.22
  333.1
```

This is how it displays on one system, where SQL strips any zeroes on the right:

SQL:
```
select *
from testfloat
```

Results:
```
one
-------------------
22.1
1.1
4444.2
22.22
333.1
```

On another system you might see something like this (and since this is a float field, the actual values will vary slightly from machine to machine):

Results:
```
one
-------------------
22.1000003814697
1.10000002384186
4444.2001953125
22.2199993133545
333.100006103516
```

The ROUND function is available on many systems (for numeric datatypes only). It allows you to specify the number of digits to the right or left of the decimal sign. The syntax is this:

```
ROUND (numeric_column, integer)
```

The *integer* value specifies the number of digits to the right (positive) or left (negative) of the decimal point. Code to limit the display to two places after the point looks like this:

SQL:
```
select round(one, 2)
from testfloat
```

Results:
```
rounded
- - - - - - - - - - - - - - - - - -
22.1
1.1
4444.2
22.22
333.1
```

The only problem with this is that trailing zeroes are stripped. Another approach is to use a series of string functions. SUBSTRING (with CONVERT, since *one* is a numeric datatype) can't do the job:

SQL:
```
select short = substring(
        convert(varchar(18), one),
            1,5), one
from testfloat
```

Results:
```
short   one
- - - - -   - - - - - - - - - - - - - - - - - -
22.10   22.1000003814697
1.100   1.10000002384186
4444.   4444.2001953125
22.21   22.2199993133545
333.1   333.100006103516
```

The results in the *short* field show that you get the first five data positions, no matter what they are.

In order to control the number of digits after the decimal point, you need to relate the third argument in SUBSTRING (the number of digits to display) to the location of the decimal point. You're not looking for an absolute number (such as 5 in the preceding query) but for something like "all of the digits on the left side of the decimal point and two digits on the right side of the decimal point."

Most database systems have a function that finds the position of one string in another. In Transact-SQL, it's CHARINDEX. The syntax is this:

```
CHARINDEX (expression1, expression2)
```

Here *expression1* is the subset (the string you are looking for) and *expression2* is the full set (the string in which the subset is embedded).

For our example, *expression1* is the decimal point (.) and *expression2* is the floating point field *one*. Because *one* will be used inside SUBSTRING, it has to be converted to a character datatype. Once you put these pieces together, the CHARINDEX segment looks like this:

```
charindex(".", convert(varchar(18),one))
```

Add 2 to this segment, and substitute the whole thing for the third SUBSTRING argument. Now SUBSTRING goes from the first character to two places after the decimal point. Here's what the query and its results look like:

```
SQL:
select short = substring(
        convert(varchar(18),one),
            1, charindex
                (".",convert(varchar(18),one)) + 2), one
from testfloat

Results:
short                 one
-----------------     -------------------
22.10                 22.1000003814697
1.10                  1.10000002384186
4444.20               4444.2001953125
22.21                 22.2199993133545
333.10                333.100006103516
```

Changing the final *+2* to *+1* will display only one digit after the decimal point. As an exercise, try right-justifying the numbers.

PLAYING WITH PATTERNS

These recipes concern retrieving data when there's lots of action in the WHERE clause but the joins are simple. The next section deals with more complex joins.

The first three queries retrieve data by matching patterns in various ways. The fourth is something of a maverick. It locates inconsistent mixtures of NULL and blank strings. Then it cleans them up with an UPDATE statement.

Read on to learn how to find

- Character data when you're not sure whether it's uppercase, lowercase, or mixed
- Character strings of (or not of) a given length
- Date data
- Null data masquerading as spaces

Matching Uppercase and Lowercase Letters

Sometimes data is stored in uppercase letters ("COMPUTER"), sometimes in lowercase letters ("computer"), and sometimes in mixed cases ("Computer"). This may reflect the lack of standards when the data was entered and thus the absence of integrity checks.

For example, let's say you want to determine the exact title of a book that is called either *Life Without Fear* or *Life without Fear.* You're unsure of the case of the word *without.* In fact, you suspect that the data is inconsistent throughout, and there is no good way to predict how book titles are stored. There are a number of ways to deal with this.

You can use LIKE, as in the following example:

```
SQL:
select title
from titles
where title
    like '%[Ww][Ii][Tt][Hh][Oo][Uu][Tt]%'
```

```
Results:
title
- - - - -
Life Without Fear
```

Each bracketed pair allows matches on either upper- or lowercase letters. Check your system for equivalent syntax.

Another option is to use the UPPER function. It converts lowercase letters in the field to uppercase letters. The syntax is this:

```
UPPER (char_expression)
```

Once the data has been changed to uppercase letters, LIKE compares it to the matching pattern:

```
SQL:
select title
from titles
where upper(title) like '%WITHOUT%'
```

This is easier to read and understand than the LIKE syntax alone. UPPER's sister function, LOWER, works the same way, but converts data to a lowercase string. Check to see how your system handles mixed-case words with these functions. Some require you to use UPPER (or LOWER) twice to match any combination of upper- and lowercase letters:

```
SQL:
select title
from titles
where upper(title) like upper("%wiTHout%)
```

It may appear that the simplest answer to the problem of casing is to enter the data in one case only and avoid this kind of work. But be careful! You may lose important information that you'll need later. Many names use both upper- and lowercase letters internally. Consider the names Blotchett-Halls, DeFrance, O'Leary, MacFeather, and del Castillo from the *bookbiz* database. You've probably seen them written with irregular distributions of capital letters. If you've stored them in a one-case style, you may find yourself trying to re-create distinctions you once had but then eliminated.

Matching Character Data of a Given Size

It doesn't seem like much of a problem to find character data of a particular length. However, even this apparently simple case has a few interesting wrinkles. For example, one query for all authors with first names of exactly four characters would look like this using the Transact-SQL range wildcards (brackets enclosing the upper and lower range characters, separated by dashes):

```
SQL:
select au_fname
from authors
where au_fname like '[A-Z][a-z][a-z][a-z]'

Results:
au_fname
------------------
Dick
Burt
Dirk
Anne
```

Check your system to see if it has similar functions.

This will work fine as long as the name starts with a capital letter and contains only alphabetic characters. To retrieve names like "A-Po" and "L'to," you'll need to try this type of strategy:

```
SQL:
select au_fname
from authors
where au_fname like '_ _ _ _'

Results:
au_fname
------------------
Dick
Burt
Dirk
Anne
```

The underscore (_) matches *any* character. However, the results of the query will depend on how your database is implemented; it may also retrieve names with fewer than four characters, so that the results look like this:

```
Results:
au_fname
------------------
Anne
Dirk
Dick
Ann
Burt
```

This occurs when two strings are compared, and the shorter string is conceptually padded with blanks to equal the longer one. To avoid potential ambiguity, use code similar to the following where the caret (^) is a negative, so [^] means "not a space":

```
SQL:
select au_fname
from authors
where au_fname like '[^ ][^ ][^ ][^ ]'
```

```
Results:
au_fname
------------------
Anne
Dirk
Dick
Burt
```

Now you'll have a list in which each name is made up of four nonspace characters. It does not include three-letter names or names of three letters and a space.

What about all the authors whose names are *not* four characters long? One solution is just the reverse of the previous one:

```
SQL:
select au_fname
from authors
where au_fname not like '[^ ][^ ][^ ][^ ]'
```

From the *bookbiz* database, nineteen rows are returned.

Locating Date Data

Date data can be hard to retrieve because of the variety of possible ways it can be stored. In Transact-SQL, date fields include the month, day, year, and time of day (the first three fields can be displayed in a number of ways).

This presents some problems in matching the time part of the field. One example is a query like this:

```
SQL:

select price, pubdate
from titles
where pubdate = 'Oct 21 1985'
```

```
Results:

price        pubdate
-----        ---------
21.59        Oct 21 1985 12:00AM
20.95        Oct 21 1985 12:00AM
```

This query will find records with a date of October 21, 1985, and a time of 12:00 A.M. To get all records from *any* time on that date, you must add some more code. To test the solutions, first change one of the dates:

```
SQL:

update titles
set pubdate = 'Oct 21 1985 2:30PM'
where pubdate = 'Oct 21 1985' and price = 20.95
update titles
```

Now the query returns only one row:

```
SQL:

select price, pubdate
from titles
where pubdate = 'Oct 21 1985'
```

```
Results:

price        pubdate
-----        ---------
21.59        Oct 21 1985 12:00AM
```

One simple method for finding all rows entered on one day is to spell out the full minimum and maximum time values for the day and use BETWEEN to find everything within those parameters:

SQL:
```
select price, pubdate
from titles
where pubdate
    between 'Oct 21 1985 00:00'
        and 'Oct 21 1985 23:59'
```

Results:
```
price        pubdate
-----        ---------
21.59        Oct 21 1985 12:00AM
20.95        Oct 21 1985  2:30PM
```

Another idea is to use the keyword LIKE to find everything that matches the known part of the date. Here, the percent sign (%) wildcard stands for whatever follows the month, day, and year part of the date:

SQL:
```
select price, pubdate
from titles
where pubdate like 'Oct 21 1985%'
```

You could also use CONVERT to change the date into a shorter character string and search for the string:

SQL:
```
select price, pubdate
from titles
where convert(char(11), pubdate) = 'Oct 21 1985'
```

A different approach involves date functions. Check to see what your system provides. This example uses DATEPART, a function that matches each known part (month, day, and year) of the full date value against its numeric representation (October is 10). The time part of the date becomes irrelevant. The syntax is this:

```
DATEPART (datepart, date)
```

Here's how the query looks:

```
SQL:
select price, pubdate
from titles
where datepart(mm, pubdate) = 10 and
    datepart(dd, pubdate) = 21 and
    datepart(yy, pubdate) = 1985
```

DATEADD is another similar function. Set it up to add one day to the known date. Then you can retrieve all the data between the parameters without worrying about the time, as shown in the following example.

```
SQL:
select price, pubdate
from titles
where pubdate between 'Oct 21 1985' and
    dateadd(day, 1, 'Oct 21 1985')
```

This finds all records with a date between 10/21/85 and one day later, 10/22/85.

Changing Spaces into Nulls

You may set up a table to allow nulls when a value is missing or unknown. Other users less knowledgeable in relational quirks may circumvent your intention by carefully typing spaces instead of letting the database insert NULL. The result is dirty data: strings of blanks in some places, nulls in others. If the only correct answer is either meaningful data or NULL, you need to convert those strings of spaces to nulls.

In the long run, you have to figure out a way to enforce your business rules. This may mean using rules, triggers, or front-end checkers to prevent spaces where you want nulls. In the short run, you need to do something about the spaces.

For example, someone has added two new writers to the *authors* table. The names and identification numbers are fine, but the phone and address information is incomplete: just strings of blanks. (All the address fields—*city*, *state*, and *zip*—and *phone* allow nulls.)

If you'd like to follow the example on your database, insert these two rows into the *authors* table:

```
SQL:
insert authors
values('123-45-6789', 'Wu', 'Amelia', ' ',
    ' ',' ',' ',     ')
insert authors
values('123-54-6789', 'Khandasamy', ' J.', ' ',
    ' ',' ',' ',     ')
```

A SELECT of first name, phone, and address fields (shortened with SUB-STRING for readability) returns results like these:

```
Results:
au_fname    phone   address   city    state   zip
--------    -----   -------   ----    -----   ---
Amelia
   J.
```

How do you make these rows consistent with the rest of the table and show NULL where the information is missing or unknown? In Sybase Transact-SQL, the RTRIM function removes trailing (right-hand) blanks. When there is nothing in the field but blanks, and the field allows NULL, RTRIM removes the spaces, and the system (abhorring a vacuum) inserts a NULL. Its syntax is this:

```
RTRIM (char_expression)
```

Check your system to determine whether you have a similar function, and whether it handles NULL in the same way (not all systems do).

Here's how an UPDATE statement with (this kind of) RTRIM looks:

```
SQL:
update authors
set phone = rtrim(phone),
    address = rtrim(address),
    city = rtrim(city),
```

```
      state = rtrim(state),
      zip = rtrim(zip)
where au_id like '123%'
```

This query produces the following results:

```
SQL:

select au_fname, phone, address, city, state, zip
from authors
where au_id like '123%'
```

```
Results:

au_fname    phone    address   city    state    zip
--------    -----    -------   ----    -----    ---
Amelia      NULL     NULL      NULL    NULL     NULL
   J.       NULL     NULL      NULL    NULL     NULL
```

If the fields you trim down to nothing don't allow NULL, the system won't insert NULL and will give an error message—but that's a different problem. This example assumes you're set up for NULL.

To tidy all your space-filled data as you convert blank fields, use LTRIM to remove leading (left-hand) spaces while RTRIM removes trailing ones. (LTRIM's syntax is identical to RTRIM's.) For example, Mr. Khandasamy's first name ("J.") was inserted into the table with two leading blanks. You can remove them by adding these lines:

```
SQL:

update authors
set au_fname = ltrim(au_fname)
```

The results show that both of the new first names are lined up on the left with no leading blanks:

```
SQL:

select au_fname, phone, address, city, state, zip
from authors
where au_id like '123%'
```

```
Results:
au_fname    phone    address    city    state    zip
--------    -----    -------    ----    -----    ---
Amelia      NULL     NULL       NULL    NULL     NULL
J.          NULL     NULL       NULL    NULL     NULL
```

Here's how you'd combine stripping meaningful data of unnecessary spaces and converting blank strings into nulls:

```
SQL:
update authors
set au_fname = rtrim(ltrim(au_fname)),
    phone = rtrim(ltrim(phone)),
    address = rtrim(ltrim(address)),
    city = rtrim(ltrim(city)),
    state = rtrim(ltrim(state)),
    zip = rtrim(ltrim(zip))
```

Before continuing, remove the two rows you added to *authors* with a DELETE statement:

```
SQL:
delete authors
where au_id like '123%'
```

FINDING DATA WITH COMPLEX JOINS AND SUBQUERIES

This section contains more query hints, the uniting theme of which is the use of more complex joins and subqueries. Here you'll find code for these contexts:

- Matching pairs of fields in different tables (using an outer join or a subquery)
- Finding rows within a range, when you know neither the top nor the bottom value (with and without subqueries)
- Displaying data in spreadsheet format (with correlated subqueries in the SELECT clause)

Matching Column Pairs in Different Tables

In two tables with similar data (such as the *city* and *state* fields in the *authors* and *publishers* tables), how do you find out if column pairs in one table occur at least once as pairs in the other?

This kind of code is handy when you perform integrity checks on data after you copy it from one table to another, or when you store subsets of a large table in separate smaller tables for efficient retrievals.

Here is a method that uses the outer join. As you'll recall, an outer join can be left (*=) or right (=*). A left outer join displays all of the selected fields in the first table in the join but only the matching fields in the second. A right outer join does the opposite: it shows the matching fields in the first table and all the selected fields in the second. An easy way to remember this is that the asterisk (*) stands for everything, so the table with the same position as the asterisk in the join (right or left) is the one that gives full results. Outer join results are very easy to scan visually.

```
SQL:
select authors.city acity, authors.state astate,
    publishers.city  pcity, publishers.state
      pstate
from authors, publishers
where authors.city *= publishers.city
    and authors.state *= publishers.state
```

```
Results:
```

acity	astate	pcity	pstate
Menlo Park	CA	NULL	NULL
Berkeley	CA	Berkeley	CA
San Jose	CA	NULL	NULL
Oakland	CA	NULL	NULL
Lawrence	KS	NULL	NULL
Berkeley	CA	Berkeley	CA
Palo Alto	CA	NULL	NULL
Covelo	CA	NULL	NULL
San Francisco	CA	NULL	NULL
Nashville	TN	NULL	NULL
Corvallis	OR	NULL	NULL
Walnut Creek	CA	NULL	NULL

```
Ann Arbor        MI      NULL        NULL
Gary             IN      NULL        NULL
Oakland          CA      NULL        NULL
Oakland          CA      NULL        NULL
Oakland          CA      NULL        NULL
Rockville        MD      NULL        NULL
Palo Alto        CA      NULL        NULL
Vacaville        CA      NULL        NULL
Salt Lake City   CA      NULL        NULL
Salt Lake City   CA      NULL        NULL
```

Another method, using EXISTS, locates the same information: Which *authors* city/state pairs also appear in *publishers*?

```
SQL:
select authors.city, authors.state
from authors
where exists
    (select *
    from publishers
    where publishers.city = authors.city
    and publishers.state = authors.state)
```

```
Results:
city            state
--------------  -----
Berkeley        CA
Berkeley        CA
```

To see the *authors* pairs that don't appear in *publishers*, use NOT EXISTS.

Finding Data within a Range When You Don't Know the Values

To find all the books with prices between $7.00 and $10.95, you can run a query like this:

```
SQL:
select title, title_id, price
from titles
where price between 7.00 and 10.95

Results:
title                title_id     price
------------------   --------     -----
Is Anger the Enemy?  PS2091       10.95
Life Without Fear    PS2106        7.00
Emotional Security   PS7777        7.99
```

If you want to see all books with prices between those of two particular books, but you don't know the prices of the books, try something like this:

```
SQL:
select title, title_id, price
from titles
where price between
   (select price
    from titles
    where title like 'Life Without%')
and
    select price
    from titles
    where title like 'Is Anger%')
```

As long as you put the book with the lower price first in the BETWEEN clause, you're fine. But if you put them in higher-to-lower order (not knowing what the prices are), you'll get zero rows returned or an error message. One way to avoid this possibility is to use an OR and include both combinations:

```
SQL:
select title, title_id, price
from titles
where price between
    (select price
     from titles
     where title like 'Life Without%')
```

```
    and
    (select price
    from titles
    where title like 'Is Anger%')
or price between
    (select price
    from titles
    where title like 'Is Anger%')
    and
    (select price
    from titles
    where title like 'Life Without%')
```

Another way to cover both cases is to find the minimum and maximum prices. As a variant, you can use the identification numbers of the books instead of the titles:

SQL:
```
select title, title_id, price
from titles
where price between
    (select min(price)
    from titles
    where title_id in ('PS2106', 'PS2091'))
and
    (select max(price)
    from titles
    where title_id in ('PS2106', 'PS2091'))
```

Without subqueries, the code is something like this:

SQL:
```
select t1.title, t1.title_id, t1.price
from titles t1, titles life, titles anger
where life.title like 'Life%'
    and anger.title like 'Is Anger%'
    and (t1.price between life.price and
    anger.price or t1.price between
        anger.price and life.price)
```

You would include the OR clause because you don't know which price is higher. The parentheses ensure that the OR works correctly: they are needed to limit the rows returned since there are no joins in this three-table query.

Displaying Data in Spreadsheet Format

Although this query could also appear in the format section, it includes a unique use of multiple correlated subqueries in the SELECT clause to generate a spreadsheet-like display.

The *titleauthors* table connects authors and titles. Because each book can have single or multiple authors, the table contains twenty-five rows for seventeen books: one row for each author-title combination. Ten books have one author, six books have two authors, and one book has three authors.

To display *title_id* with first and second authors in one row, try this correlated subquery:

```
SQL:
select distinct title_id,
(select au_id
        from titleauthors
        where au_ord = 1 and title_id = t.title_id) as au1,
(select au_id
        from titleauthors
        where au_ord = 2 and title_id = t.title_id) as au2
from titleauthors t
```

This query produces the following results:

```
Results:
title_id au1          au2
-------- ----------- ----------
BU2075   213-46-8915 NULL
BU7832   274-80-9391 NULL
MC2222   712-45-1867 NULL
PC1035   238-95-7766 NULL
PC9999   486-29-1786 NULL
PS2106   998-72-3567 NULL
```

```
PS3333    172-32-1176 NULL
PS7777    486-29-1786 NULL
TC3218    807-91-6654 NULL
TC4203    648-92-1872 NULL
BU1032    409-56-7008 213-46-8915
BU1111    724-80-9391 267-41-2394
MC3021    722-51-5454 899-46-2035
PC8888    427-17-2319 846-92-7186
PS1372    756-30-7391 724-80-9391
PS2091    998-72-3567 899-46-2035
TC7777    672-71-3249 267-41-2394
```

Depending on how your implementation handles this kind of subquery, you may find that you don't need DISTINCT.

You can display the one row with three authors by adding a third correlated subquery to the SELECT clause:

SQL:

```
select distinct title_id,
    (select au_id
        from titleauthors
        where au_ord = 1 and title_id = t.title_id) as au1,
    (select au_id
        from titleauthors
        where au_ord = 2 and title_id = t.title_id) as au2,
    (select au_id
        from titleauthors
        where au_ord = 3 and title_id = t.title_id) as au3
from titleauthors t
```

Results:

```
title_id au1          au2           au3
-------- -----------  -----------   -----------
BU2075   213-46-8915 NULL          NULL
BU7832   274-80-9391 NULL          NULL
MC2222   712-45-1867 NULL          NULL
PC1035   238-95-7766 NULL          NULL
PC9999   486-29-1786 NULL          NULL
PS2106   998-72-3567 NULL          NULL
PS3333   172-32-1176 NULL          NULL
```

```
PS7777     486-29-1786 NULL          NULL
TC3218     807-91-6654 NULL          NULL
TC4203     648-92-1872 NULL          NULL
BU1032     409-56-7008 213-46-8915 NULL
BU1111     724-80-9391 267-41-2394 NULL
MC3021     722-51-5454 899-46-2035 NULL
PC8888     427-17-2319 846-92-7186 NULL
PS1372     756-30-7391 724-80-9391 NULL
PS2091     998-72-3567 899-46-2035 NULL
TC7777     672-71-3249 267-41-2394 472-27-2349
```

Another way to do this is with a new table and three queries, one each for first, second, and third authors. You can add an annotation like "none" when the cell is empty. This example uses a temporary table, but it could be permanent.

```
SQL:
create table #au_order
(title_id char(6),
au1 char(11),
au2 char(11),
au3 char(11))
```

First, use INSERT to add all of the rows with first (or only) authors:

```
SQL:
insert #au_order
select title_id, au_id, 'none', 'none'
from titleauthors
where au_ord = 1
```

Here is what a SELECT performed on the table would produce:

```
Results:
title_id    au1           au2           au3
--------    ----------    ----------    -----------
PS3333      172-32-1176 none          none
BU2075      213-46-8915 none          none
PC1035      238-95-7766 none          none
BU7832      274-89-9391 none          none
```

```
PC9999      486-29-1786 none        none
PS7777      486-29-1786 none        none
TC4023      648-92-1872 none        none
MC2222      712-45-1867 none        none
TC3218      807-91-6654 none        none
PS2106      998-72-3567 none        none
BU1032      409-56-7008 none        none
BU1111      724-80-9391 none        none
MC3021      722-80-9391 none        none
PC8888      427-17-2319 none        none
PS1372      756-30-7391 none        none
PS2091      998-72-3567 none        none
TC7777      672-71-3249 none        none
```

In all, there are seventeen rows, each with an *au_id* in the first author column, and *none* in the second and third author columns.

Now, update the *#au_order* table with the values for the second author column:

SQL:

```
update #au_order
set au2 = au_id
from titleauthors
where au_ord = 2
    and titleauthors.title_id = #au_order.title_id
```

Seven rows are changed:

Results:

```
title_id au1          au2          au3
-------- ------------ ------------ ------------
PS3333   172-32-1176 none         none
BU2075   213-46-8915 none         none
PC1035   238-95-7766 none         none
BU7832   274-80-9391 none         none
PC9999   486-29-1786 none         none
PS7777   486-29-1786 none         none
TC4203   648-92-1872 none         none
MC2222   712-45-1867 none         none
TC3218   807-91-6654 none         none
```

```
PS2106    998-72-3567  none        none
BU1032    409-56-7008  213-46-8915 none
BU1111    724-80-9391  267-41-2394 none
TC7777    672-71-3249  267-41-2394 none
PS1372    756-30-7391  724-80-9391 none
PC8888    427-17-2319  846-92-7186 none
MC3021    722-51-5454  899-46-2035 none
PS2091    998-72-3567  899-46-2035 none
```

Finally, to fill in the third author cell, use an UPDATE:

```
SQL:
update #au_order
set au3 = au_id
from titleauthors
where au_ord = 3
      and titleauthors.title_id = #au_order.title_id
```

A query of *#au_order* shows the complete results:

```
SQL:
select *
from #au_order

Results:
title_id au1         au2          au3
-------- ----------- ------------ -----------
PS3333   172-32-1176 none         none
BU2075   213-46-8915 none         none
PC1035   238-95-7766 none         none
BU7832   274-80-9391 none         none
PC9999   486-29-1786 none         none
PS7777   486-29-1786 none         none
TC4203   648-92-1872 none         none
MC2222   712-45-1867 none         none
TC3218   807-91-6654 none         none
PS2106   998-72-3567 none         none
BU1032   409-56-7008 213-46-8915  none
BU1111   724-80-9391 267-41-2394  none
PS1372   756-30-7391 724-80-9391  none
```

```
PC8888    427-17-2319 846-92-7186 none
MC3021    722-51-5454 899-46-2035 none
PS2091    998-72-3567 899-46-2035 none
TC7777    672-71-3249 267-41-2394 472-27-2349
```

GROUP BY

GROUP BY generates so many misunderstandings that most of the examples from the Internet are in the next chapter, "Mistakes and How to Avoid Them." There you'll find a full treatment of GROUP BY and its companion, HAVING. This section includes only one code segment. It concerns using GROUP BY to retrieve data by time units.

Displaying Data by Time Units

GROUP BY is the answer to this interesting problem: How do you get statistics on event per time unit? For example, what is the distribution by month of books published during the year? Check your vendor for functions similar to DATEPART, which displays a specified date part, such as month, or year, for a complete date.

```
SQL:
select datepart(month, pubdate), count(title_id)
from titles
group by datepart(month, pubdate)
```

The results show a cluster of books published during the sixth month:

```
Results:
---------- ----------
NULL       2
6          13
10         3
```

For readability, add column names:

```
SQL:
select datepart(month, pubdate) as month#,
  count(title_id) as books
from titles
group by datepart(month, pubdate)
```

```
Results:
month#      books
----------  ----------
NULL        2
6           13
10          3
```

SEQUENTIAL NUMBERS

Sequential numbers serve many important functions: consider their value in tracking invoices, ordering checks, and identifying employees. But because sequential numbers deal with complex issues such as indexes and locking, the best way to produce and use them is not obvious.

Some database vendors provide this capability. Oracle has the Sequencer facility, Informix has a SERIAL datatype, Sybase and Microsoft have the IDENTITY property.

If your database system doesn't have an auto-numbering capability, or it isn't appropriate for your application, there are a number of other techniques at your disposal.

In this section, you'll explore some of the possible ways to add serial numbers to the *sonum* field. They include finding the current maximum *sonum* value and adding 1, and storing the maximum value in a separate table. You'll also look at one alternative to serial numbers—using a unique random value.

For simplicity, all of the following examples use *sonum* in the first five rows of the *sales* table. If you want to follow along, first delete all *sales* rows with *sonum* higher than 5. (You can store the rows in another table or put them into a script if you think you'll want to re-create the original table later.)

```
SQL:
delete
from sales
where sonum > 5
```

Here's how the data looks:

```
SQL:
select * from sales
```

```
Results:
sonum    stor_id ponum        date
-----    ------- -----        -----
    1    7066    QA7442.3     Sep 13 1985 12:00AM
    2    7067    D4482        Sep 14 1985 12:00AM
    3    7131    N914008      Sep 14 1985 12:00AM
    4    7131    N914014      Sep 14 1985 12:00AM
    5    8042    423LL922     Sep 14 1985 12:00AM
```

Finding the Maximum Value and Adding 1

The most intuitive solution is to find the current maximum value, add 1 to it, and insert the result into the *sales* table:

```
SQL:
insert sales
    select max(sonum) + 1,'8042','66', 'Apr 22 1993'
    from sales
```

Now the data looks like this:

```
SQL:
select *
from sales
```

```
Results:
sonum    stor_id ponum        date
-----    ------- -----        -----
    1    7066    QA7442.3     Sep 13 1985 12:00AM
    2    7067    D4482        Sep 14 1985 12:00AM
    3    7131    N914008      Sep 14 1985 12:00AM
    4    7131    N914014      Sep 14 1985 12:00AM
    5    8042    423LL922     Sep 14 1985 12:00AM
    6    8042    66           Apr 22 1993 12:00AM
```

This approach works fine for simple applications. It's another story, though, if you have a lot of concurrent users. How do you prevent two people from accessing the table at the same time? A unique index on *sonum* helps, but there is a performance cost.

One way to increase your chances of success is by putting the INSERT into a transaction:

```
SQL:
begin transaction
insert sales
    select max(sonum) + 1,'8042','66','Apr 22 1993'
    from sales
commit transaction
```

If your database system provides a user-controlled locking mechanism such as Transact-SQL's HOLDLOCK, experiment with it. It may provide additional protection from the possibility of generating duplicate keys when the database is under heavy use.

```
SQL:
begin transaction
insert sales
    select max(sonum) + 1,'8042', '66','Apr 22 1993'
    from sales holdlock
commit transaction
```

Conflict from two or more users is still possible. Depending on how your system is set up, you may need to write code to handle errors and deadlock.

Using a Separate Key Table

Another technique is to use a separate table to store the maximum value of the sequential field (in this case *sonum*). This lessens contention for the table lock and the danger of deadlock. First create a table to hold the current maximum sequential number:

```
SQL:
create table maxnum
(sonum int)
```

Since you'll be updating the table (changing the existing values), you need to initialize it with some value, such as 1:

SQL:
```
insert maxnum
values(1)
```

Results:
```
select *
from maxnum

sonum
-----------
          1
```

Now you can use a transaction to find the highest *sonum* in *sales*, store the value in *maxnum*, and then update *sales* (queries are included only to show the contents of the two tables during the process):

SQL:
```
begin transaction
  insert maxnum
        select  max(sonum) + 1
        from sales
  insert sales
        select max(maxnum.sonum), 'test', 'test',
              'May 1 1993'
        from maxnum
  select * from sales
commit transaction
```

Results:
```
sonum
-----------
          7

sonum    stor_id ponum      date
-----    ------- -----      -----
    1    7066    QA7442.3   Sep 13 1985 12:00AM
```

```
2    7067    D4482        Sep 14 1985 12:00AM
3    7131    N914008      Sep 14 1985 12:00AM
4    7131    N914014      Sep 14 1985 12:00AM
5    8042    423LL922     Sep 14 1985 12:00AM
6    8042    66           Apr 22 1993 12:00AM
7    test    test         May  1 1993 12:00AM
```

Using a Random Value

Both of the previous methods—retrieving *max(sonum)* from the target table and getting the value from a separate key table—have drawbacks. The first, as noted, can lead to contention among users. The second can become a bottleneck: Each INSERT needs an INSERT, SELECT, and INSERT. Your database now has a "hot spot" that may be hard to work around in a high-concurrency environment.

You can avoid this problem by using a random value, such as the date and time. If your system provides a timestamp, it may be just what you need. Another approach is the generated number: insert results from a formula that calculates a random and unique value.

The random approach has its own problems:

- If you really need a serial number, it won't meet your needs.
- Sorting may be costly, because the data is not ordered.

When you plan to generate unique identification numbers, weigh the various drawbacks against your application needs.

AVOIDING MISTAKES

The next chapter also uses material from the Internet. It contains some common mistakes, with explanations of why they occur and suggestions on work-arounds.

Chapter 12

Mistakes and How to Avoid Them

NO, YOU'RE *NOT* STUPID

SQL is an unusual computer language: it's not just for experts. There are still relatively few SQL mavens. Many users, in fact, are really C programmers, or accountants, or technical marketing whizzes. They pick up SQL on their own and learn by doing. They develop some skill but remain only occasional users. When they hit a snag, they don't have the luxury of appealing to a nearby guru, so they often turn to fellow users on the Internet.

Let's face it: SQL can be confusing. The code samples in this chapter, as in the previous one, are based on real-life problems submitted via the Internet, transposed to work on the now-familiar *bookbiz* database. But in this case they aren't examples to follow or copy—they are illustrations of common misuses and misunderstandings.

Interestingly, the same topics come up repeatedly:

- Using GROUP BY to count elements
- Confusion about when to use WHERE and HAVING
- Uncertainty about how to use DISTINCT with columns and aggregates
- Misunderstandings of what SQL can do

If you have a practical orientation to learning, you'll find it useful to look at these examples of mistakes that users often make, and to study the explanations of correct approaches. But rest assured: You're not alone. Judging by the volume on the Internet, many competent SQL programmers have problems in these areas, and they're not afraid to ask for help.

This chapter doesn't contain complete explanations or full syntax diagrams. Refer to earlier parts of the book and to your vendor's manuals when you encounter a topic for which you need more detailed information.

GROUP BY

GROUP BY is a mature element in SQL grammar. Nonetheless, many users seem unaware of it, and go through complex gyrations to calculate the number of elements that belong to given categories. Although some users simply forget that GROUP BY exists, others get confused by the many constraints connected to it or by dialectical differences in what is allowed.

Counting by Units

One anguished Internetter asked for help with the following problem. The code for finding the number of titles associated with a particular publisher was easy:

```
SQL:
select count(*)
from titles
where pub_id = '1389'

Results:

-----------
          6
```

But finding the count for each publisher was more difficult. The sample (unsuccessful) code attempts included variables, WHILE loops, transactions, and DISTINCT.

A number of helpful readers suggested strategies similar to this one:

```
SQL:
select pub_id, count(*)
from titles
group by pub_id
```

```
Results:
pub_id
------ ----------
0736   6
0877   6
1389   6
```

GROUP BY organizes the data into sets. COUNT(*) gives a summary value per set.

WHERE AND HAVING

WHERE and HAVING interactions are classic causes of confusion, particularly when you use them outside the standard context of a select list containing only aggregates and grouping columns. Here are two examples of common mix-ups:

- WHERE, GROUP BY, and HAVING without aggregates
- WHERE, GROUP BY, and HAVING with mixed aggregates and row values

Why So Many Rows?

Here's the kind of mix-up that appears periodically on the Internet, usually with two plaintive questions:

- Why do the results of this query (if your system will run it) include prices higher than $10.00?

```
SQL:
select price, type
from titles
where price < 10.00
group by type
```

Results:

```
price               type
- - - - - - - - - - - - - - - - - -    - - - - - - - - - - - - -
          19.99  business
          11.95  business
           2.99  business
          19.99  business
          19.99  mod_cook
           2.99  mod_cook
          21.59  psychology
          10.95  psychology
           7.00  psychology
          19.99  psychology
           7.99  psychology
```

• Why does repeating the WHERE condition in a HAVING clause "fix" the results?

SQL:

```
select price, type
from titles
where price < 10.00
group by type
having price < 10.00
```

Results:

```
price               type
- - - - - - - - - - - - - - - - - -    - - - - - - - - - - - - -
           2.99  business
           2.99  mod_cook
           7.00  psychology
           7.99  psychology
```

There is a basic issue here: What does the first query (a *bookbiz* version of one that appeared on the Internet) actually mean? Presumably the second ("correct") answer produces what was sought: a list of prices and types for books costing less than $10.00.

However, you'd get these same results by eliminating the GROUP BY and HAVING clauses from the query:

```
SQL:
select price, type
from titles
where price < 10.00
```

```
Results:
price               type
------------------  --------------
             2.99   business
             2.99   mod_cook
             7.00   psychology
             7.99   psychology
```

In fact, GROUP BY doesn't add anything to the first query. Since you're looking only for row values (individual prices and types), there's no need to form groups. GROUP BY, in the first query, is a mistake.

As you'll recall from previous chapters, GROUP BY is most meaningful when used with aggregates, in which case you'd find a summary value for each group. For example, this is how you'd find the average of books priced below $10.00 by type:

```
SQL:
select avg(price), type
from titles
where price < 10.00
group by type
```

```
Results:
price               type
------------------  --------------
             2.99   business
             2.99   mod_cook
             7.50   psychology
```

The puzzled Internetter may actually have been thinking of something like this. GROUP BY makes sense here, because there is an aggregate in the SELECT clause.

But back to question number one: Why *do* the results include rows with prices higher than $10.00 when it looks as if the WHERE clause should have eliminated them?

If you examine the results of the first and second queries, and those of the one without GROUP BY and HAVING, you should get an inkling of what happened. WHERE found the rows with values below $10.00. They included three types: *business, mod_cook,* and *psychology.* GROUP BY then displayed all the books in each of those groups. When you add an ORDER BY to the query, this is easier to see:

SQL:

```
select price, type
from titles
where price < 10.00
group by type
order by type
```

Results:

```
price               type
- - - - - - - - - - - - - - - - -   - - - - - - - - - - - - - -
            2.99  business
           11.95  business
           19.99  business
           19.99  business
            2.99  mod_cook
           19.99  mod_cook
            7.00  psychology
            7.99  psychology
           10.95  psychology
           19.99  psychology
           21.59  psychology
```

The query with GROUP BY can be paraphrased as "show me the prices and types of all books in the groups that have one or more books with prices below $10.00." Notice that no *popular_comp* or *trad_cook* rows appear in the results. There are no books from either group that cost under $10.00.

Since there are no aggregates in the select list, each qualifying row is displayed, rather than one row for each group's summary values.

Now on to the second question: Why does repeating the WHERE condition in a HAVING clause "fix" the results? First, WHERE finds the cheap books, and then GROUP BY fills in all the books in the groups that have one or more cheap books. Finally, HAVING selects the under-$10.00 values in that list. Since the WHERE and HAVING conditions are identical, you end up with the same four rows in the query with WHERE only and in the one that includes WHERE, GROUP BY, and HAVING. You might say that HAVING in this particular query "cancels" the GROUP BY effects.

Changing the HAVING value makes the process clearer:

```
SQL:
select price, type
from titles
where price < 10.00
group by type
having price > 20.00
```

```
Results:
price                type
- - - - - - - - - - - - - - - - - -  - - - - - - - - - - - - -
            21.59  psychology
```

After WHERE qualifies the rows and GROUP BY sets up the groups, HAVING makes the final cut. As you saw earlier, WHERE and GROUP BY together show eleven rows. HAVING eliminates all of them but the one row that has a price greater than $20.00. Since the WHERE and HAVING conditions are different, the query with HAVING finds different rows from the query with WHERE only.

Actually, in this particular query, with its unusual use of GROUP BY, a query with HAVING alone will produce the same results as a query with WHERE alone or with both WHERE and HAVING.

```
SQL:
select price, type
from titles
group by type
having price < 10.00
```

```
Results:
price                type
- - - - - - - - - - - - - - - - - -  - - - - - - - - - - - - -
             2.99  business
             2.99  mod_cook
             7.00  psychology
             7.99  psychology
```

In fact, your implementation may not allow HAVING without GROUP BY. Check your vendor's documents for more specifics about using GROUP BY and HAVING.

The best way to avoid these kinds of puzzling results is to carefully analyze what you are trying to accomplish with a query. It may turn out (as in this case) that GROUP BY is unnecessary.

Mixed Aggregate and Row Values

Here's another situation with GROUP BY and HAVING. As you'll recall, there are some stringent limitations on what is permitted in a select list when you use GROUP BY. You're generally restricted to the columns you are using for grouping and those for which you're calculating group summary (aggregate) values. The output shows the group and the aggregate value per group.

Some systems have extensions that permit additional columns or expressions in the select list—values that are neither groups nor aggregate functions. This section examines issues that can arise when you're working with such combinations of group and row values. If your system doesn't support these features, skip to "Avoiding HAVING Problems."

Here's a question that pops up all the time: How do you find the summary value of a particular column for each group, and then print out other columns from the rows containing that summary value?

As a starting point, here's a *bookbiz* version of the query, shaved down to find only the minimum price (summary value) per type (group):

```
SQL:
select type, min(price) as minprice
from titles
where type is not null
group by type
order by type
```

```
Results:
type            minprice
-----------     ----------
business            2.99
mod_cook            2.99
popular_comp       20.00
psychology          7.00
trad_cook          11.95
```

One common strategy for getting both summary and row values involves adding a nongrouping, nonaggregate column such as *title_id* (unique to each row) to the select list:

SQL:

```
select type, min(price) as minprice, title_id
from titles
where type is not null
group by type
order by type
```

Results:

type	minprice	title_id
business	2.99	BU1032
business	2.99	BU1111
business	2.99	BU2075
business	2.99	BU7832
mod_cook	2.99	MC2222
mod_cook	2.99	MC3021
popular_comp	20.00	PC1035
popular_comp	20.00	PC8888
popular_comp	20.00	PC9999
psychology	7.00	PS1372
psychology	7.00	PS2091
psychology	7.00	PS2106
psychology	7.00	PS3333
psychology	7.00	PS7777
trad_cook	11.95	TC3218
trad_cook	11.95	TC4203
trad_cook	11.95	TC7777

But this isn't what you want. It shows the groups, the minimum price for each group, and the book identification numbers, but not in a useful way. You can't find the identification numbers of the books that have the minimum price in each group in these results.

A fuller listing of the query, showing price as well as minimum price, puts you on the right track:

SQL:

```
select type, min(price) as minprice, price,
    title_id
from titles
where type is not null
group by type
order by type
```

Results:

type	minprice	price	title_id
business	2.99	19.99	BU1032
business	2.99	11.95	BU1111
business	2.99	2.99	BU2075
business	2.99	19.99	BU7832
mod_cook	2.99	19.99	MC2222
mod_cook	2.99	2.99	MC3021
popular_comp	20.00	22.95	PC1035
popular_comp	20.00	20.00	PC8888
popular_comp	20.00	NULL	PC9999
psychology	7.00	21.59	PS1372
psychology	7.00	10.95	PS2091
psychology	7.00	7.00	PS2106
psychology	7.00	19.99	PS3333
psychology	7.00	7.99	PS7777
trad_cook	11.95	20.95	TC3218
trad_cook	11.95	11.95	TC4203
trad_cook	11.95	14.99	TC7777

Now it's clear that what you really want is a display of the row (or rows) in each group in which price and minimum price are the same. You need to use the aggregate in your search condition. WHERE doesn't allow this, but HAVING does: it seems as if you can bring HAVING to the rescue again.

To see the identification numbers for the rows containing the minimum price for each group, try this:

SQL:

```
select type, min(price) as minprice, title_id
from titles
where type is not null
group by type
having price = min(price)
order by type
```

Results:

type	minprice	title_id
business	2.99	BU2075
mod_cook	2.99	MC3021
popular_comp	20.00	PC8888
psychology	7.00	PS2106
trad_cook	11.95	TC4203

Now you have a list of types, the minimum price for each type, and books that have that price.

But remember: this query won't work in all systems. Many do not allow any values in the SELECT statement except GROUP BY columns and aggregate columns. You may find that using *title_id* in this way is not permitted.

You can get the same results with a subquery:

SQL:

```
select type, price, title_id
from titles t
where price =
     (select min(price)
     from titles t2
     where t.type = t2.type
     group by t2.type)
```

Results:

type	price	title_id
business	2.99	BU2075
mod_cook	2.99	MC3021
popular_comp	20.00	PC8888
psychology	7.00	PS2106
trad_cook	11.95	TC4203

Avoiding HAVING Problems

Here are some considerations that may prevent problems with WHERE, GROUP BY, and HAVING combinations.

In queries without aggregates, WHERE restricts rows in the final result:

SQL:

```
select pub_id, type
from titles
group by pub_id, type
order by pub_id, type
```

Results:

```
pub_id  type
------  ----------
0736    business
0736    psychology
0877    NULL
0877    mod_cook
0877    trad_cook
1389    business
1389    popular_comp
```

SQL:

```
select pub_id, type
from titles
where pub_id <> '0877'
group by pub_id, type
order by pub_id, type
```

Results:

```
pub_id  type
------  ----------
0736    business
0736    psychology
1389    business
1389    popular_comp
```

In queries with aggregates, WHERE restricts the rows used in computing aggregates and groups:

SQL:

```
select pub_id, type, max(advance)
from titles
where pub_id <> '0877'
group by pub_id, type
order by pub_id, type
```

Results:

```
pub_id type
------ ------------ ----------------------
0736   business     10125.00
0736   psychology   7000.00
1389   business     5000.00
1389   popular_comp 8000.00
```

With or without aggregates, HAVING restricts the final rows returned:

SQL:

```
select pub_id, type
from titles
where pub_id <> '0877'
group by pub_id, type
having type in ('business', 'psychology')
order by pub_id, type
```

Results:

```
pub_id  type
------  -----------
0736    business
0736    psychology
1389    business
```

SQL:
```
select pub_id, type, max(advance)
from titles
where pub_id <> '0877'
group by pub_id, type
having type in ('business', 'psychology')
order by pub_id, type
```

Results:
```
pub_id  type
------  -----------    ----------
0736    business       10,125.00
0736    psychology      7,000.00
1389    business        5,000.00
```

To limit aggregate values returned, use HAVING. Remember, you can't include aggregates in a WHERE clause.

SQL:
```
select pub_id, type, max(advance)
from titles
where pub_id <> '0877'
group by pub_id, type
having type in ('business', 'psychology') and
    max(advance) > 5000.00
order by pub_id, type
```

Results:
```
pub_id  type
------  -----------    ----------
1389    business       10,125.00
0736    psychology      7,000.00
```

If your system allows columns or expressions in the select list that are neither aggregates nor in the GROUP BY clause, use HAVING to control the results:

SQL:

```
select pub_id, type, maxadv = max(advance), price
from titles
where pub_id <> '0877'
group by pub_id, type
having type in ('business', 'psychology') and
    max(advance) > 5000.00
order by pub_id, type
```

Results:

pub_id	type	maxadv	price
1389	business	10,125.00	2.99
0736	psychology	7,000.00	7.00
0736	psychology	7,000.00	7.99
0736	psychology	7,000.00	10.95
0736	psychology	7,000.00	19.99
0736	psychology	7,000.00	21.59

SQL:

```
select pub_id, type, maxadv = max(advance), price
from titles
where pub_id <> '0877' group by pub_id, type
having type in ('business', 'psychology') and
    max(advance) > 5000.00 and
    advance = max(advance)
order by pub_id, type
```

Results:

pub_id	type	maxadv	price
1389	business	10,125.00	2.99
0736	psychology	7,000.00	21.59

DISTINCT

Given a table with two identifying columns, how do you find all the unique combinations? DISTINCT seems like an obvious answer, but more than one user complained on the Internet of getting nothing but syntax errors or confusing results from what seemed like straightforward DISTINCT queries.

This is probably because DISTINCT occurs in two unique forms: with column names and with aggregates. The syntax of these two cases differs just enough to cloud the occasional user's judgment.

With column names and expressions, you use DISTINCT just once, and it applies to everything that comes after it. It is the first word in the select list and requires no parentheses. When you opt to use DISTINCT this way, you're locked in. You can't specify a non-DISTINCT value for anything in the select list.

But there are exceptions. When you use DISTINCT with an aggregate (AVG, SUM, and so on), it goes inside the aggregate parentheses and applies to the elements in that particular aggregate clause only. In some systems you can use more than one aggregate DISTINCT in a select list.

These two variants are similar enough to instill fear, uncertainty, and doubt. How many DISTINCTs can you use in a select list? Should they or shouldn't they be inside parentheses?

The safest way to avoid errors is to remember that there are really two DISTINCTs.

DISTINCT with Columns and Expressions

Here's an example that may help to clarify the difference between the two DISTINCTs. Let's say you want to look at the distribution of prices and advances in the *titles* table for books costing under $15.00. Getting separate lists of unique prices and unique advances is easy:

```
SQL:
select distinct price
from titles
where price < $15.00
```

Results:
```
price
- - - - - - - - - - - - - - - - - - - - - -
                         2.99
                         7.00
                         7.99
                        10.95
                        11.95
                        14.99
```

SQL:
```
select distinct advance
from titles
where price < 15.00
```

Results:
```
advance
- - - - - - - - - - - - - - - - - - - - - -
                     2,275.00
                     4,000.00
                     5,000.00
                     6,000.00
                     8,000.00
                    10,125.00
                    15,000.00
```

There are six distinct prices and seven different advance amounts.

To find the distinct combinations of these values, resist the temptation to use DISTINCT with each column: DISTINCT must be the first word in the SELECT clause, and it applies to everything after it.

The following query finds the unique combinations of price and advance for books under $15.00:

SQL:
```
select distinct price, advance
from titles
where price < 15.00
```

```
Results:
price                    advance
- - - - - - - - - - - - - - - -      - - - - - - - - - - - - - - - - - - - -
2.99                     10,125.00
2.99                     15,000.00
7.00                      6,000.00
7.99                      4,000.00
10.95                     2,275.00
11.95                     4,000.00
11.95                     5,000.00
14.99                     8,000.00
```

The results show eight different combinations of price and advance. Two prices ($2.99 and $11.95) appear twice, and one advance ($4,000.00) is listed twice.

DISTINCT with Aggregates

Now let's examine how DISTINCT is used in aggregates. More than one SQL neophyte has puzzled over how to get a count of distinct values in a table. The code offered for comment often resembles the following:

```
SQL:
select count(distinct *)
from titles
```

The result is syntax errors.

In this instance, DISTINCT isn't legal with COUNT(*). If you think it through, it's clear why. Since COUNT(*) tallies all rows, there's no way to distinguish which duplicates you're trying to eliminate. Copies of particular column values? Which ones? Copies of duplicate rows?

For a similar reason, DISTINCT doesn't do you much good with MIN or MAX. The minimum (or maximum) value for a column is as distinct as it's going to get.

You could get the answer with these two steps:

```
SQL:
select distinct pub_id
into temp_table
from titles

select count(*)
from temp_table

Results:
----------
          3
```

However, there is an easier way. DISTINCT works fine for counting unique values when you specify the column by name. Here's some code that'll do the job:

```
SQL:
select count(distinct pub_id)
from titles

Results:
----------
          3
```

You use DISTINCT with other aggregates in the same way. To find the average of distinct prices under $15.00, you'd write a query like this:

```
SQL:
select avg(distinct price)
from titles
where price < 15

Results:
-----------------
            9.31
```

If your system permits multiple DISTINCTs with aggregates, you can try this type of maneuver:

```
SQL:

select avg(distinct price),
    avg(distinct advance)
from titles
where price < 15
```

```
Results:

----------------    -----------------------
        9.31                    7,200.00
```

Notice that you use DISTINCT twice, once in each aggregate. If you don't, you're likely to get results of disputable meaning.

DISTINCT and DISTINCT

In some database systems, it's possible to mix the two kinds of DISTINCTs, but be alert! Combining column names and aggregates can be tricky. The mixture may be forbidden by your system unless the column name is a grouping column. Even if this is allowed, the results may not make sense at first examination. Here's an example:

```
SQL:

select distinct price, avg(distinct price)
from titles
where price < 15
```

```
Results:
price
----------------    ----------------------
         NULL                    9.31
         2.99                    9.31
         7.00                    9.31
         7.99                    9.31
        10.95                    9.31
        11.95                    9.31
        14.99                    9.31
        19.99                    9.31
        20.00                    9.31
```

20.95	9.31
21.59	9.31
22.95	9.31

The average of distinct prices ($9.31) is what you expect—it's what you found in the previous query. But why are so many prices returned? Clearly, they were not limited by the WHERE clause conditions.

As you'll recall, when there are aggregates in the select list, the WHERE clause applies to them. You need to add a HAVING clause to control the query as a whole:

SQL:

```
select distinct price, avg(distinct price)
from titles
where price < 15
having price < 15
```

Results:

```
price
----------------  ---------------------
         NULL              9.31
         2.99              9.31
         7.00              9.31
         7.99              9.31
        10.95              9.31
        11.95              9.31
        14.99              9.31
```

Now you have more meaningful results: each unique price under $15.00 and the average of all those prices. However, putting the two together isn't particularly helpful—the display is more confusing than illuminating. It might make sense to keep your DISTINCTs "distinct" and use two separate queries.

OTHER MIX-UPS

This section addresses tasks SQL "should" do, but doesn't. It includes two examples:

- Creating report-style output
- Finding the "first" value

Removing Duplicates

It's true—SQL is *not* a formatting tool. There are some things it just can't do, or can't do without expensive gyrations. Sometimes you simply have to give up and turn your results over to a good report writer. Removing duplicated elements from output to produce a nicely formatted display is one of those cases.

But hope springs eternal: more than one Internet respondent has wondered if there is any SQL method for cleaning up these kinds of results:

```
SQL:
select title_id, authors.au_id
from authors, titleauthors
where authors.au_id = titleauthors.au_id
    and titleauthors.title_id like 'P%'
order by title_id, authors.au_id

Results:
title_id    au_id
--------    -----------
PC1035      238-95-7766
PC8888      427-17-2319
PC8888      846-92-7186
PC9999      486-29-1786
PS1372      724-80-9391
PS1372      756-30-7391
PS2091      899-46-2035
PS2091      998-72-3567
PS2106      998-72-3567
PS3333      172-32-1176
PS7777      486-29-1786
```

Ideally, you'd rather have a display like this:

```
Results:
title_id    au_id
--------    -----------
PC1035      238-95-7766
PC8888      427-17-2319
            846-92-7186
```

```
PC9999         486-29-1786
PS1372         724-80-9391
               756-30-7391
PS2091         899-46-2035
               998-72-3567
PS2106         998-72-3567
PS3333         172-32-1176
               486-29-1786
```

In fact, there's no easy way to construct that display with SQL. Instead, you should turn to a front-end formatter or report writer to reformat the unwieldy results.

Finding the "First" Entry

Here's a problem based on more than a syntax error: it's a misunderstanding of what a relational database can do.

The question, like others in this chapter, is based on mail sent via the Internet. Given a table with a limited number of codes, each possibly having multiple identification entries, the submitter asked, how do you find the *first* entry for each code?

There are a couple of odd things about this question. It implies a built-in order, and it assigns a special status to the first entry for each code. Both of these concepts are foreign to relational databases and hence counter to SQL.

If you find yourself needing to construct such a query, you should probably start by reexamining your database design. Maybe the table is lacking a timestamp or some kind of sequential column that would save information about when or in what order data was entered. Once you add that, you'll be able to find entries in sequence. Without it, you have to make a series of questionable assumptions about what "firstness" means.

Appendix A

Syntax Summary for the SQL
Used in This Book

SYNTAX CONVENTIONS

	Key
BIG	Caps means it's a keyword (command).
MIXed	Caps mixed with lowercase letters means it's a keyword and you can type either the full word or just the part in caps.
little	Lowercase words are variables; supply your own.
{ }	Curly braces mean you must choose at least one of the enclosed options.
[ ]	Brackets mean choosing one or more of the enclosed options is optional.
( )	Parentheses are actually typed as part of the command (unlike curly braces and brackets, which are syntax symbols).
|	The vertical bar means you choose a maximum of one option.
,	The comma means you choose as many options as you like, and separate your choices with commas that you type as part of the command.
. . .	The ellipses mean you can do it again, whatever it was.

FORMATTING

SQL is a free-form language, meaning there are no rules about how many words you can put on a line or where you need to break a line. However, for

readability, all examples and syntax statements in this manual are formatted so that each clause of a statement begins on a new line. Clauses that
have more than one part extend to additional lines, which are indented.

Case

```
SELECT column_name
FROM table_name
WHERE search_conditions
```

In syntax statements in this book, keywords (commands) are in uppercase letters, and identifiers and user-supplied words are in lowercase letters.
Type the keywords just as you see them, disregarding case. (Keywords with
some uppercase and some lowercase letters mean you can use either the
full word or abbreviate by using only the uppercase part of it.)

```
SELECT is the same as Select is the same as select
```

Case is significant for identifiers and user-supplied words.

```
Column_name is not the same as column_name or COLUMN_NAME
```

STATEMENT LIST

The following SQL statements are discussed in *The Practical SQL
Handbook:*

ALTER DATABASE	DROP VIEW
ALTER TABLE	DUMP DATABASE
BEGIN TRANsaction	DUMP TRANsaction
COMMIT TRANsaction	GRANT
CREATE DATABASE	INSERT
CREATE INDEX	LOAD DATABASE
CREATE TABLE	LOAD TRANsaction
CREATE VIEW	REVOKE
DELETE	ROLLBACK TRANsaction
DROP DATABASE	SELECT
DROP INDEX	UPDATE
DROP TABLE	UPDATE STATISTICS

Appendix B

Industry SQL Equivalents

SYNTAX COMPARISON

In this appendix, you'll find the most common SQL commands (CREATE and DROP, SELECT, INSERT, UPDATE, DELETE, GRANT, REVOKE) for Sybase SQL Server, Sybase SQL Anywhere, Microsoft SQL Server, Informix, and Oracle. All of the versions are represented with the syntax conventions described in this book, though in some cases the syntax has been simplified to make the entries easier to read and compare. For example, we shorten all types of expressions (*constant_expression*, *non_aggregate_expression*, and so on) to "expr" and substitute "int" for "integer." In addition, we use a modified object name convention (*db, table, index, column*) instead of the completely qualified form (Sybase *database.owner.table_name* or Informix *db_name@servername;owner.table_name*). Figure B-1 shows how naming conventions compared before we stripped them down and reduced object names to their simplest forms.

Sybase SQL Server	[[db_name.]owner.]table_name.
SQL Anywhere	[creator.]table_name
Microsoft SQL Server	[[db_name.]owner.]table_name.
Informix	[[db_name[@servername];]owner.]table_name
Oracle	[user.]table

Figure B-1. Naming Conventions

Where various forms of a command are available, we have chosen the one identified as basic SQL. You'll notice that command syntax, overall, is very similar. However, there are some caveats to keep in mind when reviewing this list:

- Not all vendors offer every item in even this basic set.
- There are some differences in options in those commands that are universally present.
- There may be underlying semantic content that makes two apparently identical commands rather different in meaning (for example, the definitions of terms such as *subselect* or *expression* for particular vendors).
- Vendors do modify existing SQL commands and add new ones as they refine their products; items on this list may not represent the latest version.

In short, this appendix can help you get an idea of the similarities and differences among vendors, but you should consult your system manuals for exact, up-to-date information.

DATA DEFINITION

These commands deal with creating and dropping databases, specifying the active database, and creating and dropping database objects (indexes, tables, and views). Where possible, we've lined up similar clauses for easy comparison.

Database Statements

Most systems have commands for creating and dropping databases, though some use operating system commands.

Sybase SQL Server	Sybase SQL Anywhere	Microsoft SQL Server	Informix	Oracle
CREATE DATABASE db [ON {DEFAULT | dev} [= size] [, dev [= size]]..] [LOG ON dev [= size] [, dev [= size]]...] [WITH OVERRIDE] [FOR LOAD]	initialization utility	CREATE DATABASE db [ON {DEFAULT | dev} [= size] [, dev [= size]]..] [LOG ON dev [= size] [, dev [= size]]...] [FOR LOAD]	CREATE DATABASE db [IN dbspace] [WITH LOG IN 'pathname' [MODE ANSI]] [WITH { [BUFFERED] LOG | | LOG MODE ANSI }]	CREATE DATABASE [db] [CONTROLFILE REUSE] [LOGFILE [GROUP int] file_definition [, [GROUP int] file_def]...] [MAXLOGFILES int] [MAXLOGMEMBERS] int] [MAXLOGHISTORY] integer] [DATAFILE file_def [, file_def]...] [AUTOEXTEND file_def [, file_def] [ON | OFF] [NEXT int [K | M]]] [MAXSIZ [UNLIMITED | int [K | M]]]] [MAXDATAFILES int] [MAXINSTANCES int] [ARCHIVELOG | NOARCHIVELOG] [EXCLUSIVE] [CHARACTER SET charset]
USE db	CONNECT [TO engine] [DATABASE db] [AS connection] [USER] userid IDENTI-FIED BY password	USE db	DATABASE db [EXCLUSIVE]	CONNECT user[/pass-word] [@db]
DROP DATABASE db [,db]...	erase utility	DROP DATABASE db [,db]...	DROP DATABASE db	

Creating and Dropping Database Objects

Database objects include indexes, tables, and views. In the following comparisons, each CREATE statement is followed by its DROP. ALTER TABLE is also included, because you use it to change table constraints. CREATE TABLE syntax is as full as practicable, while ALTER TABLE is abbreviated, using terms such as "column definition" and "constraint definition," since the full syntax is available in the CREATE clause.

Sybase SQL Server	Sybase SQL Anywhere	Microsoft SQL Server	Informix	Oracle
CREATE TABLE table (column datatype [DEFAULT {expr l user l NULL}] [IDENTITY l NULL l NOT NULL] [CONSTRAINT constraint| [{[UNIQUE l PRIMARY KEY} [CLUSTERED l NONCLUS-TERED] [WITH {FILLFACTOR l MAX_ROWS_PER_PAGE}= x] [ON segment] l REFERENCES table [(col-umn)] l CHECK (condition) }]... [, next_column_definition [next_constraint_definition]...]... [[CONSTRAINT constraint| {[UNIQUE l PRIMARY KEY} [CLUSTERED l NONCLUS-TERED] (column [, column]...) [WITH { FILLFACTOR l MAX_ROWS_PER_PAGE}= x] [ON segment] l FOREIGN KEY (column [, column]...) REFERENCES table [column [, column]...) l CHECK (condition) }]...) [WITH MAX_ROWS_PER_PAGE = x] [ON segment]	CREATE [GLOBAL TEMPO-RARY] TABLE table column datatype [NOT NULL] [DEFAULT {string l number l AUTOINCREMENT l CUR-RENT DATE l CURRENT TIME l CURRENT TIMESTAMP l NULL l USER}] [l UNIQUE l PRIMARY KEY l REFERENCES table [(col-umn)] [ON {UPDATE l DELETE} {CASCADE l SET NULL l SET DEFAULT l RESTRICT}] l CHECK (condition) }]... [,next_ column_definition [next_constraint_definition]...]... [l UNIQUE (column [, col-umn|...) l PRIMARY KEY (column [, column|...) l, CHECK (condition) l [NOT NULL] FOREIGN KEY [role] [(col-umn [, column|...)] REFER-ENCES table [column [, col-umn|...]] [[ON {UPDATE l DELETE} {CASCADE l SET NULL l SET DEFAULT l RESTRICT}] [CHECK ON COMMIT] }]]... [IN dbspace] [ON COMMIT DELETE ROWS l ON COMMIT PRE-SERVE ROWS])	CREATE TABLE table (column datatype [NULL l NOT NULL l IDEN-TITY] [(seed, increment)]] [[CONSTRAINT constraint| [DEFAULT {expr l user l NULL} [FOR column] l PRIMARY KEY [CLUSTERED l NONCLUS-TERED] (column) [ON segment] l UNIQUE [CLUSTERED l NONCLUSTERED] (column) [ON segment] l l FOREIGN KEY (column)] REFERENCES table (column)] l CHECK [NOT FOR REPLICATION] (expr)}]... [,next_column_definition [next_constraint_definition]...]... [PRIMARY KEY [CLUSTERED l NONCLUS-TERED] (column [, column]...) [ON segment] l UNIQUE [CLUSTERED l NONCLUSTERED] (column [, column l...) [ON segment] l l FOREIGN KEY (column [, col-umn [, ...)] REFERENCES table[column [, column]...] l CHECK [NOT FOR REPLICATION] (expr)}]...) [ON segment]	CREATE TABLE table (column datatype [DEFAULT {literal l NULL l CURRENT l DATETIME] l USER l TODAY l SITENAME l DBSERVER}] [NOT NULL] [l UNIQUE l PRIMARY KEY l REFERENCES table [(col-umn)] l CHECK (condition) } l CONSTRAINT constraint|]... [, next_column_definition [next_constraint_definition]...]... [l UNIQUE (column [, column ...) l PRIMARY KEY (column [, col-umn l...) l FOREIGN KEY (column [, column]...) REFERENCES table (column [, column]...) l CHECK (condition) } l CONSTRAINT constraint|]...) [storage option]	CREATE TABLE table ({column datatype [DEFAULT { expr}] [CONSTRAINT constraint| [NOT] NULL| {[[UNIQUE l PRIMARY KEY} USING INDEX PCTFREE int| [INTRANS int| MAXTRANS int| [TABLESPACE tablespace] STORAGE storage]]] l REFERENCES table [(col-umn)] l ON DELETE CASCADE| l CHECK (condition)	} l EXCEPTIONS INTO table| [DISABLE]]... [, next_column_definition [next_constraint_definition]...]... [[CONSTRAINT constraint| [NOT] NULL] {[[UNIQUE l PRIMARY KEY} USING INDEX PCTFREE int| [INTRANS int| MAXTRANS int| [TABLESPACE tablespace] STORAGE storage]]] l FOREIGN KEY (column [, column) REFERENCES table [(column [,column]...) l ON DELETE CASCADE| l CHECK (condition)	} l EXCEPTIONS INTO table| [DISABLE]]... [CLUSTER cluster (column [, column]...) [INTRANS int|

Sybase SQL Server	Sybase SQL Anywhere	Microsoft SQL Server	Informix	Oracle
ALTER TABLE table {ADD column datatype [DEFAULT default_definition] [identity | NULL] column_constraint |... | next_column_definition [, column_constraint |...]... | ADD table_constraint | DROP CONSTRAINT constraint | REPLACE column DEFAULT new_default_definition | PARTITION # | UNPARTITION }	ALTER TABLE table {ADD column_definition [column_constraint]... | ADD table-constraint | MODIFY column_definition | MODIFY column DEFAULT default_value | MODIFY column [NOT] NULL | MODIFY column CHECK (condition) | DELETE column | DELETE CHECK | DELETE UNIQUE (column [, column]...) | DELETE PRIMARY KEY | DELETE FOREIGN KEY role | RENAME table | RENAME column TO column}	ALTER TABLE table [WITH NOCHECK] {ADD column_definition [column_constraint]... | next_column_definition [column_constraint]...]... | ADD table_constraint [, table_constraint]... | DROP CONSTRAINT constraint [, constraint]...}	ALTER TABLE {table | synonym} {ADD column_definition [column_constraint]... | next_column_definition [column_constraint]... | DROP column [, column]... | MODIFY column {datatype [NOT NULL]} | DEFAULT default_definition [CONSTRAINT constraint_definition} | ADD CONSTRAINT constraint_definition | CONSTRAINT constraint | DROP CONSTRAINT constraint}	ALTER TABLE table { [ADD ({column_element | table_constraint } [, { column_element | table_constraint}]...)] | [MODIFY (column_element [, column_element]...)] [DROP drop] [PCTFREE int] [PCTUSED int] [INITRANS int] [MAXTRANS int] [STORAGE storage] [ALLOCATE EXTENT ([SIZE int [K|M]] [DATAFILE file] [INSTANCE int] } [ENABLE enable | DISABLE disable] [NOCACHE | CACHE] [PARALLEL | PARALLEL [DEGREE n] [INSTANCES n]] NO
DROP TABLE table [, table]...	DROP TABLE table	DROP TABLE table [, table]...	DROP TABLE {table | synonym}	DROP TABLE table [CASCADE CONSTRAINTS]
CREATE [UNIQUE] [CLUSTERED | NONCLUSTERED] INDEX index ON table (column [, column]...) [WITH {DEFAULT FILLFACTOR PERCENT | MAX_ROWS_PER_PAGE} = x, IGNORE_DUP_KEY, SORTED_DATA, [IGNORE_DUP_ROW | ALLOW_DUP_ROW] [ON segment]	CREATE [UNIQUE] INDEX index ON table (column [ASC | DESC] [, column [ASC | DESC]]...) [IN dbspace]	CREATE [UNIQUE] [CLUSTERED | NONCLUSTERED] INDEX index ON table (column [, column]...) [WITH FILLFACTOR = x, IGNORE_DUP_KEY, {SORTED_DATA | SORTED_DATA_REORG }, {IGNORE_DUP_ROW | ALLOW_DUP_ROW} [ON segment]	CREATE [UNIQUE | DISTINCT] [CLUSTER] INDEX index ON { table | synonym } (column [ASC | DESC] [, column [ASC | DESC]] ...)	CREATE [UNIQUE] INDEX index ON table (column [ASC | DESC] [, column [ASC | DESC]]...) [CLUSTER cluster] [INITRANS int] [MAXTRANS int] [PCTFREE int] [STORAGE storage] [TABLESPACE tablespace] [NOSORT] [NOPARALLEL | PARALLEL [DEGREE n] [INSTANCES n]] [UNRECOVERABLE | RECOVERABLE]
DROP INDEX index [, index]...	DROP INDEX index	DROP INDEX index [, index]...	DROP INDEX index	DROP INDEX index

Sybase SQL Server	Sybase SQL Anywhere	Microsoft SQL Server	Informix	Oracle
CREATE VIEW view	CREATE VIEW view	CREATE VIEW view	CREATE VIEW view	CREATE [OR REPLACE] [FORCE | NOFORCE] VIEW view
[(column [, column]...)]	[(column [, column]...)]	[(column [, column]...)] [WITH ENCRYPTION]	[(column [, column]...)]	[(column [, column]...)]
AS select_subset [WITH CHECK OPTION]	AS select_subset [WITH CHECK OPTION]	AS select_subset [WITH CHECK OPTION]	AS select_subset [WITH CHECK OPTION]	AS select_subset [WITH CHECK OPTION [CON-STRAINT constraint]]
DROP VIEW view [, view]...	DROP VIEW view	DROP VIEW view [, view]...	DROP VIEW view	DROP VIEW view

DATA MANIPULATION

Data manipulation commands include SELECT, INSERT, DELETE, and UPDATE. We've used the term "label" for column and expression headings in the select list to avoid confusion with table aliases in the FROM clause.

Sybase SQL Server	SQL Anywhere	Microsoft SQL Server	Informix	Oracle
SELECT [ALL | DISTINCT] select_list [INTO new_table] FROM { table [alias] [(INDEX index [PREFETCH size][LRU | MRU])] [HOLDLOCK | NOHOLD- LOCK] |SHARED] [, table [alias] [(INDEX index [PREFETCH size][LRU | MRU])] [HOLDLOCK | NOHOLDLOCK|SHARED]]...	SELECT [ALL | DISTINCT] select_list [INTO variable_list] FROM table [alias] [[, table [alias]]... | CROSS JOIN | NATURAL | KEY] JOIN | NATURAL | KEY] INNER JOIN | NATURAL | KEY] LEFT OUTER JOIN | NATURAL | KEY] RIGHT OUTER JOIN} table [alias] [ON condition]]	SELECT [ALL | DISTINCT | select_list [INTO new_ table] FROM table [alias] [({INDEX = {name | id} | NOLOCK | HOLDLOCK | UPDLOCK | TABLOCK |PAGLOCK | TABLOCKX | FASTFIRSTROW }...)] [, table [alias] [({INDEX = {name | id} | NOLOCK | HOLDLOCK | UPDLOCK | TABLOCK | PAGLOCK | TABLOCKX | FASTFIRSTROW }...)]]...	SELECT [ALL | DISTINCT | UNIQUE] select_list [INTO variable_list] FROM {table | synonym } | [AS] alias [, {OUTER} {table | synonym } [[AS] alias]...]	SELECT [ALL | DISTINCT] select_list [INTO variable_list] FROM table [alias]} [, table [alias]]...
[WHERE conditions}	[WHERE conditions]	[WHERE conditions]	[WHERE conditions]	[WHERE conditions] [CONNECT BY condition [START WITH condition]]
[GROUP BY [ALL] {column | expr} [, column | expr]...	[GROUP BY {column | label | function} [, column | label | function] ...]	[GROUP BY [ALL] {column | expr} [, column | expr]...	[GROUP BY {column | position} [, column | position]...]	[GROUP BY {column | expr } [, column| expr}...]
[HAVING conditions]	[HAVING conditions]	[HAVING conditions]	[HAVING conditions]	[HAVING conditions] [{ UNION [ALL] | INTERSECT | MINUS} SELECT...]
[ORDER BY {column | position | expr label} [ASC | DESC] [,{column | position | expr| label} [ASC | DESC]]...] [COMPUTE row_aggregate (col- umn) [, row_aggregate (col- umn)]...] [BY column [, column]...]] [FOR {READ ONLY | UPDATE [OF column_list]}] [AT ISOLATION {READ UNCOMMITTED | READ COMMITTED | SERIALIZ- ABLE }] [FOR BROWSE]	[ORDER BY {column | position | label} [ASC | DESC] [,{column | position | label}] [ASC | DESC]]...]	[ORDER BY {column | position | expr label} [ASC | DESC] [,{column | position| expr| label} [ASC | DESC]]...] [COMPUTE row_aggregate (col- umn) [, row_aggregate (col- umn)]...] [BY column [, column]...]]	[ORDER BY {column | position | label} [ASC | DESC] [,{column | position label} [ASC | DESC]]...] [INTO TEMP temptable [WITH NOLOG]]	[ORDER BY {expr | position | label } [ASC | DESC] [,{expr | position | label} [ASC | DESC]]...]
[FOR BROWSE]		[FOR BROWSE]		[FOR UPDATE [OF {table. | view.}column [, {table. | view.}column]...] [NOWAIT]]

Sybase SQL Server	SQL Anywhere	Microsoft SQL Server	Informix	Oracle
INSERT [INTO] {table	view } [(column_list)] {VALUES (values_list)	 select_statement}	INSERT INTO table [(column_list)] {VALUES ([expr	DEFAULT] [, expr	DEFAULT]...)	 select_statement}	INSERT [INTO] {table	view } [(column_list)] { DEFAULT VALUES 	VALUES {DEFAULT	expr} [, DEFAULT	expr]...	 select_statement}	INSERT INTO {table	view	 synonym} [(column_list)] { VALUES (values_list) 	select_statement 	EXECUTE PROCEDURE procedure [(parameter [, param- eter]...) }	INSERT INTO table [(column_list)] { VALUES (values_list) 	select_statement }
DELETE {[FROM] {table	view} 	FROM {view	table [(INDEX index [PREFETCH size][LRU	MRU])]]} [, { view	table [(INDEX index [PREFETCH size] [LRU	MRU])]]}... } [WHERE conditions]	DELETE [FROM] table [FROM table [, table	...] [WHERE conditions]	DELETE [FROM] {table	view} [WHERE conditions]	DELETE FROM {table	view	 synonym} [WHERE conditions]	DELETE FROM table [alias] [WHERE conditions]
UPDATE { table	view } SET column = {expr	NULL | select_statement } [, column = {expr	NULL	select_statement }]... [FROM {view	table [(INDEX index [PREFETCH size][LRU | MRU])]]} [, [view	table [(INDEX index [PREFETCH size] [LRU | MRU])]]...]...] [WHERE conditions]	UPDATE {table	view } [,{table | view }]... SET column = expr [, column = expr]... [FROM {table	view } [,{table | view }]...] [WHERE conditions] [ORDER BY expr [ASC	DESC] [, expr [ASC	DESC]]...]	UPDATE { table	view } SET column = {expr	NULL | DEFAULT } [, column = {expr | NULL	DEFAULT}]... [FROM {view	table } [, view | table]... [WHERE conditions]	UPDATE {table	view| syn- onym} SET column = {expr | select_statement } [, column = {expr | select_statement }]... [WHERE conditions]	UPDATE table [alias] SET { column = expr [, column = expr]... | (column [, column]...) = (sub- query) } [WHERE conditions]

DATA ADMINISTRATION

Data administration commands include GRANT and REVOKE.

Sybase SQL Server	Sybase SQL Anywhere	Microsoft SQL Server	Informix	Oracle
Object permissions GRANT { ALL [PRIVILEGES] | {SELECT | INSERT | DELETE | UPDATE | REFER-ENCES | EXECUTE} | SELECT | INSERT | DELETE | UPDATE | REFERENCES | EXECUTE]...} ON { table [(column [, column]...)] | view [(column [, column]...)] | procedure } TO { PUBLIC | user [, user]...| role } [WITH GRANT OPTION]	*Object permissions* GRANT { ALL [PRIVILEGES] | { SELECT | INSERT | DELETE | UPDATE [(column [, column]...)] | REFERENCES | ALTER} | SELECT | INSERT | DELETE | UPDATE [(column [, column]...)] | REFERENCES | ALTER]...} ON table TO userid [, userid]... [WITH GRANT OPTION]	*Object permissions* GRANT { ALL | {SELECT | INSERT | DELETE | UPDATE | REFERENCES | EXECUTE} | SELECT | INSERT | DELETE | UPDATE | REFERENCES | EXECUTE]...} ON { table [(column [, col-umn]...)] | view [(column [, column]...)] | procedure | extended-procedure} TO { PUBLIC | user [, user]...}	*Object permissions* GRANT { ALL [PRIVILEGES] | { SELECT [(column [, column]...)] | INSERT | DELETE | UPDATE [(column [, column]...)] | REFERENCES [(column [, column]...)] | ALTER | INDEX} | SELECT [(column [, column]...)] | INSERT | DELETE | UPDATE [(column [, column]...)] | REFERENCES [(column [, column]...)] | ALTER | INDEX]...} ON { table | view | synonym } TO {PUBLIC | user [, user]...} [WITH GRANT OPTION] [AS GRANTOR]	*Object permissions* GRANT {SELECT [(column [, column]...)] | INSERT | DELETE | UPDATE [(column [, column]...)] | REFERENCES [(column [, column]...)] | ALTER | INDEX} [, SELECT [(column [, column]...)] | INSERT | DELETE | UPDATE [(column [, column]...)] | REFERENCES [(column [, column]...)] | ALTER | INDEX]...} ON {table | view | procedure}
Database permissions GRANT { ALL [PRIVILEGES] | CREATE_commands} TO { PUBLIC | user [, user]... | role}	*Database permissions* GRANT {DBA | RESOURCE | GROUP | MEMBERSHIP IN GROUP userid } [DBA | RESOURCE | GROUP | MEMBERSHIP IN GROUP userid]... TO userid	*Database permissions* GRANT { ALL | CREATE/DUMP_commands} TO { PUBLIC | user [, user]...}	*Database permissions* GRANT { CONNECT | RESOURCE | DBA} [, CON-NECT | RESOURCE | DBA]... TO {PUBLIC | user [, user]...}	TO { PUBLIC | user [, user]... | role [, role] ...} [WITH GRANT OPTION]
	Procedure permission GRANT EXECUTE ON procedure TO userid [, userid]...		*Procedure permission* GRANT EXECUTE ON procedure TO {PUBLIC | user [, user]...}	*Database permissions* GRANT{ system_privilege [, system_privilege]... | role [, role] ...} TO {PUBLIC | user [, user]... | role [, role]...}, | PUBLIC | user [, user]... | role [, role]...]... [WITH ADMIN OPTION]
	New user (connection) permis-sion GRANT CONNECT TO userid [, userid]... IDENTIFIED BY password [, password]...			

Sybase SQL Server	Sybase SQL Anywhere	Microsoft SQL Server	Informix	Oracle
Object permissions REVOKE [GRANT OPTION FOR] { ALL [PRIVILEGES] | {SELECT | INSERT | DELETE | UPDATE | REFER- ENCES | EXECUTE} [, SELECT | INSERT | DELETE | UPDATE | REFERENCES | EXECUTE] ...}	*Object permissions* REVOKE {SELECT | INSERT | DELETE | UPDATE [(column [, column]...)] | REFERENCES | ALTER} [, SELECT | INSERT | DELETE | UPDATE [(column [, col- umn]...)] | REFERENCES | ALTER]...}	*Object permissions* REVOKE { ALL | {SELECT | INSERT | DELETE | UPDATE | REFER- ENCES | EXECUTE} [, SELECT | INSERT | DELETE | UPDATE | REFERENCES | EXECUTE] ...}	*Object permissions* REVOKE {SELECT | INSERT | DELETE | UPDATE | REFER- ENCES}| ALTER | INDEX} [, SELECT | INSERT | DELETE | UPDATE | REFERENCES | ALTER | INDEX]...	*Object permissions* REVOKE {SELECT [(column [, column]...)} | INSERT | DELETE | UPDATE [(column [, column]...)] | REFERENCES [(column [, column]...)] | ALTER | INDEX} [, SELECT [(column [, col- umn]...)] | INSERT | DELETE | UPDATE [(column [, col- umn]...)] | REFERENCES [(col- umn [, column]...)] | ALTER | INDEX]...}
ON { table [(column [, col- umn]...)] | view [(column [, column]...)] | procedure } FROM { PUBLIC | user [, user]...| role [, role] ...} [CASCADE]	ON table FROM userid [, userid]...	ON { table [(column [, column]...)] | view [(column [, column]...)] | procedure | extended_procedure} FROM { PUBLIC | user [, user]... ...}	ON { table | view | synonym } FROM {PUBLIC | user [, user]...}	ON {table | view | procedure} FROM { PUBLIC | user [, user]...| role [, role]...} [CASCADE CONSTRAINTS]
Database permissions REVOKE { ALL [PRIVILEGES] | CREATE_commands} FROM { PUBLIC | user [, user]...| role [, role] ...}	*Database permissions* REVOKE {DBA | RESOURCE | GROUP | MEMBERSHIP IN GROUP userid } [,DBA | RESOURCE | GROUP | MEMBERSHIP IN GROUP userid]... FROM userid	*Database permissions* REVOKE { ALL | CREATE/DUMP_commands} FROM { PUBLIC | user [, user]...}	*Database permissions* REVOKE { CONNECT | RESOURCE | DBA}, [, CON- NECT | RESOURCE | DBA]... FROM {PUBLIC | user [, user]...}	*Database permissions* REVOKE { system_privilege [, system_privilege]...| role [, role]...} FROM {PUBLIC | user [, user]... | role [, role]...}| PUBLIC | user [, user]...| role [, role]...}...
	Procedure permission REVOKE EXECUTE ON procedure TO userid [, userid]...			

Glossary

access strategy
  The method by which a database management system locates physical data.

aggregate functions
  Often used with the GROUP BY and HAVING clauses, aggregate functions generate one summary value from a group of values in a specified column. Aggregate functions include AVG, COUNT, COUNT(*), MIN, and MAX.

alias
  A temporary name given to a table (in the FROM clause). Here are two examples of how it can be used:

```
select au_id, a.city, p.city, pub_id
from authors a, publishers p
where au_lname like 'P%'

select a.au_id, b.au_id
from authors a, authors b
where a.zip = b.zip
```

  In the first example, the alias eliminates the need to type the whole table name as a qualifier for each column name that could belong to either table in the FROM clause. In the second example, aliases allow a self-join—the *authors* table takes on two identities, *a* and *b*.

argument
  A value (also called "parameter") supplied to a function.

arithmetic operators

Addition (+), subtraction (–), multiplication (*), and division (/) are arithmetic operators. They can be used with all numeric columns. Some systems also supply modulo (%), for finding the integer remainder after a division operation on two integers.

association

A many-to-many relationship between entities.

attribute

A data value that describes one characteristic of an entity. It is also called a "field" or a "column."

base table

A permanent database table on which a view (also called a virtual table) is based.

benchmarking

The process of testing a piece of hardware or software to determine its general or specific performance characteristics.

binary datatype

A datatype provided by some systems for storing bit patterns.

bit datatype

A datatype provided by some systems for storing true/false data.

Boolean expressions

Expressions that evaluate as "true" or "false" rather than return a specific value.

Boolean operators

The logical operators AND, OR, and NOT.

buffer cache

Memory allocated for data storage.

Cartesian product

All the possible combinations of rows from the tables. Such a result is generally caused by not including all the necessary joins.

cascade
Propagation of an update or delete through related tables in a database.

character datatype
A datatype used to store character data such as letters, numbers, and special characters.

character set
A list of letters and special characters (repertoire) and its internal mapping to computer codes (form-of-use).

clustered index
An index in which the bottom, or leaf, level is the data itself. A table can have only one clustered index.

collating sequence
See **sort order**.

collation
See **sort order**.

column
One particular attribute or characteristic of the entity that is the subject of a table; also called a "field."

command
Any SQL statement, such as INSERT or CREATE DATABASE.

comparison operators
Operators used for comparing one expression to another in a WHERE or HAVING clause. Comparison operators include equal to (=), greater than (>), less than (<), greater than or equal to (>=), less than or equal to (<=), and not equal to (!= or <>).

composite indexes
Indexes based on more than one column in a table.

comprehensive data sublanguage
A single language that handles all communications with the database.

concurrency control

Strategies such as locking that prevent two or more users from changing the same piece of data concurrently.

connecting column

A column that participates in a join, allowing one table to link with another or with itself. Connecting columns are columns from one or more tables that contain similar values.

constraints

Clauses in the CREATE TABLE statement (CHECK, PRIMARY KEY, UNIQUE, REFERENCES, FOREIGN KEY) that help enforce referential integrity and business rules.

correlated subquery

A subquery that cannot be evaluated independently, but that depends on the outer query for its results. Also called a "repeating subquery," since the subquery is executed once for each row that might be selected by the outer query.

data administration

One of the three general categories for which SQL is used. The other two are data definition and data manipulation. Data administration includes activities such as granting and revoking permissions to users.

data cache

The area of memory allocated for data storage.

data control

Another term for data administration.

data definition

The process of creating (or removing) a database and its objects.

data dictionary

The system tables that contain descriptions of the database objects and how they are structured.

data manipulation

Retrieving and modifying data, through SQL statements SELECT, INSERT, DELETE, and UPDATE.

data modification

Changing data, through SQL statements   INSERT, DELETE, and UPDATE.

data retrieval

Finding and displaying data in the database via queries (SELECT statements).

data structure diagram

A diagram that shows how the objects in a database fit together. It is also called an "entity-relationship (E-R) diagram."

database

A collection of related tables containing data and definitions of database objects.

database administrator

See **system administrator**.

database design

The process of setting up the objects in the database (principally, but not exclusively, tables and their columns).

database device

The physical or logical device on which a database is stored.

database owner

The creator or owner of a database, a concept most useful in systems that allow more than one database.

date datatype

A datatype used for storing date information.

decimal datatype

A datatype used for storing decimal data.

default

A value entered by the system for specified columns when the user supplies no explicit value.

derived tables
A name sometimes applied to views, which are also known as "virtual tables."

designations
One-to-many relationships among data.

detail table
See **master table**.

difference
A set operation that displays rows that two tables do not have in common.

distinguished nulls
Unknown pieces of information whose values are not precisely known, but some things about the values are known.

domain
The set of all legal or valid values for a particular column.

dummy values
False values you enter as placeholders or tests.

entity
The object or thing that a table describes; the subject of the table.

entity integrity
An integrity rule requiring that each row have a primary key and that no primary key allow nulls.

entity-relationship diagram
See **data structure diagram**.

entity-relationship modeling
Identifying the important subjects about which information will be stored; identifying their attributes; and identifying the relationships among these entities. Also known as "entity modeling."

equijoin
Joining columns on the basis of equality, where values match exactly; see also **natural join**.

escape character
A character used in a LIKE clause with the ESCAPE keyword to strip a wildcard of its magic meaning and force SQL to interpret it as a literal.

exclusive lock
Sometimes called a "write" lock, it gives one user exclusive use of a row, page, or table during data modification activities.

expression
A constant, column name, function, or any combination thereof connected by arithmetic (and sometimes bitwise) operators.

field
An attribute of an entity, a column of a table.

file
Often used as equivalent to "table."

fillfactor
An indexing option provided by Transact-SQL that allows you to control how full to make each page of a new index. This number affects performance because of the time it takes for the system to split index pages when they become 100 percent full.

first normal form
First of the five normal forms. It requires that tables have a fixed number of columns and that there be no repeating groups.

fixed length
Some datatypes can have either fixed or variable length. Choosing the correct one may have storage and performance implications.

foreign key
A column in a table that matches a primary key column in another table.

form-of-use
See **character set**.

form system
A user-interface screen with places where you can type data.

free-form language
A computer language with no requirements for line length or line breaks.

grouped view
A view with a GROUP BY clause in its definition.

identifier
The name of a database or database object.

inclusive range
A range, specified with the keyword BETWEEN, in which you search for the lower value and upper value of the range as well as the values included in the range.

index
A mechanism for locating data.

instance
Each row in a table represents an occurrence, or instance, of the entity.

integrity
Data consistency and correctness.

intersection
A set operation that displays rows that two or more tables have in common.

join
Selecting from more than one table by comparing values in specified columns.

join column
A column used to set conditions for a join.

join-compatible columns
Columns holding similar kinds of data values.

key values

Primary keys uniquely identify a row, while foreign keys provide a way to refer to those unique values from another table.

keyword

A word used as part of SQL syntax, also called a "reserved word."

locking

A concurrency-control mechanism to protect data both from being modified by more than one user at a time and from being read while a transaction is in progress.

logical independence

The concept that relationships among tables, columns, and rows can change without impairing the function of application programs and ad hoc queries.

logical operators

AND (joins two or more conditions and returns results when all the conditions are true), OR (connects two or more conditions and returns results when any of the conditions is true), and NOT (negates a condition).

lookup table

A table used primarily for reference purposes, rather than for data entry or modification.

lost-update problem

Multiuser updates can overwrite each other if a database has no concurrency control.

LRU-MRU

Least recently used, most recently used: An algorithm often used in data caching. Most recently used items are put in the cache, displacing least recently used ones.

many-to-many

Relationships such as those between *authors* and *titles*, in which an author can have several books and a book can have several authors.

master table

A database table that holds the top level of information (such as the *bookbiz sales* table) for a particular activity and is associated with one or more detail tables (such as the *bookbiz salesdetails* table).

MIS specialist

See **system administrator**.

modulo

An arithmetic operator that gives the integer remainder after a division operation on two integers. For example, 21 modulo 9 is 3, because 21 divided by 9 equals 2 with a remainder of 3.

money datatype

A datatype used for representing decimal currency values.

natural join

A display of only one from each pair of columns whose matching values created the join on the basis of equality. See also **equijoin**.

nested query

See **subquery**.

nested sort

A sort within another sort.

nonrelated subquery

A subquery that can be evaluated independently of the outer SQL statement.

non-loss decomposition

The process of splitting a table into smaller tables without losing any information.

nonprocedural language

A language that allows you to specify the results you want without describing the method for getting them.

normal forms

See **normalization**.

normalization
Normalization guidelines are a set of data design standards called the **normal forms**. Five normal forms are widely accepted, although more have been proposed.

null
A null represents a missing or inapplicable value in a column of a database table.

occurrence
Each row in a table is an occurrence or instance of the entity.

one-to-many
A master-detail relationship in which one row in the first table may relate to many in the second, but a row in the second table can relate to only one row in the first.

outer join
A join that displays nonjoining rows from either one or the other of a pair of joined tables.

owner
The creator of a database object is the owner of that object and usually has full privileges on that object.

permissions
Authority to run certain actions on certain database objects or to run certain commands.

physical data independence
The independence of the physical storage of data from a database's logical design.

precompiled queries
In Transact-SQL, named collections of SQL statements for which execution plans have already been figured out.

primary key
The column or columns whose values uniquely identify a row in a table.

privileges
See **permissions**.

projection
Listing the columns that will be included in the results of a selection from the database.

qualifications
Conditions on the rows to be retrieved, described in the WHERE or HAVING clause.

queries
Requests for retrieval of data from the database; sometimes also used to refer to SQL statements in general.

query optimizer
The part of the DBMS that calculates the most efficient way to perform a given query.

record
A set of related fields that describes a specific entity. Also called "tuple" or "row."

recovery
Restoring the database to a consistent state after a software or hardware failure.

referential integrity
The rules governing data consistency, specifically the requirement that a foreign key must either match its primary key exactly or else be completely null.

relation
Synonym for table.

repeating subquery
See **correlated subquery**.

repertoire
See **character set**.

restrict

See **restriction**.

restriction

One of the basic query operations in a relational system, also called selection. A restriction determines which rows will be selected from a table.

rows

The set of data values associated with one instance of the entity that the table describes: one set of columns.

rule

A specification that controls what data may be entered in a particular column.

scalar aggregate

An aggregate function that produces a single value from a SELECT statement. See also **vector aggregate**.

schema

In SQL-92 terms, a collection of database objects belonging to a single user. The term is also used for the overall database design ("Let me see the schema.").

second normal form

Requires that all the non–primary key columns relate to the entire primary key and not just to one of its components.

selection

Specifying conditions for retrieving rows from a table. See also **restriction**.

select list

The asterisk (for all columns) or a list of columns and expressions to be included in the query results.

self-join

Selecting from a table by comparing values in one or more columns of the same table.

serial datatype or property
A facility to maintain a sequentially increasing number.

sets
Groups of rows to which aggregates apply.

shared lock
A lock created by non-update ("read") operations. Other users may read the data concurrently, but no transaction can acquire an exclusive lock on the data until all the shared locks have released.

sort order
A collating sequence (or collation) for a character set, determining which characters come before and after other characters.

SQL
A unified language for defining, querying, modifying, and controlling the data in a relational database (originally an acronym for Structured Query Language).

statement
A SQL data definition, data manipulation, or data administration command.

stored procedures
See **precompiled queries**.

strings
Groups of one or more letters, numbers, or special characters (such as the question mark or asterisk).

subquery
A SELECT statement that nests inside the WHERE clause of another SELECT statement.

system administrator
The person who has overall responsibility for the data in the database, and for its consistency and integrity.

system catalog
The system tables containing descriptions of the database objects and how they are structured.

system tables
See **system catalog**.

table
A rectangular display of data values as rows and columns.

table list
The list of tables, views, or both following the FROM keyword in a SELECT statement.

table scan
Reading each row in a table rather than using an index to locate a particular data element. (For small tables, a table scan can be the most efficient access method.)

terminator
A character, word, or menu option marking the end of a SQL statement.

theta join
A join based on any valid comparison operator, such as equal (=), greater than (>), or not less than (!<).

third normal form
Third normal form requires that each nonkey column give information about the key column. A nonkey column may not describe another nonkey column.

time datatype
A datatype that stores time information.

transaction
A mechanism for ensuring that a set of actions is treated as a single unit of work.

transaction log
A log in which changes to the database are recorded (usually for recovery purposes). The method is implementation dependent.

transaction management

Ensuring that transactions are either completed or canceled so that the database is never left in an inconsistent state.

trigger

Meaning can vary from system to system. In Transact-SQL, a special form of stored procedure that goes into effect when a user gives a data modification command on a specified table or column.

trigger actions

In Transact-SQL, the actions for which a trigger is specified.

trigger conditions

In Transact-SQL, the conditions that cause a trigger to take effect.

tuple

A set of related attributes that describes a specific entity. Also called "row" or "record."

unique indexes

An index with no duplicate primary keys.

unmodified comparison operator

A comparison operator not followed by ANY or ALL.

user-defined datatypes

In Transact-SQL, datatypes created by the user, defined in terms of the system datatypes, with characteristics such as null status and length (where appropriate). Users can apply rules and defaults to these datatypes.

user-defined transaction

Transactions you define with transaction commands such as BEGIN TRANSACTION and COMMIT TRANSACTION.

user tables

Tables that contain the information that is the database management system's reason for existing.

validation rules

A rule specifies what data may be entered in a particular column: it is a way of defining the domain of the column. Rules are sometimes referred to as "validation rules," since they allow the system to check whether a value being entered in a column falls within the column's domain.

value
A single data element, such as the contents of one column-row intersection.

vector aggregate
An aggregate that returns an array of values, one per set.

view
An alternative way of looking at the data in one or more tables.

viewed table
Another term for "view" (as opposed to "base" table).

virtual table
See **view**.

whole number
A number with no fraction or decimal value.

whole-number datatype
A datatype that holds whole numbers (*number, integer, int, smallint*).

wildcards
Characters used with the SQL LIKE keyword that can represent one character (underscore, _) or any number of characters (percent sign, %).

Appendix D

The *bookbiz* Sample Database

This is the sample database *bookbiz*. The names of the tables are *authors, publishers, roysched, titleauthors, titles, editors, titleditors, sales,* and *salesdetails*. The information is shown in a table format and then as a script, with CREATE and INSERT statements.

TABLE CHARTS

The header for each column lists the datatypes and the column null/not null status. Indexes are noted where they apply.

publishers				
pub_id char(4) not null	*pub_name* varchar(40) null	*address* varchar(40) null	*city* varchar(20) null	*state* char(2) null
unique index pubind				
0736 0877 1389	New Age Books Binnet & Hardley Algodata Infosystems	1 1st St 2 2nd Ave. 3 3rd Dr.	Boston Washington Berkeley	MA DC CA

authors							
au_id char(11) not null	*au_lname* varchar(40) not null	*au_fname* varchar(20) not null	*phone* char(12) null	*address* varchar(40) null	*city* varchar(20) null	*state* char(2) null	*zip* char(5) null
unique index auidind	composite index aunmind						
172-32-1176	White	Johnson	408 496-7223	10932 Bigge Rd.	Menlo Park	CA	94025
213-46-8915	Green	Marjorie	415 986-7020	309 63rd St.	Oakland	CA	94618
238-95-7766	Carson	Cheryl	415 548-7723	589 Darwin Ln.	Berkeley	CA	94705
267-41-2394	O'Leary	Michael	408 286-2428	22 Cleveland Av.	San Jose	CA	95128
274-80-9391	Straight	Dick	415 834-2919	5420 College Av.	Oakland	CA	94609
341-22-1782	Smith	Meander	913 843-0462	10 Misisipi Dr.	Lawrence	KS	66044
409-56-7008	Bennet	Abraham	415 658-9932	6223 Bateman St.	Berkeley	CA	94705
427-17-2319	Dull	Ann	415 836-7128	3410 Blonde St.	Palo Alto	CA	94301
472-27-2349	Gringlesby	Burt	707 938-6445	PO Box 792	Covelo	CA	95428
486-29-1786	Locksley	Chastity	415 585-4620	18 Broadway Av.	San Francisco	CA	94130
527-72-3246	Greene	Morningstar	615 297-2723	22 Graybar Rd.	Nashville	TN	37215
648-92-1872	Blotchet-Halls	Reginald	503 745-6402	55 Hillsdale Bl.	Corvallis	OR	97330
672-71-3249	Yokomoto	Akiko	415 935-4228	3 Silver Ct.	Walnut Creek	CA	94595
712-45-1867	del Castillo	Innes	615 996-8275	2286 Cram Pl.	Ann Arbor	MI	48105
722-51-5454	DeFrance	Michel	219 547-9982	3 Balding Pl.	Gary	IN	46403
724-08-9931	Stringer	Dirk	415 843-2991	5420 Telegraph Av.	Oakland	CA	94609
724-80-9391	MacFeather	Stearns	415 354-7128	44 Upland Hts.	Oakland	CA	94612
756-30-7391	Karsen	Livia	415 534-9219	5720 McAuley St.	Oakland	CA	94609
807-91-6654	Panteley	Sylvia	301 946-8853	1956 Arlington Pl.	Rockville	MD	20853
846-92-7186	Hunter	Sheryl	415 836-7128	3410 Blonde St.	Palo Alto	CA	94301
893-72-1158	McBadden	Heather	707 448-4982	301 Putnam	Vacaville	CA	95688
899-46-2035	Ringer	Anne	801 826-0752	67 Seventh Av.	Salt Lake City	UT	84152
998-72-3567	Ringer	Albert	801 826-0752	67 Seventh Av.	Salt Lake City	UT	84152

titles									
title_id char(6) not null	*title* varchar(80) not null	*type* char(12) null	*pub_id* char(4) null	*price* money null	*advance* money null	*ytd_sales* int null	*contract* bit not null	*notes* varchar(200) null	*pubdate* date null
unique index titleidind	index titleind								
BU1032	The Busy Executive's Database Guide	business	1389	$19.99	$5000.00	4095	1	An overview of available database systems with emphasis on common business applications. Illustrated.	Jun 12 1985 12:00AM
BU1111	Cooking and Computers: Surreptitious Balance Sheets	business	1389	$11.95	$5000.00	3876	1	Helpful hints on how to use your electronic resources to the best advantage.	Jun 9 1985 12:00AM

titles, continued									
title_id char(6) not null	*title* varchar(80) not null	*type* char(12) null	*pub_id* char(4) null	*price* money null	*advance* money null	*ytd_sales* int null	*contract* bit not null	*notes* varchar(200) null	*pubdate* date null
unique index titleidind	**index** **titleind**								
BU2075	You Can Combat Computer Stress!	business	0736	$2.99	$10125.00	18722	1	The latest medical and psychological techniques for living with the electronic office. Easy-to-understand explanations.	Jun 30 1985 12:00AM
BU7832	Straight Talk About Computers	business	1389	$19.99	$5000.00	4095	1	Annotated analysis of what computers can do for you: a no-hype guide for the critical user.	Jun 22 1985 12:00AM
MC2222	Silicon Valley Gastronomic Treats	mod_cook	0877	$19.99	$0.00	2032	1	Favorite recipes for quick, easy, and elegant meals, tried and tested by people who never have time to eat, let alone cook.	Jun 9 1985 12:00AM
MC3021	The Gourmet Microwave	mod_cook	0877	$2.99	$15000.00	22246	1	Traditional French gourmet recipes adapted for modern microwave cooking.	Jun 18 1985 12:00AM
MC3026	The Psychology of Computer Cooking	NULL	0877	NULL	NULL	NULL	0	NULL	NULL
PC1035	But Is It User Friendly?	popular_comp	1389	$22.95	$7000.00	8780	1	A survey of software for the naive user, focusing on the "friendliness" of each.	Jun 30 1985 12:00AM

titles, continued									
title_id char(6) not null	title varchar(80) not null	type char(12) null	pub_id char(4) null	price money null	advance money null	ytd_sales int null	contract bit not null	notes varchar(200) null	pubdate date null
unique index titleidind	index titleind								
PC8888	Secrets of Silicon Valley	popular_ comp	1389	$20.00	$8000.00	4095	1	Muckraking reporting by two coura- geous women on the world's largest com- puter hardware and software manufacturers.	Jun 12 1985 12:00AM
PC9999	Net Etiquette	popular_ comp	1389	NULL	NULL	NULL	0	A must-read for computer con- ferencing debu- tantes!	NULL
PS1372	Computer Phobic and Non-Phobic Individuals: Behavior Variations	psychology	0736	$21.59	$7000.00	375	1	A must for the specialist, this book examines the difference between those who hate and fear computers and those who think they are swell.	Oct 21 1985 12:00AM
PS2091	Is Anger the Enemy?	psychology	0736	$10.95	$2275.00	2045	1	Carefully researched study of the effects of strong emotions on the body. Met- abolic charts included.	Jun 15 1985 12:00AM
PS2106	Life Without Fear	psychology	0736	$7.00	$6000.00	111	1	New exercise, meditation, and nutritional techniques that can reduce the shock of daily interac- tions. Popular audience. Sam- ple menus included, exer- cise video available sepa- rately.	Oct 5 1985 12:00AM

titles, continued									
title_id char(6) not null	*title* varchar(80) not null	*type* char(12) null	*pub_id* char(4) null	*price* money null	*advance* money null	*ytd_sales* int null	*contract* bit not null	*notes* varchar(200) null	*pubdate* date null
unique index titleidind	index titleind								
PS3333	Prolonged Data Deprivation: Four Case Studies	psychology	0736	$19.99	$2000.00	4072	1	What happens when the data runs dry? Searching evaluations of information-shortage effects on heavy users.	Jun 12 1985 12:00AM
PS7777	Emotional Security: A New Algorithm	psychology	0736	$7.99	$4000.00	3336	1	Protecting yourself and your loved ones from undue emotional stress in the modern world. Use of computer and nutritional aids emphasized.	Jun 12 1985 12:00AM
TC3218	Onions, Leeks, and Garlic: Cooking Secrets of the Mediterranean	trad_cook	0877	$20.95	$7000.00	375	1	Profusely illustrated in color, this makes a wonderful gift book for a cuisine-oriented friend.	Oct 21 1985 12:00AM
TC7777	Sushi, Anyone?	trad_cook	0877	$14.99	$8000.00	4095	1	Detailed instructions on improving your position in life by learning how to make authentic Japanese sushi in your spare time. 5-10% increase in number of friends per recipe reported from beta test.	Jun 12 1985 12:00AM

titles, continued									
title_id char(6) not null	title varchar(80) not null	type char(12) null	pub_id char(4) null	price money null	advance money null	ytd_sales int null	contract bit not null	notes varchar(200) null	pubdate date null
unique index titleidind	index titleind								
TC4203	Fifty Years in Bucking-ham Palace Kitchens	trad_cook	0877	$11.95	$4000.00	15096	1	More anecdotes from the Queen's favorite cook describing life among English royalty. Recipes, techniques, tender vignettes.	Jun 12 1985 12:00AM

titleauthors			
au_id char(11) not null	title_id char(6) not null	au_ord tinyint null	royaltyshare float null
unique composite index taind			
172-32-1176	PS3333	1	1.000000000
213-46-8915	BU1032	2	0.400000000
213-46-8915	BU2075	1	1.000000000
238-95-7766	PC1035	1	1.000000000
267-41-2394	BU1111	2	0.400000000
267-41-2394	TC7777	2	0.300000000
274-80-9391	BU7832	1	1.000000000
409-56-7008	BU1032	1	0.600000000
427-17-2319	PC8888	1	0.500000000
472-27-2349	TC7777	3	0.300000000
486-29-1786	PC9999	1	1.000000000
486-29-1786	PS7777	1	1.000000000
648-92-1872	TC4203	1	1.000000000
672-71-3249	TC7777	1	0.400000000
712-45-1867	MC2222	1	1.000000000
722-51-5454	MC3021	1	0.750000000
724-80-9391	BU1111	1	0.600000000
724-80-9391	PS1372	2	0.250000000
756-30-7391	PS1372	1	0.750000000
807-91-6654	TC3218	1	1.000000000
846-92-7186	PC8888	2	0.500000000
899-46-2035	MC3021	2	0.250000000
899-46-2035	PS2091	2	0.500000000
998-72-3567	PS2091	1	0.500000000
998-72-3567	PS2106	1	1.000000000

sales			
sonum int not null	**stor_id** char(4) not null	**ponum** varchar(20) not null	**sdate** date null
1	7066	QA7442.3	Sep 13 1985 12:00AM
2	7067	D4482	Sep 14 1985 12:00AM
3	7131	N914008	Sep 14 1985 12:00AM
4	7131	N914014	Sep 14 1985 12:00AM
5	8042	423LL922	Sep 14 1985 12:00AM
6	8042	423LL930	Sep 14 1985 12:00AM
7	6380	722a	Sep 13 1985 12:00AM
8	6380	6871	Sep 14 1985 12:00AM
9	8042	P723	Mar 11 1988 12:00AM
19	7896	X999	Feb 21 1988 12:00AM
10	7896	QQ2299	Oct 28 1987 12:00AM
11	7896	TQ456	Dec 12 1987 12:00AM
12	8042	QA879.1	May 22 1987 12:00AM
13	7066	A2976	May 24 1987 12:00AM
14	7131	P3087a	May 29 1987 12:00AM
15	7067	P2121	Jun 15 1987 12:00AM

salesdetails				
sonum int not null	**qty_ordered** smallint not null	**qty_shipped** smallint null	**title_id** char(6) not null	**date_shipped** date null
1	75	75	PS2091	Sep 15 1985 12:00AM
2	10	10	PS2091	Sep 15 1985 12:00AM
3	20	20	PS2091	Sep 18 1985 12:00AM
4	25	20	MC3021	Sep 18 1985 12:00AM
5	15	15	MC3021	Sep 14 1985 12:00AM
6	10	3	BU1032	Sep 22 1985 12:00AM
7	3	3	PS2091	Sep 20 1985 12:00AM
8	5	5	BU1032	Sep 14 1985 12:00AM
9	25	5	BU1111	Mar 28 1988 12:00AM
19	35	35	BU2075	Mar 15 1988 12:00AM
10	15	15	BU7832	Oct 29 1987 12:00AM
11	10	10	MC2222	Jan 12 1988 12:00AM
12	30	30	PC1035	May 24 1987 12:00AM
13	50	50	PC8888	May 24 1987 12:00AM
14	20	20	PS1372	May 29 1987 12:00AM
14	25	25	PS2106	Apr 29 1987 12:00AM
14	15	10	PS3333	May 29 1987 12:00AM
14	25	25	PS7777	Jun 13 1987 12:00AM
15	40	40	TC3218	Jun 15 1987 12:00AM
15	20	20	TC4203	May 30 1987 12:00AM
15	20	10	TC7777	Jun 17 1987 12:00AM

editors								
ed_id char(11) not null	ed_lname varchar(40) not null	ed_fname varchar(20) not null	ed_pos varchar(12) null	phone char(12) null	address varchar(40) null	city varchar(20) null	state char(2) null	zip char(5) null
unique index edind	composite index ednmind							
234-88-9720	Hunter	Amanda	acquisition	617 432-5586	18 Dowdy Ln.	Boston	MA	02210
321-55-8906	DeLongue	Martinella	project	415 843-2222	3000 6th St.	Berkeley	CA	94710
723-48-9010	Sparks	Manfred	copy	303 721-3388	15 Sail	Denver	CO	80237
777-02-9831	Samuelson	Bernard	project	415 843-6990	27 Yosemite	Oakland	CA	94609
777-66-9902	Almond	Alfred	copy	312 699-4177	1010 E. Devon	Chicago	IL	60018
826-11-9034	Himmel	Eleanore	project	617 423-0552	97 Bleaker	Boston	MA	02210
885-23-9140	Rutherford-Hayes	Hannah	project	301 468-3909	32 Rockbill Pike	Rockbill	MD	20852
943-88-7920	Kaspchek	Chistof	acquisition	415 549-3909	18 Severe Rd.	Berkeley	CA	94710
993-86-0420	McCann	Dennis	acquisition	301 468-3909	32 Rockbill Pike	Rockbill	MD	20852

titleditors		
ed_id char(11) not null	title_id char(6) not null	ed_ord tinyint null
unique composite index teind		
321-55-8906	BU1032	2
321-55-8906	BU1111	2
321-55-8906	BU2075	3
321-55-8906	BU7832	2
321-55-8906	PC1035	2
321-55-8906	PC8888	2
777-02-9831	PC1035	3
777-02-9831	PC8888	3
826-11-9034	BU2075	2
826-11-9034	PS1372	2
826-11-9034	PS2091	2
826-11-9034	PS2106	2
826-11-9034	PS7777	2
885-23-9140	MC2222	2
885-23-9140	MC3021	2
885-23-9140	TC3218	2
885-23-9140	TC4203	2
885-23-9140	TC7777	2
943-88-7920	BU1032	1
943-88-7920	BU1111	1

titleditors, continued		
ed_id **char(11)** **not null**	**title_id** **char(6)** **not null**	**ed_ord** **tinyint** **null**
unique composite index **teind**		
943-88-7920	BU2075	1
943-88-7920	BU7832	1
943-88-7920	PC1035	1
943-88-7920	PC8888	1
993-86-0220	MC2222	1
993-86-0220	MC3021	1
993-86-0220	PS1372	1
993-86-0220	PS2091	1
993-86-0220	PS2106	1
993-86-0220	PS3333	1
993-86-0220	PS7777	1
993-86-0220	TC3218	1
993-86-0220	TC4203	1
993-86-0220	TC7777	1

roysched			
title_id **char(6)** **not null**	**lorange** **int** **null**	**hirange** **int** **null**	**royalty** **float** **null**
index **rstidind**			
BU1032	0	5000	0.100000
BU1032	5001	50000	0.120000
PC1035	0	2000	0.100000
PC1035	2001	4000	0.120000
PC1035	4001	50000	0.160000
BU2075	0	1000	0.100000
BU2075	1001	5000	0.120000
BU2075	5001	7000	0.160000
BU2075	7001	50000	0.180000
PC9999	0	50000	0.100000
PS2091	0	1000	0.100000
PS2091	1001	5000	0.120000
PS2091	5001	50000	0.140000
PS2106	0	2000	0.100000
PS2106	2001	5000	0.120000
PS2106	5001	50000	0.140000
MC3021	0	1000	0.100000
MC3021	1001	2000	0.120000
MC3021	2001	6000	0.140000
MC3021	6001	8000	0.180000
MC3021	8001	50000	0.200000
TC3218	0	2000	0.100000
TC3218	2001	6000	0.120000
TC3218	6001	8000	0.160000

rosysched, continued			
title_id char(6) not null	lorange int null	hirange int null	royalty float null
index rstidind			
TC3218	8001	50000	0.180000
PC8888	0	5000	0.100000
PC8888	5001	50000	0.120000
PS7777	0	5000	0.100000
PS7777	5001	50000	0.120000
PS3333	0	5000	0.100000
PS3333	5001	50000	0.120000
MC3026	0	1000	0.100000
MC3026	1001	2000	0.120000
MC3026	2001	6000	0.140000
MC3026	6001	8000	0.180000
MC3026	8001	50000	0.200000
BU1111	0	4000	0.100000
BU1111	4001	8000	0.120000
BU1111	8001	50000	0.140000
MC2222	0	2000	0.100000
MC2222	2001	4000	0.120000
MC2222	4001	8000	0.140000
MC2222	8001	12000	0.160000
TC7777	0	5000	0.100000
TC7777	5001	15000	0.120000
TC4203	0	2000	0.100000
TC4203	2001	8000	0.120000
TC4203	8001	16000	0.140000
BU7832	0	5000	0.100000
BU7832	5001	50000	0.120000
PS1372	0	50000	0.100000

CREATE AND INSERT STATEMENTS
FOR THE *bookbiz* DATABASE

The CREATE and INSERT statements for creating the *bookbiz* database with Sybase SQL Anywhere are provided for your reference in re-creating this database on your system. They are not guaranteed to work with the SQL you are using.

```
set option date_format='Mmm dd yyyy hh:mmaa'
go
set option date_order = 'MDY'
go
set option scale = 2
```

```
go
drop table authors
go

create table authors
    (au_id char(11) not null,
    au_lname varchar(40) not null,
    au_fname varchar(20) not null,
    phone char(12) null,
    address varchar(40) null,
    city varchar(20) null,
    state char(2) null,
    zip char(5) null)
go
grant select on authors to public
go
drop table publishers
go
create table publishers
    (pub_id char(4) not null,
    pub_name varchar(40) null,
    address varchar(40) null,
    city varchar(20) null,
    state char(2) null)
go
grant select on publishers to public
go
drop table roysched
go
create table roysched
    (title_id char(6) not null,
    lorange int null,
    hirange int null,
    royalty float null)
go
grant select on roysched to public
go
drop table titleauthors
go
create table titleauthors
    (au_id char(11) not null,
```

```
      title_id char(6) not null,
      au_ord tinyint null,
      royaltyshare float null)
go
grant select on titleauthors to public
go
drop table titles
go
create table titles
      (title_id char(6) not null,
      title varchar(80) not null,
      type char(12) null,
      pub_id char(4) null,
      price money null,
      advance money null,
      ytd_sales int null,
      contract bit not null,
      notes varchar(200) null,
      pubdate date null)
go
grant select on titles to public
go
drop table editors
go
create table editors
      (ed_id char(11) not null,
      ed_lname varchar(40) not null,
      ed_fname varchar(20) not null,
      ed_pos varchar(12) null,
      phone char(12) null,
      address varchar(40) null,
      city varchar(20) null,
      state char(2) null,
      zip char(5) null)
go
grant select on editors to public
go
drop table titleditors
go
create table titleditors
      (ed_id char(11) not null,
```

```
       title_id char(6) not null,
       ed_ord tinyint null)
go
grant select on titleditors to public
go
drop table sales
go
create table sales
    (sonum int not null,
    stor_id char(4) not null,
    ponum varchar(20) not null,
    sdate date null)
go
grant select on sales to public
go
drop table salesdetails
go
create table salesdetails
    (sonum int not null,
    qty_ordered smallint not null,
    qty_shipped smallint null,
    title_id char(6) not null,
    date_shipped date null)
go
grant select on salesdetails to public
go
create unique index pubind on publishers
(pub_id)
go
create unique index auidind on authors
(au_id)
go
create index aunmind on authors
(au_lname, au_fname)
go
create unique index titleidind on titles
(title_id)
go
create index titleind on titles
(title)
go
```

```
create unique index taind on titleauthors
(au_id, title_id)
go
create unique index edind on editors
(ed_id)
go
create index ednmind on editors
(ed_lname, ed_fname)
go
create unique index teind on titleditors
(ed_id, title_id)
go
create index rstidind on roysched
(title_id)
go
insert into authors
values('409-56-7008', 'Bennet', 'Abraham',
'415 658-9932', '6223 Bateman St.', 'Berkeley', 'CA', '94705')
go
insert into authors
values ('213-46-8915', 'Green', 'Marjorie',
'415 986-7020', '309 63rd St. #411', 'Oakland', 'CA', '94618')
go
insert into authors
values('238-95-7766', 'Carson', 'Cheryl',
'415 548-7723', '589 Darwin Ln.', 'Berkeley', 'CA', '94705')
go
insert into authors
values('998-72-3567', 'Ringer', 'Albert',
'801 826-0752', '67 Seventh Av.', 'Salt Lake City', 'UT', '84152')
go
insert into authors
values('899-46-2035', 'Ringer', 'Anne',
'801 826-0752', '67 Seventh Av.', 'Salt Lake City', 'UT', '84152')
go
insert into authors
values('722-51-5454', 'DeFrance', 'Michel',
'219 547-9982', '3 Balding Pl.', 'Gary', 'IN', '46403')
go
insert into authors
values('807-91-6654', 'Panteley', 'Sylvia',
```

```
'301 946-8853', '1956 Arlington Pl.', 'Rockville', 'MD', '20853')
go
insert into authors
values('893-72-1158', 'McBadden', 'Heather',
'707 448-4982', '301 Putnam', 'Vacaville', 'CA', '95688')
go
insert into authors
values('724-08-9931', 'Stringer', 'Dirk',
'415 843-2991', '5420 Telegraph Av.', 'Oakland', 'CA', '94609')
go
insert into authors
values('274-80-9391', 'Straight', 'Dick',
'415 834-2919', '5420 College Av.', 'Oakland', 'CA', '94609')
go
insert into authors
values('756-30-7391', 'Karsen', 'Livia',
'415 534-9219', '5720 McAuley St.', 'Oakland', 'CA', '94609')
go
insert into authors
values('724-80-9391', 'MacFeather', 'Stearns',
'415 354-7128', '44 Upland Hts.', 'Oakland', 'CA', '94612')
go
insert into authors
values('427-17-2319', 'Dull', 'Ann',
'415 836-7128', '3410 Blonde St.', 'Palo Alto', 'CA', '94301')
go
insert into authors
values('672-71-3249', 'Yokomoto', 'Akiko',
'415 935-4228', '3 Silver Ct.', 'Walnut Creek', 'CA', '94595')
go
insert into authors
values('267-41-2394', 'O''Leary', 'Michael',
'408 286-2428', '22 Cleveland Av. #14', 'San Jose', 'CA', '95128')
go
insert into authors
values('472-27-2349', 'Gringlesby', 'Burt',
'707 938-6445', 'PO Box 792', 'Covelo', 'CA', '95428')
go
insert into authors
values('527-72-3246', 'Greene', 'Morningstar',
'615 297-2723', '22 Graybar House Rd.', 'Nashville', 'TN', '37215')
```

```
go
insert into authors
values('172-32-1176', 'White', 'Johnson',
'408 496-7223', '10932 Bigge Rd.', 'Menlo Park', 'CA', '94025')
go
insert into authors
values('712-45-1867', 'del Castillo', 'Innes',
'615 996-8275', '2286 Cram Pl. #86', 'Ann Arbor', 'MI', '48105')
go
insert into authors
values('846-92-7186', 'Hunter', 'Sheryl',
'415 836-7128', '3410 Blonde St.', 'Palo Alto', 'CA', '94301')
go
insert into authors
values('486-29-1786', 'Locksley', 'Chastity',
'415 585-4620', '18 Broadway Av.', 'San Francisco', 'CA', '94130')
go
insert into authors
values('648-92-1872', 'Blotchet-Halls', 'Reginald',
'503 745-6402', '55 Hillsdale Bl.', 'Corvallis', 'OR', '97330')
go
insert into authors
values('341-22-1782', 'Smith', 'Meander',
'913 843-0462', '10 Misisipi Dr.', 'Lawrence', 'KS', '66044')
go
insert into publishers
values('0736', 'New Age Books', '1 1st St', 'Boston', 'MA')
go
insert into publishers
values('0877', 'Binnet & Hardley', '2 2nd Ave.', 'Washington', 'DC')
go
insert into publishers
values('1389', 'Algodata Infosystems', '3 3rd Dr.', 'Berkeley', 'CA')
go
insert into roysched
values('BU1032', 0, 5000, .10)
go
insert into roysched
values('BU1032', 5001, 50000, .12)
go
insert into roysched
```

```
values('PC1035', 0, 2000, .10)
go
insert into roysched
values('PC1035', 2001, 4000, .12)
go
insert into roysched
values('PC1035', 4001, 50000, .16)
go
insert into roysched
values('BU2075', 0, 1000, .10)
go
insert into roysched
values('BU2075', 1001, 5000, .12)
go
insert into roysched
values('BU2075', 5001, 7000, .16)
go
insert into roysched
values('BU2075', 7001, 50000, .18)
go
insert into roysched
values('PS9999', 0, 50000, .10)
go
insert into roysched
values('PS2091', 0, 1000, .10)
go
insert into roysched
values('PS2091', 1001, 5000, .12)
go
insert into roysched
values('PS2091', 5001, 50000, .14)
go
insert into roysched
values('PS2106', 0, 2000, .10)
go
insert into roysched
values('PS2106', 2001, 5000, .12)
go
insert into roysched
values('PS2106', 5001, 50000, .14)
go
```

```
insert into roysched
values('MC3021', 0, 1000, .10)
go
insert into roysched
values('MC3021', 1001, 2000, .12)
go
insert into roysched
values('MC3021', 2001, 6000, .14)
go
insert into roysched
values('MC3021', 6001, 8000, .18)
go
insert into roysched
values('MC3021', 8001, 50000, .20)
go
insert into roysched
values('TC3218', 0, 2000, .10)
go
insert into roysched
values('TC3218', 2001, 6000, .12)
go
insert into roysched
values('TC3218', 6001, 8000, .16)
go
insert into roysched
values('TC3218', 8001, 50000, .16)
go
insert into roysched
values('PC8888', 0, 5000, .10)
go
insert into roysched
values('PC8888', 5001, 50000, .12)
go
insert into roysched
values('PS7777', 0, 5000, .10)
go
insert into roysched
values('PS7777', 5001, 50000, .12)
go
insert into roysched
values('PS3333', 0, 5000, .10)
```

```
go
insert into roysched
values('PS3333', 5001, 50000, .12)
go
insert into roysched
values('MC3026', 0, 1000, .10)
go
insert into roysched
values('MC3026', 1001, 2000, .12)
go
insert into roysched
values('MC3026', 2001, 6000, .14)
go
insert into roysched
values('MC3026', 6001, 8000, .18)
go
insert into roysched
values('MC3026', 8001, 50000, .20)
go
insert into roysched
values('BU1111', 0, 4000, .10)
go
insert into roysched
values('BU1111', 4001, 8000, .12)
go
insert into roysched
values('BU1111', 8001, 50000, .14)
go
insert into roysched
values('MC2222', 0, 2000, .10)
go
insert into roysched
values('MC2222', 2001, 4000, .12)
go
insert into roysched
values('MC2222', 4001, 8000, .14)
go
insert into roysched
values('MC2222', 8001, 12000, .16)
go
insert into roysched
```

```
values('TC7777', 0, 5000, .10)
go
insert into roysched
values('TC7777', 5001, 15000, .12)
go
insert into roysched
values('TC4203', 0, 2000, .10)
go
insert into roysched
values('TC4203', 2001, 8000, .12)
go
insert into roysched
values('TC4203', 8001, 16000, .14)
go
insert into roysched
values('BU7832', 0, 5000, .10)
go
insert into roysched
values('BU7832', 5001, 50000, .12)
go
insert into roysched
values('PS1372', 0, 50000, .10)
go
insert into titleauthors
values('409-56-7008', 'BU1032', 1, .60)
go
insert into titleauthors
values('486-29-1786', 'PS7777', 1, 1.00)
go
insert into titleauthors
values('486-29-1786', 'PC9999', 1, 1.00)
go
insert into titleauthors
values('712-45-1867', 'MC2222', 1, 1.00)
go
insert into titleauthors
values('172-32-1176', 'PS3333', 1, 1.00)
go
insert into titleauthors
values('213-46-8915', 'BU1032', 2, .40)
go
```

```
insert into titleauthors
values('238-95-7766', 'PC1035', 1, 1.00)
go
insert into titleauthors
values('213-46-8915', 'BU2075', 1, 1.00)
go
insert into titleauthors
values('998-72-3567', 'PS2091', 1, .50)
go
insert into titleauthors
values('899-46-2035', 'PS2091', 2, .50)
go
insert into titleauthors
values('998-72-3567', 'PS2106', 1, 1.00)
go
insert into titleauthors
values('722-51-5454', 'MC3021', 1, .75)
go
insert into titleauthors
values('899-46-2035', 'MC3021', 2, .25)
go
insert into titleauthors
values('807-91-6654', 'TC3218', 1, 1.00)
go
insert into titleauthors
values('274-80-9391', 'BU7832', 1, 1.00)
go
insert into titleauthors
values('427-17-2319', 'PC8888', 1, .50)
go
insert into titleauthors
values('846-92-7186', 'PC8888', 2, .50)
go
insert into titleauthors
values('756-30-7391', 'PS1372', 1, .75)
go
insert into titleauthors
values('724-80-9391', 'PS1372', 2, .25)
go
insert into titleauthors
values('724-80-9391', 'BU1111', 1, .60)
```

```
go
insert into titleauthors
values('267-41-2394', 'BU1111', 2, .40)
go
insert into titleauthors
values('672-71-3249', 'TC7777', 1, .40)
go
insert into titleauthors
values('267-41-2394', 'TC7777', 2, .30)
go
insert into titleauthors
values('472-27-2349', 'TC7777', 3, .30)
go
insert into titleauthors
values('648-92-1872', 'TC4203', 1, 1.00)
go
insert into titles
values ('PC8888', 'Secrets of Silicon Valley',
'popular_comp', '1389', $20.00, $8000.00, 4095, 1,
'Muckraking reporting on the world''s largest computer hardware
and software manufacturers.',
'06/12/85')
go
insert into titles
values ('BU1032', 'The Busy Executive''s Database Guide',
'business', '1389', $19.99, $5000.00, 4095, 1,
'An overview of available database systems with emphasis on
common business applications.  Illustrated.',
'06/12/85')
go
insert into titles
values ('PS7777', 'Emotional Security: A New Algorithm',
'psychology', '0736', $7.99, $4000.00, 3336, 1,
'Protecting yourself and your loved ones from undue emotional
stress in the modern world.  Use of computer and nutritional
aids emphasized.',
'06/12/85')
go
insert into titles
values ('PS3333', 'Prolonged Data Deprivation: Four Case Studies',
'psychology', '0736', $19.99, $2000.00, 4072,1,
```

```
'What happens when the data runs dry?  Searching evaluations of
information-shortage effects.',
'06/12/85')
go
insert into titles
values ('BU1111', 'Cooking with Computers: Surreptitious Balance
Sheets',
'business', '1389', $11.95, $5000.00, 3876, 1,
'Helpful hints on how to use your electronic resources to the
best advantage.', '06/09/85')
go
insert into titles
values ('MC2222', 'Silicon Valley Gastronomic Treats',
'mod_cook', '0877', $19.99, $0.00, 2032, 1,
'Favorite recipes for quick, easy, and elegant meals tried and
tested by people who never have time to eat, let alone cook.',
'06/09/85')
go
insert into titles
values ('TC7777', 'Sushi, Anyone?',
'trad_cook', '0877', $14.99, $8000.00, 4095, 1,
'Detailed instructions on improving your position in life by
learning how to make authentic Japanese sushi in your spare
time. 5-10% increase in number of friends per recipe reported
from beta test.',
'06/12/85')
go
insert into titles
values ('TC4203', 'Fifty Years in Buckingham Palace Kitchens',
'trad_cook', '0877', $11.95, $4000.00, 15096, 1,
'More anecdotes from the Queen''s favorite cook describing life
among English royalty.  Recipes, techniques, tender
vignettes.',
'06/12/85')
go
insert into titles
values ('PC1035', 'But Is It User Friendly?',
'popular_comp', '1389', $22.95, $7000.00, 8780, 1,
'A survey of software for the naive user, focusing on the
''friendliness'' of each.',
'06/30/85')
```

```
go
insert into titles
values('BU2075', 'You Can Combat Computer Stress!',
'business', '0736', $2.99, $10125.00, 18722, 1,
'The latest medical and psychological techniques for living
with the electronic office.  Easy-to-understand explanations.',
'06/30/85')
go
insert into titles
values('PS2091', 'Is Anger the Enemy?',
'psychology', '0736', $10.95, $2275.00, 2045, 1,
'Carefully researched study of the effects of strong emotions
on the body. Metabolic charts included.',
'06/15/85')
go
insert into titles
values('PS2106', 'Life Without Fear',
'psychology', '0736', $7.00, $6000.00, 111, 1,
'New exercise, meditation, and nutritional techniques that can
reduce the shock of daily interactions. Popular audience.  Sample
menus included, exercise video available separately.',
'10/05/85')
go
insert into titles
values('MC3021', 'The Gourmet Microwave',
'mod_cook', '0877', $2.99, $15000.00, 22246, 1,
'Traditional French gourmet recipes adapted for modern microwave
cooking.',
'06/18/85')
go
insert into titles
values('TC3218',
'Onions, Leeks, and Garlic: Cooking Secrets of the Mediterranean',
'trad_cook', '0877', $20.95, $7000.00, 375, 1,
'Profusely illustrated in color, this makes a wonderful gift
book for a cuisine-oriented friend.',
'10/21/85')
go
insert into titles (title_id, title, pub_id, contract)
values('MC3026', 'The Psychology of Computer Cooking', '0877', 0)
go
```

```
insert into titles
values ('BU7832', 'Straight Talk About Computers',
'business', '1389', $19.99, $5000.00, 4095, 1,
'Annotated analysis of what computers can do for you: a no-hype
guide for the critical user.',
'06/22/85')
go
insert into titles
values('PS1372',
'Computer Phobic and Non-Phobic Individuals: Behavior Variations',
'psychology', '0736', $21.59, $7000.00, 375, 1,
'A must for the specialist, this book examines the difference
between those who hate and fear computers and those who think
they are swell.',
'10/21/85')
go
insert into titles (title_id, title, type, pub_id, contract, notes)
values('PC9999', 'Net Etiquette', 'popular_comp', '1389', 0,
'A must-read for computer conferencing debutantes!.')
go
insert into editors
values ('321-55-8906', 'DeLongue', 'Martinella', 'project',
'415 843-2222', '3000 6th St.', 'Berkeley', 'CA', '94710')
go
insert into editors
values ('723-48-9010', 'Sparks', 'Manfred', 'copy',
'303 721-3388', '15 Sail', 'Denver', 'CO', '80237')
go
insert into editors
values ('777-02-9831', 'Samuelson', 'Bernard', 'project',
'415 843-6990', '27 Yosemite', 'Oakland', 'CA', '94609')
go
insert into editors
values ('777-66-9902', 'Almond', 'Alfred', 'copy',
'312 699-4177', '1010 E. Devon', 'Chicago', 'IL', '60018')
go
insert into editors
values ('826-11-9034', 'Himmel', 'Eleanore', 'project',
'617 423-0552', '97 Bleaker', 'Boston', 'MA', '02210')
go
```

```
insert into editors
values ('885-23-9140', 'Rutherford-Hayes', 'Hannah',
'project',
'301 468-3909', '32 Rockbill Pike', 'Rockbill', 'MD', '20852')
go
insert into editors
values ('993-86-0420', 'McCann', 'Dennis', 'acquisition',
'301 468-3909', '32 Rockbill Pike', 'Rockbill', 'MD', '20852')
go
insert into editors
values ('943-88-7920', 'Kaspchek', 'Christof', 'acquisition',
'415 549-3909', '18 Severe Rd.', 'Berkeley', 'CA', '94710')
go
insert into editors
values ('234-88-9720', 'Hunter', 'Amanda', 'acquisition',
'617 432-5586', '18 Dowdy Ln.', 'Boston', 'MA', '02210')
go
insert into titleditors values
('826-11-9034', 'BU2075', 2)
go
insert into titleditors values
('826-11-9034', 'PS2091', 2)
go
insert into titleditors values
('826-11-9034', 'PS2106', 2)
go
insert into titleditors values
('826-11-9034', 'PS3333', 2)
go
insert into titleditors values
('826-11-9034', 'PS7777', 2)
go
insert into titleditors values
('826-11-9034', 'PS1372', 2)
go
insert into titleditors values
('885-23-9140', 'MC2222', 2)
go
insert into titleditors values
('885-23-9140', 'MC3021', 2)
go
```

```
insert into titleditors values
('885-23-9140', 'TC3281', 2)
go
insert into titleditors values
('885-23-9140', 'TC4203', 2)
go
insert into titleditors values
('885-23-9140', 'TC7777', 2)
go
insert into titleditors values
('321-55-8906', 'BU1032', 2)
go
insert into titleditors values
('321-55-8906', 'BU1111', 2)
go
insert into titleditors values
('321-55-8906', 'BU7832', 2)
go
insert into titleditors values
('321-55-8906', 'PC1035', 2)
go
insert into titleditors values
('321-55-8906', 'PC8888', 2)
go
insert into titleditors values
('321-55-8906', 'BU2075', 3)
go
insert into titleditors values
('777-02-9831', 'PC1035', 3)
go
insert into titleditors values
('777-02-9831', 'PC8888', 3)
go
insert into titleditors values
('943-88-7920', 'BU1032', 1)
go
insert into titleditors values
('943-88-7920', 'BU1111', 1)
go
insert into titleditors values
('943-88-7920', 'BU2075', 1)
```

```
go
insert into titleditors values
('943-88-7920', 'BU7832', 1)
go
insert into titleditors values
('943-88-7920', 'PC1035', 1)
go
insert into titleditors values
('943-88-7920', 'PC8888', 1)
go
insert into titleditors values
('993-86-0420', 'PS1372', 1)
go
insert into titleditors values
('993-86-0420', 'PS2091', 1)
go
insert into titleditors values
('993-86-0420', 'PS2106', 1)
go
insert into titleditors values
('993-86-0420', 'PS3333', 1)
go
insert into titleditors values
('993-86-0420', 'PS7777', 1)
go
insert into titleditors values
('993-86-0420', 'MC2222', 1)
go
insert into titleditors values
('993-86-0420', 'MC3021', 1)
go
insert into titleditors values
('993-86-0420', 'TC3218', 1)
go
insert into titleditors values
('993-86-0420', 'TC4203', 1)
go
insert into titleditors values
('993-86-0420', 'TC7777', 1)
go
```

```
insert into sales
values(1, '7066', 'QA7442.3', '09/13/85')
go
insert into sales
values(2, '7067', 'D4482', '09/14/85')
go
insert into sales
values(3, '7131', 'N914008', '09/14/85')
go
insert into sales
values(4, '7131', 'N914014', '09/14/85')
go
insert into sales
values(5, '8042', '423LL922', '09/14/85')
go
insert into sales
values(6, '8042', '423LL930', '09/14/85')
go
insert into sales
values(7, '6380', '722a', '09/13/85')
go
insert into sales
values(8, '6380', '6871', '09/14/85')
go
insert into sales
values(9, '8042', 'P723', '03/11/88')
go
insert into sales
values(19, '7896', 'X999', '02/21/88')
go
insert into sales
values(10, '7896', 'QQ2299', '10/28/87')
go
insert into sales
values(11, '7896', 'TQ456', '12/12/87')
go
insert into sales
values(12, '8042', 'QA879.1', '5/22/87')
go
insert into sales
values(13, '7066', 'A2976', '5/24/87')
go
```

```
insert into sales
values(14, '7131', 'P3087a', '5/29/87')
go
insert into sales
values(15, '7067', 'P2121', '6/15/87')
go
insert into salesdetails
values(1, 75, 75, 'PS2091', '9/15/85')
go
insert into salesdetails
values(2, 10, 10, 'PS2091', '9/15/85')
go
insert into salesdetails
values(3, 20, 720, 'PS2091', '9/18/85')
go
insert into salesdetails
values(4, 25, 20, 'MC3021', '9/18/85')
go
insert into salesdetails
values(5, 15, 15, 'MC3021', '9/14/85')
go
insert into salesdetails
values(6, 10, 3, 'BU1032', '9/22/85')
go
insert into salesdetails
values(7, 3, 3, 'PS2091', '9/20/85')
go
insert into salesdetails
values(8, 5, 5, 'BU1032', '9/14/85')
go
insert into salesdetails
values(9, 25, 5, 'BU1111', '03/28/88')
go
insert into salesdetails
values(19, 35, 35, 'BU2075', '03/15/88')
go
insert into salesdetails
values(10, 15, 15, 'BU7832', '10/29/87')
go
insert into salesdetails
values(11, 10, 10, 'MC2222', '1/12/88')
```

```
go
insert into salesdetails
values(12, 30, 30, 'PC1035', '5/24/87')
go
insert into salesdetails
values(13, 50, 50, 'PC8888', '5/24/87')
go
insert into salesdetails
values(14, 20, 20, 'PS1372', '5/29/87')
go
insert into salesdetails
values(14, 25, 25, 'PS2106', '4/29/87')
go
insert into salesdetails
values(14, 15, 10, 'PS3333', '5/29/87')
go
insert into salesdetails
values(14, 25, 25, 'PS7777', '6/13/87')
go
insert into salesdetails
values(15, 40, 40, 'TC3218', '6/15/87')
go
insert into salesdetails
values(15, 20, 20, 'TC4203', '5/30/87')
go
insert into salesdetails
values(15, 20, 10, 'TC7777', '6/17/87')
go
create view titleview
as
select title, au_ord, au_lname,
price, ytd_sales, pub_id
from authors, titles, titleauthors
where authors.au_id = titleauthors.au_id
and titles.title_id = titleauthors.title_id
go
/*end of bookbiz script*/
```

Appendix E

Bibliography

ANSI SQL Standard.
The 1992 ISO-ANSI SQL standard is available through ANSI as document X3.135-1992 and through ISO as document ISO/IEC 9075:1992. ANSI is located at 11 West 42nd Street, New York, N.Y., 10036; 212-642-4900.

Codd, E. F.
"A Relational Model of Data for Large Shared Data Banks," *Communications of the ACM* 13, no. 6 (June 1970) 377–87.

———.
"Is Your DBMS Really Rational?" *Computerworld*, October 14, 1985, 1–9. Author proposes twelve criteria for testing relational database management systems.

———.
"Does Your DBMS Run by the Rules?" *Computerworld*, October 21, 1985, 49–55. Details on the thirty essential features of the relational model.

Date, C. J.
Database: A Primer. Reading, Mass.: Addison-Wesley Publishing Company, 1983.

———.
An Introduction to Database Systems, Volume 2, Reading, Mass.: Addison-Wesley Publishing Company, 1983.

———.
An Introduction to Database Systems, vol. 1, 4th ed., Reading, Mass.: Addison-Wesley Publishing Company, 1986.

———.
Relational Database: Selected Writings. Reading, Mass.: Addison-Wesley Publishing Company, 1986.

———.
A Guide to the SQL Standard. Reading, Mass.: Addison-Wesley Publishing Company, 1987. The third edition (1993) is written with Hugh Darwin and includes SQL-92.

Epstein, Robert
Relational Performance: Understanding the Performance of Relational DBMSs. Emeryville, Calif.: Sybase, Inc., 1986. Photocopy.

Gane, Chris
Developing Business Systems in SQL Using ORACLE on the IBM-PC. New York: Rapid System Development, Inc., 1986.

IBM Corporation
SQL/Data System Terminal User's Reference for VSE. Endicott, N.Y.: IBM Corporation, 1984.

Informix Software, Inc.
Informix Guide to SQL: Reference. Englewood Cliffs, N.J.: Informix Press, Prentice-Hall, Inc., 1995.

Kent, William
"A Simple Guide to Five Normal Forms in Relational Database Theory," in *Communications of the ACM* 20, no. 2 (February 1983): 120–25.

Koch, George, and Kevin Loney
ORACLE: The Complete Reference, 3rd ed. Berkeley, Calif.: Osborne McGraw-Hill, 1995.

Larson, Bruce L.
The Database Expert's Guide to Database 2. New York: McGraw-Hill Book Company, 1988.

Melton, Jim and Alan R Simon
Understanding the New SQL: A Complete Guide. San Mateo, Calif.: Morgan Kaufmann Publishers, 1993.

Microsoft Corporation
Transact-SQL Reference: Microsoft SQL Server Version 6.0. Redmond, Wash.: Microsoft Corporation, 1995.

Perkinson, R. C.
Data Analysis: The Key to Data Base Design. Wellesley, Mass.: QED Information Sciences, Inc., 1984.

Relational Database Systems, Inc.
INFORMIX-SQL Reference Manual. Menlo Park, Calif.: Relational Database Systems, Inc., 1986.

Relational Technology
INGRES Quick Reference Summary SQL Release 5.0. Alameda, Calif.: Relational Technology, 1986

Ross, Ronald G.
Entity Modeling: Techniques and Application. Boston: Database Research Group, Inc., 1987.

Sachs, Jonathon, et al.
SQL* Plus Reference Guide. Belmont, Calif.: ORACLE Corporation, 1987.

Sybase, Inc.
Sybase SQL Server Reference Manual, vols. 1 and 2. Emeryville, Calif.: Sybase, Inc., 1995.

————.

Sybase SQL Anywhere: User's Guide, vols. 1 and 2. Emeryville, Calif.: Sybase, Inc., 1995.

van der Lans, Rick E.
Introduction to SQL. Reading, Mass.: Addison-Wesley Publishing Company, 1988.

Index

Sybase SQL Anywhere Runtime Version

Included on the CD-ROM that accompanies this book are the Windows 3.x, Windows 95, and Windows NT Runtime Versions of Sybase SQL Anywhere.

The runtime version of the Sybase SQL Anywhere database engine does not include all of the functionality of the regular Sybase SQL Anywhere product. Specifically, it does not allow ALTER, CALL, COMMENT, CREATE, DROP, user defined trigger commands, stored procedures, data replication, or graphical database administration to be performed. GRANT and REVOKE allow you to add new users and change passwords, but the runtime database engine prevents a user from changing the permission on tables. In addition, to simplify database administration the runtime product has an integrated transaction log.

The regular Sybase SQL Anywhere product has networking features which are beyond the scope of Sybase SQL Anywhere Runtime. As a result, features such as DBWATCHW, DBCLIENW, and DBSERVEW are not included in the runtime product.

The Sybase SQL Anywhere product included on the CD-ROM is provided without support or maintenance from Sybase. Please read the software license carefully before opening the sealed media package.

Please contact Sybase directly to obtain more information regarding the full-function version of Sybase SQL Anywhere:

Sybase, Inc.
6475 Christie Avenue
Emeryville, CA 94608
Telephone: 1-800-8-SYBASE in the USA and Canada
Fax: 1-510-922-3210

LICENSE

IMPORTANT – READ CAREFULLY BEFORE OPENING

PLEASE READ THIS LICENSE CAREFULLY BEFORE USING THIS SOFTWARE. BY OPENING THE SEALED MEDIA PACKAGE YOU INDICATE YOUR ACCEPTANCE OF THE FOLLOWING LICENSE AGREEMENT. IF YOU DO NOT ACCEPT OR AGREE WITH THESE TERMS, YOU SHOULD PROMPTLY RETURN THIS BOOK AND THE <u>UNOPENED</u> MEDIA PACKAGE TO THE PLACE WHERE YOU PURCHASED IT AND YOUR MONEY WILL BE REFUNDED.

SYBASE SQL ANYWHERE RUNTIME LICENSE AGREEMENT

(THIS IS A LICENSE AND NOT A SALE)

1. LICENSE AND SUPPORT. Addison Wesley Longman ("Addison-Wesley") hereby grants you a non-exclusive, royalty-free license to reproduce the SQL Runtime Distributable Components, as specified in the "Read Me First" document included in the product package, subject to the following additional terms and conditions:

You:

- may distribute copies of the SQL Runtime Distributable Components only in conjunction with and as part of your stand-alone database application written using your properly licensed copy of SYBASE SQL ANYWHERE. Notwithstanding the foregoing, you explicitly agree not to distribute SQL Runtime Distributable Components in conjunction with and as part of a general purpose database development system without the express written permission of SYBASE, which permission may be denied at SYBASE's sole and arbitrary discretion.
- shall include the following copyright notice on the diskette or other physical media containing SQL Runtime Distributable Components: "SYBASE SQL Runtime, Copyright (c) SYBASE, INC. 1992-5; Portions Copyright (c) Rational Systems, Inc. 1992-4".
- and not SYBASE shall be solely responsible for providing technical assistance and other support services to your customers.

This agreement does not entitle you to any maintenance or new release of the Programs, which releases must be separately licensed. If you purchase telephone support for any Programs in use on a computer or in a network, you must purchase support for all products provided by Sybase in use on such computer or network.

2. COPYRIGHT AND OWNERSHIP. The Programs are owned by Sybase or its suppliers and are protected by United States and Canadian copyright laws and international treaty provisions. You acquire only the right to use the Programs as specified herein and do not acquire any rights of ownership in the Programs or the media on which they are provided.

3. COPY RESTRICTIONS AND OTHER RESTRICTIONS. Except as expressly permitted in this Agreement, you may not copy the Programs except to make one (1) copy for backup or archival purposes. You may not copy, modify or adapt, in whole or in part including but not limited to translating or creating derivative works, the written materials and manuals accompanying the Programs ("Documentation"). You may not modify, reverse engineer, decompile or dissemble the Programs. The Program may not be transferred, sold, leased, assigned, or otherwise conveyed (whether by operation of law or otherwise) to another party without Sybase's prior written consent. You may not modify, delete, alter or obscure any of the proprietary rights notices or markings included in the SQL Runtime code or which appear during execution. Transfer of a Program outside the country in which it was originally delivered to you is not permitted without Sybase's prior written consent and is subject to compliance with all applicable export restrictions. You may not use the Programs for timesharing, rental or service bureau purposes. Results of benchmarking or other performance tests run on the Programs may not be disclosed to any third party without Sybase's prior written consent. Upon reasonable notice to you, Sybase may audit the number of copies of the Programs in use by you. If this product package is an "upgrade", you must have a valid license for the qualifying product that is being upgraded for the Programs to be licensed hereunder and the Programs must be used to replace such qualifying product.

4. U.S. GOVERNMENT RESTRICTED RIGHTS. If this license is acquired under a U.S. Government contract, use, duplication or disclosure by the U.S. Government is subject to restrictions as set forth in DFARS 252.227-7013(c)(ii) for Department of Defense contracts and as

set forth in FAR 52.227-19(a)-9d) for civilian agency contracts. Sybase reserves all unpublished rights under the United States copyright laws.

5. FEES. In addition to the license fees and support fees for the Programs, you shall pay all applicable shipping charges, and sales, use, personal property; or similar taxes , tariffs or governmental charges, exclusive of Sybase's not income and corporate franchise taxes.

6. TERMINATION. This agreement and your license to copy and redistribute the SQL Runtime Distributable Components will automatically terminate without notice if you fail to comply with any provision of this Agreement or upon the termination of your license to use SYBASE SQL ANYWHERE with which your application was developed. Upon termination you shall immediately cease the reproduction of SQL Runtime Distributable Components and destroy all copies of SQL Runtime Distributable Components in your possession. All disclaimers of warranties and limitation of liability set forth in this Agreement shall survive any termination of this Agreement. Sybase may terminate this Agreement upon written notice if you fail to make any payment when due.

7. INDEMNIFICATION. You shall indemnify, hold harmless and defend SYBASE and its suppliers from and against any claims or lawsuits, including attorney's fees, that arise or result from this license or the use or distribution of your application which includes SQL Runtime Distributable Components.

8. LIMITED WARRANTY AND LIABILITY. Sybase warrants that the Programs, as updated and when properly used, will operate in all material respects in conformity with Sybase published specifications for the applicable version, and the Program media shall be free of defects, for ninety (90) days from the date of shipment of such version to you. In the event of a failure to meet the foregoing limited warranty, provided you return the item with a copy of your receipt within the 90 day period, your sole remedy, at Sybase's option, shall be replacement of the defective materials or a refund of the license fees paid for the affected Program. This limited warranty gives you specific legal rights. You may have other rights, which vary among states/provinces. Some states/provinces do not allow limitation on the duration of implied warranties so the above limitation may not apply to you.

SYBASE DISCLAIMS ALL OTHER WARRANTIES AND CONDI-TIONS, EXPRESS OR IMPLIED, INCLUDING WITHOUT LIMITATION THE IMPLIED WARRANTIES OR CONDITIONS OF MERCHANTABLE QUALITY AND FITNESS FOR A PARTICULAR PURPOSE, AND WHETHER ARISING BY STATUTE OR IN LAW OR AS A RESULT OF A COURSE OF DEALING OR USAGE OF TRADE, WITH RESPECT TO THE PROGRAMS, THE DOCUMENTATION, THE SUPPORT OR OTHER SERVICES RELATED TO THE PROGRAMS. NO WARRANTY IS MADE REGARDING THE RESULTS OF ANY PROGRAM OR SERVICES OR THAT ALL ERRORS IN THE PROGRAMS WILL BE CORRECTED, OR THAT THE PROGRAMS' FUNCTIONALITY WILL MEET YOUR REQUIREMENTS. YOU ACKNOWLEDGE YOUR RESPONSIBILITY TO (i) REGULARLY BACK UP DATA MAINTAINED ON ANY COMPUTER SYSTEM USING THE PROGRAMS AND (ii) ADEQUATELY TEST PRIOR TO DEPLOYMENT EACH PRODUCTION VERSION OF THE PRO-GRAMS IN A CONFIGURATION WHICH REASONABLY SIMULATES YOUR PLANNED PRODUCTION ENVIRONMENT.

IN NO EVENT WILL SYBASE OR ITS SUPPLIERS BE LIABLE FOR ANY LOSS OR INACCURACY OF DATA, LOSS OF PROFITS OR INDIRECT, SPECIAL, INCIDENTAL OR CONSEQUENTIAL DAMAGES, EVEN IF SY-BASE HAS BEEN ADVISED OF THE POSSIBILITY OF SUCH DAMAGES. SYBASE'S TOTAL LIABILITY, IF ANY, ARISING OUT OF OR RELATING TO THIS AGREEMENT SHALL NOT EXCEED THE LICENSE FEES PAID BY YOU FOR THE PROGRAMS. THE FOREGOING RESTRICTIONS, DISCLAIMERS AND LIMITATIONS SHALL APPLY AND REMAIN IN FORCE EVEN IN THE EVENT OF A BREACH WHICH CONSTITUTES A FUNDAMENTAL BREACH. SOME STATES/PROVINCES DO NOT ALLOW THE EXCLUSION OR LIMITATION OF INCIDENTAL OR CON-SEQUENTIAL DAMAGES, SO THE ABOVE LIMITATION OR EXCLU-SION MAY NOT APPLY TO YOU.

No oral or written information given by Sybase, its agents or employees shall create a warranty. This Agreement shall inure to the benefit of Sybase's suppliers.

Addison-Wesley warrants the enclosed CD-ROM to be free of defects in materials and faulty workmanship under normal use for a period of ninety days after purchase. If a defect is discovered in the disk during this warranty period, a replacement disk can be obtained at no charge by sending the defective disk, postage prepaid, with proof of purchase to:

Addison-Wesley Longman
Developers Press
Editorial Department
One Jacob Way
Reading, MA 01867

After the ninety-day period, a replacement will be sent upon receipt of the defective disk and a check or money order for $10.00, payable to Addison-Wesley Publishing Company.

Addison-Wesley makes no warranty, either express or implied, with respect to this software, its quality, performance, merchantability, or fitness for a particular purpose. In no event will Addison-Wesley, its distributors, or dealers be liable for direct, indirect, special, incidental, or consequential damages arising out of the use or inability to use this software. The exclusion of implied warranties is not permitted in some states. Therefore, the above exclusion may not apply to you. This warranty provides you with specific legal rights. There may be other rights that you may have that vary from state to state.

9. GOVERNING LAW; COMPLETE AGREEMENT. THIS AGREEMENT CONSTITUTES THE COMPLETE AGREEMENT BETWEEN THE PARTIES WITH RESPECT TO THE PROGRAMS AND IS GOVERNED BY THE LAWS OF THE STATE OF CALIFORNIA IF THE USER IS LOCATED IN THE UNITED STATES, AND BY THE LAWS OF THE PROVINCE OF ONTARIO IF THE USER IS LOCATED IN CANADA. The terms of this Agreement supersede the terms of any purchase order, order letter or other document issued or signed by you to authorize your license of the Programs. If any provision of this Agreement is held to be unenforceable, such provisions shall be limited, modified or severed as necessary to eliminate its unenforceability, and all other provisions shall remain unaffected.

10. WAIVERS. The failure or delay of either party to exercise any of its rights shall not be deemed a waiver thereof and no waiver by either party of any breach of this Agreement shall constitute a waiver of any other or subsequent breach.

11. TRANSLATION. The parties have requested that this Agreement and all documents contemplated hereby be drawn up in English. Les parties aux présentes ont exigeè que cette entente et tous autres documents envisagés par les présentes soient rédigés en anglais.

222-8513 (E)

Momtute